Alternatives to Freedom:
Arguments and Opinions

LONGMAN
London and New York

Longman Group Limited,
Longman House, Burnt Mill,
Harlow, Essex CM20 2JE, England
and Associated Companies throughout the world.

Published in the United States of America
by Longman Publishing, New York

© Longman Group Limited 1995

First published 1995

ISBN 0 582 25130 3 PPR

British Library Cataloguing-in-Publication Data

A catalogue record for this book is
available from the British Library

Library of Congress Cataloging-in-Publication Data

Alternatives to freedom : arguments and opinions / edited by William
   L. Miller.
      p.   cm.
   Includes bibliographical references and index.
   ISBN 0–582–25130–3
   1. Freedom of the press.   2. Press and politics.   3. Civil rights.
   I. Miller, William Lockley, 1943–   .
   PN4736.A47   1994   94–289
   323.44'5 – – dc20   C

Transferred to digital print on demand 2002

Printed and bound by Antony Rowe Ltd, Eastbourne

CONTENTS

WESTMINSTER KINGSWAY COLLEGE

00049186

LIST OF CONTRIBUTORS

Amongst many other activities, past and present:

Lord (Robert) Armstrong of Ilminster is a former Cabinet Secretary and Head of the Home Civil Service.

Fedor Burlatsky is former Chairman of the USSR Supreme Soviet's Human Rights Committee and editor of *Literaturnaya gazeta*.

Elemer Hankiss is former President of Hungarian Television.

Roy Hattersley is former Deputy Leader of the Labour Party.

Lord (Roy) Jenkins of Hillhead is a former Deputy Leader of the Labour Party, President of the European Commission and first leader of the Social Democratic Party.

Arnold Kemp is editor of the (Glasgow) *Herald*.

Michael Lessnoff is Reader in Politics at the University of Glasgow.

Daniel Patrick Moynihan is Senior Senator for New York State.

William L. Miller is Edward Caird Professor of Politics at the University of Glasgow, and a fellow of the British Academy.

Annis May Timpson is a Lecturer in the School of English and American Studies, University of Sussex.

Writers and Readers

Two themes have persistently arisen during my 30 years and more in journalism, of which the last 13 have been as editor of the (Glasgow) *Herald*. One concerns the constitutional future of Scotland, the second the freedom of the press and the tension between it and government or political parties.

In 1979 Scotland came very close to Home Rule. The Scotland Act, setting up a Scottish Assembly, reached the statute book after a tortuous parliamentary progress. But in the referendum it was endorsed with insufficient conviction by an electorate which had become confused and increasingly apprehensive. When the Callaghan government fell soon afterwards, the devolutionary industry went into recession: those in the media who had become somewhat obsessed by devolution felt that winter had come, and as members of the 'chattering classes' they reflected that perhaps they had lost touch with the real sentiments of a more sceptical public.

In a similar way, it is easy for journalists to think that the public will automatically endorse a libertarian view of press freedom. Yet this is not necessarily the case. In the early 1980s the *Herald* published a valedictory letter from the British ambassador to Saudi Arabia. Its release was unauthorised and its contents highly embarrassing to the Foreign Office. At about 5 a.m. I was awakened by a call from a sheriff's officer who told me that the government had secured an interdict (or 'injunction' in English parlance) forbidding distribution, by us or our agents, of the edition of the paper carrying the article. The presses had already completed their print-run, and for 10 minutes or so I faced the horrifying prospect that I would have to pull back the entire print from the distributive and retail trades. That would have made me really popular in the board room! However, our astute legal adviser was able to point out that the newspaper distributors were not our servants, but a company in their own right; and since the papers had already been despatched from our building, we could do nothing further. The government's lawyers had slipped up and I breathed a sigh of relief.

But in the morning we were somewhat taken aback by many calls from our readers who, almost without exception, strongly disapproved of our action. Those readers who called – I think what Professor Miller would call a self-selecting sample – clearly placed the interests of the British government higher than the rights of the *Herald* on this matter at least.

The issues discussed in this fascinating volume, therefore, are not theoretical. They are encountered in everyday life by journalists, politicians, lawyers and, not least, citizens.

In the last few years, there has been renewed debate both about Scotland's place in the UK as it enters more fully, if still often reluctantly, into the European Union, and about whether new laws are required to restrain the more intrusive aspects of press behaviour, a string of scandals having destabilised the government.

The British press enjoys no entrenched rights, as it does in the United States: it is free *before the law* like everyone else. Yet a whole raft of restrictive legislation or practice now inhibits serious journalism to the point where investigative reporting has many obstacles to overcome and the International Press Institute no longer regards Britain as near the top of the league for press freedom. The freedom of the press has to be balanced against other freedoms, of course, and the reconciliation of all in some sort of hierarchy is a difficult if not impossible prospect. This is just one aspect of the debate about freedom conducted so eloquently in this book, which I have much pleasure in commending.

Arnold Kemp

Glasgow, 1994

ACKNOWLEDGEMENTS

All but one of the 'Arguments' chapters in this volume were made possible through the generosity of Glasgow University's Stevenson Citizenship Fund and the (Glasgow) *Herald*. As well as the authors of those chapters, I must thank the Principal of Glasgow University, Sir William Kerr Fraser, and the editor of the *Herald*, Arnold Kemp, for their personal involvement and encouragement. Eileen Reynolds was enormously helpful in establishing and maintaining contacts with the authors of the 'Arguments' chapters. The *American Scholar* kindly gave permission to reprint, with minor modifications, Senator Daniel Patrick Moynihan's contribution.

The 'Opinions' chapters are based upon the British Rights Survey which was funded by the British ESRC (Economic and Social Research Council) under grant number R000232637 to William L. Miller, Annis May Timpson and Michael Lessnoff. Malcolm Dickson and Morag Brown acted as principal research assistants on that project and trained a team of over 120 interviewers. To them, and to the 4,354 local political leaders and ordinary members of the public who submitted to a long, searching, and challenging interview, many thanks. This book is not a comprehensive account of the views expressed in those interviews. Wide-ranging though it is, it deals only with those parts of the interviews which directly relate to the issues raised in the 'Arguments' chapters.

Thanks are also due to Professors Paul Sniderman (Stanford), Peter Russell and Joseph Fletcher (Toronto), and Philip Tetlock (Berkeley) who directed the Canadian Charter Study, and who provided the intellectual inspiration and a great deal of technical assistance for this whole project.

Finally I must thank Elspeth Shaw and Avril Johnston for their exceedingly prompt and efficient secretarial and administrative work on the British Rights Study and in the preparation of this manuscript.

William L. Miller

CHAPTER 1

Introduction: Alternative values

WILLIAM L. MILLER

'Englishmen never will be slaves: they are free to do whatever the Government and public opinion allow them to do.'
George Bernard Shaw, *Man and Superman* (1903), Act 3.

Defining freedom

This book is concerned with freedom, and with 'alternatives to freedom' including some important and seductive ones. It combines and connects explicit and implicit arguments for freedom, or the alternatives to freedom, with the judgements of public opinion on these issues. Throughout this book, alternate chapters present the arguments of distinguished political figures and detail the opinions of the people. It is a revealing exercise to confront the carefully argued views of distinguished political figures, arrived at after lengthy and practical consideration of such questions, with the more immediate reactions of the British people to the same or similar questions.

The arguments are put by experienced politicians and civil servants based on key civil rights issues they have had to face during what has often been a lifetime in politics and government. They argue from a variety of political standpoints but each argues his particular case with the understanding and passion that comes from direct practical experience. They focus on issues of practical politics not mere political theory, though these same issues have intrigued political theorists for long enough.

By contrast, our analyses of public opinion are necessarily dispassionate. Public opinion cannot prove or disprove arguments. Majorities need not be right: they may be ill-informed, perverse, prejudiced, or easily swayed by plausible demagogues. Nonetheless, we need to connect arguments with opinions if we are to understand public debate fully. Particularly in a democracy, it matters how many people hold a view as well as whether they are right or wrong. After all, the object of democratic debate is not just to present well-informed and logically sound arguments but to convince a majority. And conversely, although majorities may well be wrong, a fundamental tenet of the democratic faith is that majorities are less likely to be consistently wrong than minorities; that even when we disagree profoundly with majority opinion we should listen to it and take it into account; that debates with public opinion must – and should – be a two-way process. Public debate in a democracy must include a voice for the public as well as for the experts, intellectuals and top politicians. From that perspective, the contours of public opinion are more than facts: they too are arguments.

But what is freedom? Notoriously, there is no agreement among philosophers on this question, and different definitions are frequently linked with different political ideologies. Freedom may or may not be what philosophers call an 'essentially contested' concept, but that it is actually contested there is no doubt. Nor can there be much doubt as to why this is so. The term 'freedom' is almost universally taken to refer to something good, even to one of the greatest goods of human life. There is therefore an obvious motive for philosophers and politicians to define the term in such a way as to attach it to something they value highly. Furthermore, freedom is an idea sufficiently general and abstract to allow considerable scope for 'persuasive definition', so there is opportunity as well as motive.

For the purposes of this book, it is not necessary to decide which definition of freedom is 'correct', but rather to select a definition suitable for our purposes, and to make as clear as possible what that is and what it is not. For our purposes here, we need a definition of freedom which is both relatively simple and relatively narrow. It needs to be simple, so that it can be embodied in questionnaires put to a general public unfamiliar with complex philosophical concepts and arguments. It needs to be relatively narrow, because our purpose is to discuss the relation of freedom to other, alternative and competing, values. Broad definitions of freedom (as well as philosophically complex ones) have a tendency to incorporate these competing values into freedom itself, and would thus tend to frustrate, or at least confuse, our enterprise. For these reasons, we adopt what Isaiah Berlin called the 'negative' concept of freedom. It so happens that this definition is generally favoured by liberal and libertarian thinkers. However, by adopting the 'negative' concept of freedom we do not intend to indicate agreement with the views of such thinkers, only to facilitate and clarify discussion of the issues. Thus, for example, the argument advanced by Roy Hattersley in his chapter is not an argument for freedom as defined for our present analytic purpose, but for other values. This does not mean, of course, that Hattersley is wrong, either in his attempt to broaden the definition of freedom, or in his substantive views. Our choice of definition is analytic, not moral.

Berlin's 'Two Concepts of Liberty', in *Four Essays on Liberty* (1969: 118–72), is the classic analysis of different ideas of freedom. Despite its title, it deals with considerably more than two concepts. Some consideration of its themes will serve to make clearer the usage we adopt in this book, the alternatives we do not adopt, and why. According to Berlin, the two concepts of liberty (or freedom) are the 'negative' and 'positive' concepts. 'Negative' freedom is defined thus: people are free to the extent that their actions are *not interfered with* by other persons, or insofar as they are *not prevented* by others from performing actions, or *not coerced* by other persons. Berlin claims, correctly, that this is the normal meaning of the word. It follows from this definition that every law (however desirable or justified) reduces freedom (though it may also increase freedom, if it prohibits interference or coercion), and that inaction (however deplorable) does not by itself reduce freedom.

What of Berlin's 'positive' concept of freedom? This, he says, 'consists in being one's own master' (p. 131). What is the difference between being one's own master, and not being interfered with or coerced by others? The difference is that other things besides interference by other people can prevent one from being one's own master, from being in control of one's life – for example, poverty, ill health, lack of education. Looked at in this light, legislation aimed at attacking these evils can be looked on (as by Roy Hattersley) as increasing the sum of freedom, and failure of governments so to act can be described as reducing freedom. From the standpoint of the negative conception of freedom, however, to say this is to confuse not being *free* to do something with being *unable* to do it. Interference by others is only one of several possible causes of people's inability to do what they want.

There is no need to adjudicate this dispute. Suffice it to say that, for our present purpose, the negative concept is more convenient, in that it allows us to treat (economic) equality as an alternative value to freedom, which may conflict with it. This is preferable to (because simpler than) treating the conflict as being between two kinds of freedom.

There are other, more esoteric ways in which theorists of 'positive' freedom have argued that people may fail to be their own master. They may, for example, be unable to master their 'passions', or their desires, but instead be mastered by them. In that case, it is argued, they are not free. Such a conception, of course, implies that the passions, or desires, are somehow external to the person's true (or higher) self or will. What, then constitutes human beings' true (or higher) self? An answer is frequently given in terms of the faculty that supposedly distinguishes the human race from the rest of creation – reason. Thus, people are free insofar as their actions conform to reason, insofar as their reason masters their 'irrational' passions, impulses or desires. This, as Berlin tells us, was the view of Kant, among many others. Berlin calls it 'freedom as rational self-direction' (p. 145). But what does this mean? How do people act if they act rationally (and thus freely)? Perhaps this question cannot and should not be answered, but many philosophers have tried to answer it, in various ways. Kant's answer is of particular interest: to act rationally is to act in accordance with the moral law. To act freely, therefore, is to act morally, controlling one's passions, desires, and interests. However subtle this argument may be, and however desirable it may be to act rationally and morally, this definition of freedom is not suitable for our purposes. For one thing, it is too far removed from the everyday understanding of the idea, and for another, by identifying freedom and morality, it makes it impossible to treat them as alternative and possibly conflicting values, or to investigate relations between them. We need a concept of freedom according to which freedom can, in principle, be misused.

One further version of Berlin's 'positive' liberty deserves mention. If individuals are thought of primarily as members of a group, their self-mastery (or self-direction, or self-government) may be identified with – become merged into – that of the group. Then, the individual is free if the group to which he or she belongs is self-governing. In this way, freedom can become identified with democracy. The classic example is Rousseau (though he did not put it exactly in this way). In Rousseau's social contract, individuals give up their 'natural liberty' in exchange for 'civil liberty', that is, for a share equal to that of all other citizens in the sovereign law-making power. To be free in this sense is to be governed by the General Will. It is not clear to what extent this idea of Rousseau's derives from what Berlin defines as the 'positive' concept of liberty, and to what extent it is a democratisation of the classical republican concept of 'free' (i.e. non-monarchical) government; that is, what Benjamin Constant (1988: 307–28) called the 'liberty of the ancients'. What is clear, however, is that a concept of freedom which identifies it with democracy is not suited to present purposes. We want to be able to examine tensions between individual freedom and democracy, just as we wish to look at tensions between freedom and morality, and between freedom and equality.

Alternatives to freedom

In principle, there is near universal support for freedom. It has, in the words of de Tocqueville, an 'intrinsic glamour, a fascination in itself, apart from all practical considerations' (de Tocqueville 1966: 188). In principle, freedom is not just a means to an end – though it may, happily, encourage innovation, initiative, efficiency and prosperity in the long run – but it is an end in itself.

In practice, however, there is much less support for freedom. When practical choices have to be made, many people, often a majority, take sides against freedom. Why do they do so? Hypocrisy is one explanation: they never were really committed to freedom in the first place. Intellectual incapacity is another: they lack the ability to connect principles and practice, they simply fail to appreciate the relevance of their general principles to the particular issues at hand.

There is some truth in both these explanations but there is a third, less critical, explanation. As de Tocqueville himself realised, people have other values and goals apart from freedom which may or may not be compatible with it. He instanced two: first, a concern for order and good government; second, a concern for equality. Traditionally, those on the right of the political spectrum have valued order highly, while those on the left have valued equality. Both have valued freedom. So those on the right have to weigh their concern for freedom against their concern for order and efficiency while those on the left have to weigh their concern for freedom against their concern for equality. We shall show that despite elite scepticism, principles – and combinations of principles – really do influence attitudes to citizens' rights and freedoms in particular scenarios and influence them strongly, even amongst the general public, though more so amongst politicians.

De Tocqueville's alternatives to freedom – order and equality – were not new even in his time. Indeed popular concern for order and good government almost certainly pre-dates popular concern for freedom. Without modern methods of opinion research we can never be sure of that of course, but de Tocqueville confidently asserts that half a century before the Revolution the 'French people, if consulted' (which they were not) would have shown little enthusiasm for liberty:

> What they wanted was not so much a recognition of the rights of man as reforms in the existing system, and had there been on the throne a monarch of the calibre and temperament of Frederick the Great, he would certainly have initiated many of the sweeping changes made by the Revolution in social conditions and the government of the country, and thus not only preserved his crown but greatly added to his power.
>
> (de Tocqueville 1966: 185)

This same concern for strong central government and administrative efficiency is evident in contemporary politics. Professor Raymond Plant (1986: 9) wrote of the 'sense that across parties there seems to be a tacit admission of the failure of the British state to govern efficiently, justly and authoritatively'. Insofar as Thatcherism had any ideological coherence[1] it seemed to aim at reducing the scope of government while increasing its authority (Kavanagh 1990: 13) – though as time went by there seemed more stress on increasing its authority than reducing its scope (*ibid*: 284). To her admirers, Mrs Thatcher was twentieth-century Britain's Frederick the Great. Her governments recognised only 'high politics' and 'no politics': government should either withdraw altogether from certain areas of policy, handing them over to private companies or individuals operating in the market place, or insist upon its absolute and unchecked right to govern.

In pursuit of a dominant role in the steadily widening field designated as 'high politics', central government in the 1980s either abolished or curtailed the power of what de Tocqueville called 'deliberative assemblies, secondary organisations vested with local powers and generally speaking, all those counterpoises which have been devised by free peoples at various stages of their history to curb the domination of a central authority' (1966: 180). In Britain that meant that such 'secondary' or 'intermediate organisations' as the Greater London Council (GLC) and the Metropolitan County Councils were abolished, functions and powers were switched from the remaining elected councils to appointed boards, proposals (some would say promises) to set up devolved regional assemblies for Scotland and Wales were abandoned, the powers of the trade unions were curbed by law and by unemployment, the BBC was roundly attacked and subjected to further legal controls, and outspoken clerics were brusquely told to stick to religion and keep out of politics. The press was harried by government in the courts, and the police raided the BBC studios in Glasgow to prevent the Corporation revealing government secrets. In the 1990s, the process of centralising authority by abolishing elected local governments or curtailing their powers continues, and the scope of 'high politics' has been extended downwards to include even the details of primary-school curricula.

In opposition, Lord Hailsham attacked the centralisation of unchecked power as an 'elective dictatorship'. He wrote: 'I have never suggested that freedom is dead in Britain. But it has diminished, and a principal cause of its impairment has been the absolute legislative power confided in Parliament, concentrated in the hands of a government armed with a parliamentary majority' (1978: 127).

How can anyone accuse an elected Parliament of being opposed to freedom? Surely parliamentary sovereignty is the cornerstone of English liberty? Rousseau claimed, 'The English people think they are free but in this belief they are profoundly wrong. They are free only when they are electing members of Parliament. Once the election has been completed, they revert to a condition of slavery: they are nothing' (1947: 373). When Rousseau wrote that, he was (in our terms) arguing for participatory rather than representative democracy, with the whole people involved in far more decisions, taken far more frequently than every five years. But his words could be levelled with equal force against any kind of majoritarian democracy. Public choice theorists such as Buchanan and Tullock (Buchanan and Tullock 1962; Buchanan 1975) have resensitised us to the potential tyranny of majorities which so worried J. S. Mill. Conformity to *any* corporate decision, no matter how recently taken, no matter by how large a majority, necessarily restricts the freedom of the dissenting minority. More authority for government – however that government is chosen – means less liberty for dissenting citizens.

It would be quite wrong, however, to suggest that only prime ministers and cabinets value order and good government. Ordinary citizens do so too. Respect for authority is almost as widespread as love of freedom. Indeed both are so widespread that the public cannot be divided into those whose goal is freedom and those whose goal is order: most people want both though in particular circumstances, of course, they have to weigh the one against the other before deciding on a course of action. In general it would even be wrong to suggest that politicians value authority more, and freedom less, than the general public. Prime ministers and cabinets aside, the social and educational background necessary to prosper in electoral politics, coupled with personal experience of participation in a democratic process, tend to select and mould politicians whose respect for freedom is higher, and whose respect for authority is lower, than that of the general public.

New ways to assess public opinion on freedom

Public opinion is a notoriously elusive concept and notoriously difficult to measure on such complex and abstract topics as rights and freedoms. All too often opinion polls offer easy, abstract, cost-free options which appear to win overwhelming support but do not reflect the actual choices people would make in real-world situations. So we have asked about both abstract principles and the application of those principles in concrete scenarios which often involve conflicts of principle. We look at the influence of principle on practice and, especially, at the influence of conflicting principles: of freedom and its alternatives.

What should 'public' opinion mean in this context: the knee-jerk reactions of people uninvolved with practical decisions on the issues, or the considered opinions of people who have to face the issues regularly? Which 'public' best represents 'public opinion'? The opinions of the informed and involved public may best represent the opinions that the uninformed and uninvolved would have, if only they had to confront the issues more closely or more often.

We investigated public opinion on two levels using 2,060 interviews with a representative sample of the British electorate and 1,244 interviews with a sample of senior local politicians (mainly leaders of party groups, including independent groups, on local government councils throughout Britain).[2] We shall refer to these as the 'general public' and 'local politicians' respectively. These senior 'local politicians' were chosen as representative of a more informed and experienced public opinion than the 'general public', and were likely to have made policies or taken decisions that would affect the rights and freedoms of ordinary citizens. Together these two samples give us an insight into the complex structure of public opinion in British society. (We shall also make very occasional reference to a third sample of 1,255 Scots, where social or constitutional differences between Scotland and England make that appropriate.) We shall show that abstract principles influence attitudes to rights in particular scenarios more strongly among politicians than among the general public; that, paradoxically perhaps, politicians are more favourable to citizens' rights than the general public itself; but, at the same time, even local politicians have a 'governing perspective' and are more favourable towards government prerogatives than the general public.

The validity and significance of these differences might be challenged on the grounds that our samples of public and politicians differed in terms of partisanship: our sampling procedure produced proportionately more Liberals in our sample of politicians than in our sample of the general public, simply because a small Liberal Party group of a few councillors and a large Labour or Conservative group each had one leader available for inclusion in the politicians sample. Now, if the politicians sample is disproportionately Liberal (with a capital 'L') compared to the public, that alone might make politicians seem more liberal (with a small 'l'). To meet that challenge we have weighted our sample of politicians to have the same voting preferences as the general public, by downweighting Liberals and upweighting Labour slightly and Conservatives a little more. Consequently none of the differences between public and politicians in this volume owe anything to differences in the party balance, since there are none. Weighting in this way is a standard statistical technique, but to any reader who is suspicious of it we should report that we have recalculated all our results with and without this weighting; usually it alters opinion percentages amongst politicians by only 1 or 2 per cent, never by more than 5; and it never alters our conclusions in any significant way.

Neither set of interviews should be dismissed as a 'snap poll' of unconsidered opinions. Individual interviews averaged over 45 minutes in length in order to research opinion in depth, and interviewing was spread over a 10-month period from November 1991 to August 1992 to avoid findings based upon transient emotional reactions to particular current events. Despite the extended interviewing period, all reported party percentage votes in the sample of the British electorate were within 2 per cent of the actual 1992 General Election figures.

All the interviews were carried out using our own very flexible version of the CATI technique (Computer Assisted Telephone Interviewing). Our questionnaire was so much more complex than usual that it could not have been administered without CATI. One critical feature was that many questions appeared in several variant forms. For some questions there were only two variants, for others as many as a dozen. When the computer controlling the interview reached a particular question it used a random-number generator to decide, randomly, which one of the several versions of that question it would display on the screen. The interviewer read out the question as it appeared and the computer recorded on its disc which variant of the question was used on that occasion along with the answer given by the interviewee. There were 50 such references to the random-number generator in each interview.

This system of randomly varying question wording had several advantages. First, it allowed us to research more questions than even a high-pressure 45-minute telephone interview would normally allow, because each interview contained only one variant of each question. Second, because the different variants were randomly assigned to interviews, any differences in the answers could be attributed to variations in the wording (subject to the usual caveats about sampling error). To take one example which is discussed further in Chapter 11, we asked about employment quotas:

Do you think the law should require [large private companies/the government and civil service] to hire a fixed percentage of [women/blacks and Asians/disabled people] or should [women/blacks and Asians disabled people] get no special treatment?

This question involved two references to the random-number generator: first to decide whether the question should ask about private companies or government employment; and second to decide whether it should ask about gender, race or disability. This system allows us to compare support for employment quotas for different social groups and in different sectors of employment. That could be done in a conventional interview by asking all variants of the question, but in addition to taking six times as long, that approach would generate spurious consistency between answers to one variant and another: people would feel under social and psychological pressure to give consistent answers. Given the reputed reluctance of people to admit to racial prejudice, people who had just agreed to quotas for the disabled might feel particularly reluctant to oppose racial quotas for fear of being accused of racial prejudice. But since each interview with our randomised CATI method used only one variant of the question, no-one we interviewed could have felt under any pressure, logical or psychological, to give consistent answers about employment quotas for different social groups. Our strategy eliminates this potentially significant source of spurious consistency as well as researching opinion about several different kinds of employment quota in the time taken by a single question.

Let us take a one more example. As part of a battery of Agree/Disagree questions we asked:

Newspapers which get hold of confidential government documents about [defence / economic / health service] plans should *not* be allowed to publish them [(*null*)/because publication might damage our national interests].
    Agree/Disagree? Strongly or Not?

This question came in six different versions depending upon whether the question asked about defence, economic, or health plans; and upon whether it did or did not add the argument that publication 'might damage our national interests'. Again, with all the usual caveats about sampling errors, we can attribute differences in the answers to differences in question wording. We can see how far support for censorship depends upon the topic (defence, economic, or health plans); how much it depends upon an explicit reference to the 'national interest'; and how much it depends upon the interaction between the two, that is, how much influence references to the 'national interest' have in different topic areas. Answers to this question are analysed in Chapter 5.

We shall use this system of controlled variations in question wording to show that appeals to rational arguments are effective, though appeals to authority less so; that it is easier to influence the opinions of the general public than those of (even local) politicians; and indeed that there is occasional evidence of politicians actually reacting against attempts to pressure them towards certain viewpoints.

Parliamentary sovereignty

Chapter 2 argues the case against elective dictatorship. In it, Roy Jenkins advocates a new People's Bill of Rights in contrast to Parliament's Bill of Rights which was passed in 1688. That Bill affirmed the rights of Parliament against the crown: a new, People's Bill of Rights would affirm the rights of citizens against Parliament. Chapter 3 looks at the degree of public support for this argument. One of the most telling counter-arguments against either a new Bill of Rights or a written constitution is that it would shift power out of the hands of elected politicians and into the hands of unelected judges. At least the people can vote an unpopular government out of office but they have no means of bringing judges to heel; so a written constitution could ultimately leave citizens with less power and fewer rights than before.

This fear of unelected and unaccountable judges has restrained left-wing calls for a written constitution throughout most of this century. But as Roy Jenkins argues, and public opinion seems to agree, the European dimension has changed British perceptions of judges and courts. He would put more power into the hands of British judges in the hope that they would behave more like the European courts than traditional British courts. Public opinion remains suspicious of British courts, but leans towards letting European courts overrule British parliaments. Informed public opinion – as represented by our sample of local politicians – is especially suspicious of British courts yet especially willing to give European courts power over the British Parliament. Public support for the idea of parliamentary sovereignty is weak.

Secrecy

Chapter 4 raises another issue of order and good government: the need for secrecy. It is an unfashionable cause amongst the chattering classes. Lord Armstrong, formerly Cabinet Secretary to Mrs Thatcher, admits that it is very easy to voice the 'simple and loaded slogans' of open government and much less easy to defend secrecy. Yet, he argues, no one can really support totally open government. To a greater or lesser extent almost everyone accepts the need to restrict openness either to promote the efficient management of public affairs or to defend the national interest, or both.

Chapter 5 reveals widespread public support for the principles of 'free speech' and 'freedom of information'. A Freedom of Information Act tops the public's list of mechanisms for protecting citizens' rights and liberties. Nonetheless a majority of the general public would ban publication of government secrets that fell into the hands of the press. All three principles – respect for authority, for free speech, and for a right to know – clearly influence support for banning publication of government secrets 'in the national interest'. The informed public of local politicians are significantly more able than the general public to apply these principles to concrete situations in a discriminating way and, overall, they support censorship of government secrets significantly less than the general public. Paradoxically perhaps, those closest to government are the most committed to the rights of citizens on this issue, both in theory and in practice.

Freedom from the press

Freedom of the press is one of the great classic freedoms, important in its own right, and perhaps even more as a means by which other freedoms are preserved. It is enshrined along with freedom of speech in the First Amendment to the United States Constitution (i.e. the first clause of the American Bill of Rights). It was *glasnost* rather than *perestroika* that blew the old communist systems apart. De Tocqueville tells us that Voltaire 'envied the English above all for their freedom to write as they liked, while their political freedom left him indifferent' (de Tocqueville 1966: pp. 178–9). In the contemporary world, however, many now seek freedom *from the press*, rather than *for the press*. Both governments and citizens frequently allege that the press is irresponsible, that it distorts the news, spreads lies or half-truths, and intrudes into private lives where it has no right to be. There is, as Lord Armstrong claims, a right to privacy as well as a right to free speech.

Concentrations of power and influence in the media come in for particular criticism. In a speech during the 1931 Westminster by-election, the prime minister of the day, Stanley Baldwin, denounced press barons who used their papers as engines of propaganda to further their political ambitions: 'what the proprietorship of these papers is aiming at is power, and power without responsibility – the prerogative of the harlot through the ages'.[3] More recently press barons have been accused of devastating the lives of private citizens in pursuit of no greater ambition than commercial profits.

Chapter 6 adds an international perspective to the debate about press irresponsibility by chronicling the role of the Russian press in the downfall of Gorbachev. Feydor Burlatsky, a distinguished Russian journalist and chairman of Gorbachev's Human Rights Commission, accuses the press of repaying Gorbachev for its freedom by pushing him from office and encouraging the collapse of the USSR, lapsing into intemperate abuse and intolerance, mistaking its right to criticise for a licence to denounce and, in the end, sliding back to its old role of being the poodle of the regime. Despite these monumental faults however, Feydor Burlatsky sees no better long-run alternative than a free press. Many in Britain do not agree.

The times are not so heroic in contemporary Britain and issues of press freedom and responsibility are less sharply drawn than in Russia. The consequences of failure may be less severe; they are certainly less obvious. But the issues are there. Chapter 7 reveals widespread public support – on both right and left – for censorship of disreputable or irresponsible journalism. Obviously no two people will agree exactly on what is, or is not, disreputable and irresponsible. We covered a range of possibilities in our interviews, including incitement to racial or religious hatred, abusive attacks on Christianity or other religions, interviews with terrorist supporters, pictures of extreme violence, lies or distortions of the truth, sensational crime stories, reports that might encourage prejudice even if true, and intrusions into the private lives of ordinary citizens and leading politicians. On these topics commitment to the principles of order and free speech both have a significant influence on support for censorship but – quite properly – commitment to freedom of information does not. Support for censorship on these topics is lower than for a ban on publication of government secrets and there is no overall difference between politicians and the general public. In making up their minds, politicians give more weight than the general public to principles of order and free speech but – at the same time – they are more clearly able to see the irrelevance of the third principle (freedom of information) in particular circumstances.

Government control of broadcasting

Chapter 8 raises the issue of government control of the media, especially radio and television broadcasting. Even in the age of the satellite, control of broadcasting remains more concentrated than control of the print press, often with dominant channels under direct state control. Throughout Eastern Europe new 'democratic' governments have insisted on their right to control broadcasting: 'freedom of the press' has been interpreted quite literally as 'freedom of the print-press' even to the limited extent that it has been conceded at all. The 'BBC solution' to freedom of the press despite monopoly government control was to require 'balanced broadcasting' within the channel rather than a wide range of different channels offering alternative viewpoints. It is, of course, notoriously difficult to define balance, and an essential feature of the 'BBC solution' is that the Broadcasting Authority should operate 'at arm's length' from the government of the day, in much the same way as law courts. Both are ultimately under the control of successive governments but can resist day-to-day pressures from a particular cabinet. As President of Hungarian Television, Elemer Hankiss fought a bitter, sometimes farcical, and ultimately unsuccessful battle to implement the 'BBC solution' in post-Communist Hungary. He was opposed by well-meaning democrats who admired Thatcher and, like her, wished to strengthen the authority of central government over all intermediate organisations including state radio and television. Dr Hankiss chronicles Hungarian Radio and Television's 'war of independence'.

In its ideal form the 'BBC solution' was never implemented anywhere. In Britain itself it remained an intention rather than a reality. It originated in the political deal to get Labour to join the war-time Coalition. It came under increasing attack during the 1980s. But Chapter 9 shows it remains popular while government control of either press or broadcasting remains massively unpopular. Opposition to government control of the press or broadcasting is strongest on the left but extends right across the ideological spectrum. While Chapters 5 and 7 show there is widespread support for a ban on various kinds of publication, Chapter 9 shows that a majority of those who call for a ban on particular news items nonetheless oppose direct government control of broadcasting. It may be a paradox to call for censorship yet oppose government control, yet that is what people want: censorship without a state censor. Any discussion that fails to take account of this simply misrepresents the subtlety of public opinion.

Equality

Equality was one of the slogans of the French Revolution though de Tocqueville (1966: 184–5) notes it was already popular amongst some of those who advised the *ancien régime*. Different conceptions of equality have been popular at different times and with different ideological tendencies. Three kinds of equality are important: first, *equality before the law* – including the laws that affect elections and politics; second, *equality of opportunity* – including opportunities in education and employment; and third, *equality of outcome*, including equality of income and wealth. There is now a broad consensus in favour of legal and political equality at least for native-born citizens if not for 'guest-workers', immigrants and resident non-citizens. Today, no one seriously proposes that the franchise be restricted to men or to the well-educated or to the well-off, as they did in Victorian Britain, nor to the free-born, as they did in nineteenth century America.

The conflicts between freedom and equality of opportunity or outcome remain more visible. De Tocqueville was scathing about equality of outcome, the 'subversive theories of what today is known as socialism' (1966: 184). Equality of income, wealth and consumption could only be achieved and maintained with a large dose of coercion. Even equality of opportunity has implications for freedom if taken at all seriously. We can imagine opening the doors of a public library to all-comers: that seems to provide both freedom and opportunity for all. But libraries cost money. A charitable library provided by a philanthropic Andrew Carnegie might reasonably be described as increasing equality of opportunity without restricting freedom of choice, but not a public library financed by taxation. If educational or job opportunities have to be provided by the state and financed by public taxation then equality of opportunity is bought at the expense of restricting the taxpayers' freedom to spend their wealth as they choose. If equality of educational or job opportunities is increased by legally imposed minimum quotas, however low, then the freedom of selection boards is necessarily diminished, even if it is only their freedom to be prejudiced that is diminished. And if the quotas are set high enough to provide equality of outcome, they may curtail the freedom of well-qualified potential applicants to compete as well as the freedom of selection boards to select.

Consequently, it is usually assumed that freedom and equality (at least beyond legal and political equality) must necessarily be in conflict. In Chapter 10 Roy Hattersley argues that equality promotes liberty: that more equality would increase the 'sum of liberty'. It is certainly a collectivist view, but one that focuses on freedom rather than relegating it to the status of a second priority. Equality becomes a part of Hattersley's positive definition of freedom. But even though Hattersley is not proposing an alternative (equality) to freedom in terms of his own expanded definition of freedom, he is nonetheless arguing for an alternative to the purely negative definition of freedom which we use – for analytic clarity and nothing more – throughout this book.

Chapter 11 shows there is near universal support for equality of opportunity, though far less for equality of outcome. Surprisingly, for those who adhere to the conventional wisdom, there is a modest positive correlation between commitment to freedom and commitment to equality – that is, the people with the greatest commitment to freedom also have the greatest commitment to equality, no matter how equality is defined. And this correlation extends to practical policies: those who value freedom the most support high taxation for public services more than those who value freedom less.

But there are limits to this paradox. There is a large majority against employment quotas for women or ethnic minorities, and a complex relationship between commitment to equality and support for quotas. Commitment to freedom increases support for the goal of better representation of women and minorities in Parliament but decreases support for the use of legal quotas to achieve it. So although there is a positive correlation between commitment to freedom and commitment to equality, the two principles themselves have conflicting influences on support for the more adventurous egalitarian policies.

The moral community

The third slogan of the French revolutionaries, 'fraternity', also conflicts with the first. Fraternity, or brotherhood, raises notions of citizenship and community, ideas that place the individual in a complex web of support and duty. Conceptions of community are as varied and as ideologically driven as conceptions of equality. To some, membership of a community means the right to call upon others for help, to others it means the duty to help other individuals within the community, or to give service to the community as a collective whole. To some, community rights and duties are purely economic or defensive, to others they include standards of behaviour: there are moral communities as well as economic communities and defence communities. We might expect a monastery to be a moral rather than an economic or defence community, though historians might regard that expectation as naive. We think of the European Union in terms of its former title, the European Economic Community, though it now has wider ambitions that include a defence community.

The state has certainly claimed to be an economic and defence community, but traditionally it has also claimed to be a moral community. That is why there are established state churches or (equivalently) state campaigns against religion. In this respect, there was no fundamental difference between the revolutionaries who persecuted priests and the *ancien régime* that employed them. The language of 'moral standards', 'community standards', 'traditional values' implies that those who use these terms do not accept that morals are a private matter. Non-conformists, in the fundamental sense of that term, reject this language and insist that state and community (except for voluntary sub-communities) should not impose community standards of moral or religious behaviour on their (involuntary) citizens.

In Chapter 12, Senator Daniel Patrick Moynihan puts the case for community standards of some kind. He suggests that contemporary Americans are 'defining deviancy down'. Similar arguments have been advanced by government ministers in Britain, though with less style or passion. He suggests that society is coping with surging levels of moral deviance by simply redefining it as 'normal'. Unfortunately linguistic redefinitions seldom change realities. Redefinition is often an attempt to escape from problems rather than find a solution to them. He offers three categories of redefinition: *altruistic* redefinitions, *opportunistic* redefinitions, and *normalising* redefinitions. Altruistic redefinitions are attempts to solve a problem by correcting the mistaken perceptions and perspectives of the past, and restating the problem in terms that evoke effective action. Opportunistic redefinitions are designed to benefit the definers in one way or another, usually financial. Normalising redefinitions simply cope with deviance by defining it as normal. Without the cover-up of fraudulent redefinitions, he claims there is clearly an explosion of deviance and a 'manifest decline of the civic order'.

In Chapter 13, we look at the British public's tolerance for private freedom. Do the public subscribe to the notion of 'community standards' and 'traditional values'? Do they believe that the state should impose community standards on individuals? Two-thirds of the public, though only half our sample of local politicians, feel that government does have a duty 'to uphold morality'. While those on the left back the community against individual self-interest, those on the right back the community against individual rights. In practical terms we look at sex issues such as abortion and homosexuality, issues of drink and drugs, and religious issues such as tolerance for 'fanatical and weird religions', religious teaching in state schools and ritual slaughter of animals. The views of the public, and especially the politicians, on these practical issues prove to be strongly influenced by general principles. But general principles of moral enthusiasm conflict with general principles of tolerance. In the secular 1990s commitment to tolerance is not surprising, but we find remarkably widespread commitment to 'traditional ideas' and the importance of 'following God's will'. It is the tension between this pervasive moral enthusiasm on the one hand, and tolerance of immorality on the other, that determines public attitudes to private freedom.

Constitution and culture

Finally, Chapter 14 poses the question: how well does the British constitution fit British political culture? It is a commonplace to attribute the characteristics of a nation's history and institutions to its people, but people need not be democrats simply because they live in a democracy, republicans because they live in a republic, nor traditionalists simply because they happen to live in a state with an unbroken history and an unreformed constitution. We now know, if we ever doubted it, that people certainly were not communists just because they lived under communist regimes. So it is worth asking whether British political institutions now fit British political culture. To the extent that they do not, there is a case for reform here as elsewhere. It is still possible to argue against reform on the grounds that public opinion is ill-informed, uneducated and mis-guided – in short that it is wrong – but harder to do so when the fit between political culture and political institutions is even worse amongst the more informed and politically experienced part of the public who routinely confront policy choices that affect the civil and political liberties of British citizens.

Notes

1 Some suggest it had little coherence. See King (1987: 130).
2 The British Rights Study was funded by the Economic and Social Research Council (ESRC) and directed by W. L. Miller, A. M. Timpson and M. Lessnoff with Morag Brown and Malcolm Dickson as principal research assistants.
3 Curran and Seaton (1991: 49). See also Butler and Sloman (1980: 249).

References

Berlin, I. (1969) *Four Essays on Liberty*, Oxford: Oxford University Press.
Buchanan, J. M. (1975) *The Limits of Liberty: Between Anarchy and Leviathan*, Chicago: University of Chicago Press.
Buchanan, J. M. and Tullock, G. (1962) *The Calculus of Consent*, Ann Arbor, Michigan: Michigan University Press.
Butler, D. and Sloman, A. (1980) *British Political Facts 1900–1979*, London: Macmillan.
Constant, B. (1988) *Political Writings*, ed. B. Fontana, Cambridge: Cambridge University Press.
Curran J. and Seaton J. (1991) *Power Without Responsibility: The Press and Broadcasting in Britain*, London: Routledge.
Hailsham (Lord) (1978) *The Dilemma of Democracy: Diagnosis and Pre-scription*, London: Collins.
Kavanagh, D. (1990) *Thatcherism and British Politics: The End of Consen-sus?*, Oxford: Oxford University Press.
King, D (1987) *The New Right: Politics, Markets and Citizenship*, London: Macmillan.
Plant, R. (1986) 'Ideology', in H. Drucker, P. Dunleavy, A. Gamble and G. Peele (eds) *Developments in British Politics 2*, London: Macmillan.
Rousseau, J. J. (1947) *The Social Contract*, Oxford: Oxford University Press.
Tocqueville, A. de (1966) *The Ancien Régime and the French Revolution*, Glasgow: Collins Fontana.

PART ONE

Freedom versus Parliament

CHAPTER 2

Argument: The case for a People's Bill of Rights [1]

LORD JENKINS OF HILLHEAD

In the past decade, we have passed through some major centenaries in three of the principal Western countries. 1987 was the 200th anniversary of the United States Constitution, the first definition and enactment of universal and inalienable individual rights. The French followed suit in 1791, although the bicentenial of the Declaration of the Rights of Man was not much celebrated in 1991, mainly because the Revolution which paved the way to it had been so exhaustively – and exhaustingly and expensively – commemorated in July 1989, that there was not much energy or money left for a fresh round. In the meantime, since the American bicentenary, the 300th anniversary of the English Bill of Rights had passed in 1988. This was not much marked either, partly because, in contrast to the French, any retrospective fervour was reserved for the following year and the tercentenary of the so-called Glorious Revolution.

But this was not regarded as very glorious in Scotland (still less so in Ireland), and even in England it was well past the heyday of the Whig historians, from Macaulay to his great-nephew G. M. Trevelyan, for whom it was the epitome of good (he even had 1689 as his Cambridge telephone number). 1688 never had this degree of resonance – and rightly so – for the English Bill of Rights was not comparable as a proclamation of the rights of the individual with either the American Constitution or the French Declaration of the Rights of Man. Typically and importantly it was essentially about the rights of Parliament against the Crown and not about the protection of individuals against the Crown, still less against Parliament, except for some vague declaration against arbitrary and excessive punishment.

So much for anniversaries. Let me now outline my view of the British tradition of human rights, which I describe as empirical and insufficient. Essentially it is Dicey's dogma. A. V. Dicey, Professor of Law at Oxford for 30 years and Fellow of All Souls, was the dominant constitutional pundit of late Victorian and Edwardian Britain. He was partnered by Sir William Anson, Warden of All Souls and MP for Oxford University, but Dicey was the more certain and more the fount of doctrine. In 1885 he proclaimed 'the one fundamental dogma of English constitutional law' to be 'the absolute legislative sovereignty or despotism of the Crown in Parliament': *constitutional* because it required the enactment of the two Houses of Parliament as well as the formal topping out of the

Royal Assent, but *despotic* because, once made, no law was subject to any subsequent challenge. The principle of parliamentary sovereignty means that Parliament has the right to make or unmake any law whatsoever.

Dicey explicitly treated all law as equal. For some reason or other he chose the Dentists Act, then a fairly recently enacted piece of minor legislation, as his 'poorest he that is in England' (to quote Colonel Rainborough of the Levellers) on which to found his theory of equal laws, and set it out in a famous passage:

There are indeed important statutes, such as the Act embodying the Treaty of Union with Scotland, with which it would be political madness to tamper gratuitously; there are utterly unimportant statutes, such for example, as the Dentists Act, 1878, which may be repealed or modified at the pleasure or caprice of Parliament; but neither the Act of Union with Scotland nor the Dentists Act ... has more claim than the other to be considered a supreme law. Each embodies the will of the sovereign legislative power; each can be legally altered or repealed by Parliament; neither tests the validity of the other. Should the Dentists Act ... unfortunately contravene the terms of the Act of Union, the Act of Union would be *pro tanto* repealed, but no judge would dream of maintaining that the Dentists Act was thereby rendered invalid or unconstitutional. The one fundamental dogma of English constitutional law is the absolute legislative sovereignty or despotism of the King in Parliament.

(Dicey 1959: 145)

It should be said that this Dicey dogma was never quite as widely and freely accepted by judicial and political opinion north of the border as it was in England, and the reason for this is obvious. If the English were prepared to see Magna Carta, the Bill of Rights, the Act of Union with Scotland, the Protestant Succession and the Petition of Rights put on a par with the Dentists Bill, there was less enthusiasm in Scotland for putting the Act of Union in the same category. If the Union was a takeover of one country by another it was perfectly logical that the terms should be subject to subsequent variation by the ordinary processes of the combined parliament. But if it was a voluntary coming together of two countries of equal legal status, even if not of equal size and power, then the terms on which it was done were bound to have some special status above that of the Dentists Act. Hence the greater coolness towards Dicey's doctrine in Scotland. But even in Scotland there was not much direct challenge to it for the best part of three-quarters of a century after its enunciation.

Dicey's second and less interesting (because more trite) constitutional doctrine was the supremacy of the law and the obligation upon everybody to obey it. Curiously enough however he himself reneged on that at the time of the third Home Rule Bill and the Ulster crisis of 1912–14. So partisan a Unionist was he that he supported all the illegal threats and published a pamphlet entitled *A Fool's Paradise*.

Nevertheless the influence of his first doctrine survived his betrayal of his second and ran on to provide much of the basis for Britain's traditional hostility to international law-making bodies, whether they be the European Community, the Council of Europe or the United Nations. Hence there has persisted the unwillingness to incorporate the European Convention on Human Rights (which is of course a Council of Europe, Strasbourg-based and not a European Community, Brussels- or Luxembourg-based system) into British law. This is despite the fact that, since the right of individual petition for British citizens came to be allowed in the late 1960s, British governments have been forced to recognise the jurisdiction of the Strasbourg Court. Britain has indeed provided a large bulk of the cases and the British government has established the record for the number of times it has been found against (with the verdict going in favour of its citizens) in the Court. It would have been not only much cheaper, for the taxpayer as well as the litigant, but also less humiliating, to have incorporated the Convention into our domestic law and settled the matters in our own courts. But this would mean edging towards a supreme, constitutional and overriding law of the land.

With us the law of the constitution, the rules which in other countries naturally form part of a constitutional code, are *not the source, but the consequence* of the rights of individuals as defined and enforced in the courts.

Dicey separates law from morality. 'Law is concerned with acts, morality with character.' He does however recognise that law must reflect public opinion but only because it would be impossible otherwise to enforce obedience to the law. Furthermore the main safeguards against the abuse of power by the government in Parliament are essentially conventions and not legally enforceable. These constitutional conventions he saw as dependent upon:

1. The sense of fair play of ministers and civil servants;
2. The vigilance of the opposition and individual MPs;
3. The influence of the free press, and of an informed public opinion;
4. The periodic opportunity to change the government through free and secret elections.

Under Dicey's interpretation of the constitution, which is still essentially our present system, the role of an independent and impartial judiciary is of course important in interpreting and applying the common law and in deciding where state power ends and the rights of individuals begin. But in the protection of human rights, however, the role of British judges is circumscribed both by the subordinate role which the courts are perceived to enjoy in relation to the all-powerful role of the legislature and, until recently at least, public support for the narrowness of the judicial mandate.

In sharp contrast with the system in the United States and most of our European neighbours, our present system is based on a philosophy which is sceptical of:

1. The democratic credentials of the judiciary and the competence of judges to act as law-makers or to interpret sufficiently independently controversial issues of policy;
2. The validity of written constitutions (or international conventions).

In the last decade or so the accepted British wisdom has been subject to two contrary pulls. On the one hand the too frequent and damaging arraignment of the British government before the Strasbourg Court has led to increasing pressure not only for incorporation of the Human Rights Convention in British law but also for a Bill of Rights and a move towards some fundamental constitutional law and guarantees of rights based on more than unwritten habits and hopes. On the other hand the reputation of the judiciary (for which this would necessarily involve a greater and more sensitive role) has undoubtedly suffered from the series of major miscarriages of justice and from the inability of the Court of Criminal Appeal and in particular the former Lord Chief Justice of England to consider that he might be mistaken. There have however been considerable changes of personnel recently; and whether more civil and still higher tribunals, which like the United States Supreme Court would be more concerned in the interpretation of a constitutional law, should have visited upon them the sins of the Court of Criminal Appeal is open to question.

And there is the third factor: that adherence to Dicey's dogma not only increasingly isolates Britain in this respect from nearly every other Western democracy, but also makes it difficult for us to be a fully participating member of the international community. It has also thrown up anomalies which reveal worrying lacunae in the protection of the individual against the state. These relate to such disparate subjects as prisoners' rights and to the continuing ability of the government to exclude those in Crown employment both from some civil rights of their own and from answerability before the normal processes of law in their dealings with the public.

It must be made clear that the arguments in favour of a modern Bill of Rights or the enshrinement in the constitution of a legally enforceable Citizen Rights' Bill is far from assuming that this guarantees the pursuit by a government of a humane and liberal policy. There are no fewer than 24 British Commonwealth countries which have incorporated the Strasbourg Convention in their independence constitutions. No one would suggest however that in the majority of these countries human rights are in practice better secured than in Britain and New Zealand, the two Commonwealth countries which conspicuously do not have written and general declarations of rights. But that is not the point. A high respect for individual liberty is in practice, regrettably but realistically, mostly a function of relatively rich, pluralistic Western democracies. India provides a massive semi-exception to the rule. It has shown that free if dangerous elections and a choice of parties do not need the cushion of a high average national income. But it remains very much an exception, and I do not think that even there the rights of the citizen against, say, arbitrary arrest are well secured. Most of the rest of Asia and most of Africa are effectively one party states with the liberty of the individual much more dependent upon the whim of those in charge of that party than upon any fine declarations in the constitution. The true comparison is not therefore between Britain, without any written protection of individual rights, and, say, Ghana, with a resonant preamble to its declaration of independence. The true comparison is between Britain with its empirical 'muddling through' approach and an equally advanced Western democracy, whether in Europe or the United States, which does have certain built-in constitutional safeguards for the individual. In that perspective, the records of the Strasbourg Court strongly suggest that human rights are at somewhat greater risk under the British system.

To illustrate further the conflict between the British tradition and the continental, and indeed between an insular and an international approach to law, it is worth looking back to 1950. That was the year when the European Convention on Human Rights was going through the pangs which preceded its birth in 1951. The now published Cabinet and other state papers show precisely how ambivalent – if not positively hostile – certain of our senior politicians were to this creature of the Council of Europe (which was described by Ernest Bevin in 1951 as 'the Council's only positive achievement to date'). It is made a more striking illustration of the persistence of Dicey's dogma and the legal insularity which it bred by the fact that several of the politicians whose somewhat obscurantist remarks I am about to quote were amongst those for whom at the time and subsequently I felt considerable admiration and/or affection. The position was also made more ironic by the part played within the Council of Europe by British lawyers in the drafting of the Convention.

When it came before the Consultative Assembly at Strasbourg, leading British proponents of the Convention included two future Conservative Prime Ministers, Churchill and Macmillan, Lord Layton for the Liberals, and a somewhat less enthusiastic Sir Lynn (later Lord Justice) Ungoed-Thomas for Labour. Within the Attlee Government, the Foreign Secretary, Ernest Bevin, already in failing health, supported the project, which was looked upon even more enthusiastically by his Minister of State, Kenneth Younger. Equally, if not more, passionate in their opposition were the Lord Chancellor Earl Jowitt, the Colonial Secretary James Griffiths, and the Chancellor of the Exchequer Sir Stafford Cripps.

Their principal objections were to the proposed right of individuals and others to petition the European Commission on Human Rights alleging violations of the Convention by the United Kingdom and to the acceptance of the jurisdiction of the European Court of Human Rights in such cases. At this stage, it should be noted, the draft Convention made the acceptance of the proposed right of individual petition mandatory rather than optional, although it later became optional with the government of a member state able to decide whether or not it wished its citizens to have this right. The United Kingdom government decided that it did not until 1967.

When in July 1950 Kenneth Younger circulated a memorandum recommending adoption of the Convention as it then was drafted, the Colonial Secretary, in reply, circulated his own memorandum objecting to the right of individual petition. His prime argument against the proposal was that it was 'likely to cause considerable misunderstanding and political unsettlement in many Colonial territories . . . where . . . the bulk of the people were still politically immature'. His fear, so he argued, was that the right of petition to an international body would suggest to these colonies either that the ultimate authority lay not in the Crown, as they had been taught to believe by their colonial masters, or that there was 'more than one ultimate authority'. And he concluded: 'This confusion would undoubtedly be exploited by extremist politicians in order to undermine the authority of the Colonial Government concerned. Loyalty would be shaken: administration would be made more difficult and agitation more easy.' King George III, when dealing with the North American colonists, could not have expressed it better.

Cripps, on the other hand, at one of the Cabinet meetings which discussed the matter, objected on the grounds that a government committed to a policy of planning could not ratify the Convention as drafted. For example, the Article on powers of entry into private premises was inconsistent with the powers of economic control which were essential to the operation of a planned economy. From the point of view of the judiciary, represented by the Lord Chancellor, the objection was that if individuals had a right to take alleged infractions from British courts to a European court, the effect on our judicial system might be undermining. Furthermore it was intolerable that the code of common law, built up over many years, should be made subject to review by an international court administrating no defined system of law.

The Foreign Secretary, absent (in Strasbourg appropriately enough) from the Cabinet meeting which agreed to instruct him to persuade the Committee of Ministers to send back the draft Convention for reconsideration by member governments, responded by suggesting that the right of individual petition should be made optional – a suggestion to which the Prime Minister gratefully clung.

Justifying the Cabinet decision opposing the right of individual petition, the Lord Chancellor wrote: 'We were not prepared, just to encourage our European friends, to jeopardise our whole system of law . . . in favour of some half-baked scheme to be administered by some unknown court.'

The Committee of Ministers accepted the British proposal to make both the right of individual petition and also the Court's jurisdiction optional, thus seriously weakening the original draft.

In spite of these concessions, the Lord Chancellor continued to fulminate against the Convention. It was eventually agreed by Cabinet that the Foreign Secretary could continue to support the draft Convention on the clear understanding that the British government could not accept:

1. The right of individual petition;
2. The proposed European Court of Human Rights;
3. Provisions which included the rights relating to property, free choice of education and political freedom.

This was a little like agreeing to support Chelsea Football Club provided that they were not allowed to score any goals. And it also set a pattern which has been the harbinger of every subsequent British approach to Europe: in, but not far in, like a doorstep caller on a cold January day, who will neither come in and allow the door to be closed, nor go away, thereby driving those fully inside demented with cold and frustration.

The Convention was eventually signed in this watered-down state to satisfy British objections on 4 November 1950. Ironically, and not a little sardonically, the British Government was then the first member state to ratify it – on 8 March 1951. There was of course no acceptance of the right to petition or of the Court's jurisdiction; nor was there any legislation to alter domestic law, still less to incorporate the rights and freedoms of the Convention into United Kingdom law. And this last deficiency, although not the others, still persists.

Since those in many ways far-off days (although they are well within the adult memory of many of us), there has been a significant sea-change in attitudes among people in Britain towards our constitutional arrangements. Until that time they were considered as a fine and enviable example of a flexible and adaptable method of governing a modern democracy with the consent of the governed and with freedom for the individual under the law. Indeed we were all taught – and mostly tended to believe in – the virtue of *not* having a written constitution.

What then has gradually changed people's attitudes in the second half of this century, and particularly in the last 15 years or so? Specifically, why are more and more people now convinced that our so-called empirical tradition is not adequate in the protection of the individual's rights?

First of all, the make-up of the nation has changed considerably. The best conditions for the working of the system were those of Victorian Britain: a society self-satisfied in its homogeneity and insularity, relatively rich, and presiding confidently over a vast empire. Now many of those areas of the law which are now being questioned directly affect the lives of minority groups who either in the past did not live in the United Kingdom in any significant numbers, or who were not organised to think of themselves as being entitled to any rights. These groups included the ethnic minorities; and indeed women who, though never a minority, were denied equal rights at work and elsewhere; also groups such as homosexuals who, even when no longer outlawed, found themselves discriminated against within the law.

It was generally believed till recently that the 'natural and inalienable' or 'fundamental' rights for all written into the constitution in post-revolutionary France or the United States two hundred years ago were simply not a necessary part of our system. Such rights were surely protected more effectively by traditional methods from the vigilance of MPs, through the integrity of skilled and dedicated administrators, to an independent judiciary.

I began to feel considerable doubts about this during my second period as Home Secretary from 1974–76. Towards the end of this I circulated a Green Paper on possible legislation on Human Rights, with particular reference to the European Convention. In the foreword to that Green Paper I cautiously wrote:

Respect for individual freedom and for the rights of the citizen against the State is central to our constitutional traditions. We rightly attach great importance to the way in which this tradition is expressed in our political and legal institutions; and the extent of the protection afforded to basic rights in this country today can indeed stand comparison with the standard set in earlier periods of our own history or by the general practice of other States. Nevertheless we cannot afford to take for granted the protection of our liberties. It is not enough that our freedoms have merely survived the assaults made on them. We need constantly to question their ability to withstand new and more subtle stresses. ... There has recently been growing public debate about the adequacy of existing safeguards for fundamental human rights and freedoms.

(Home Office 1976)

In the event the Green Paper, which leant heavily towards incorporation of the European Convention in our own law or of domestic enactment, though useful as a discussion document, did not spawn any legislation. I myself left the Home Office and the Government in September of that year to become President of the European Commission and nothing more was done about the subject.

Since then public concern about 'the adequacy of existing safeguards for fundamental human rights and freedoms' has swollen. Over the Thatcherite decade, in my view, it multiplied itself several times. It is part of a wider scepticism about the constitutional and institutional arrangements which, almost uniquely in the world, have held us in a constricting rigidity for a hundred years and more.

The doctrine of the unlimited power of a temporary majority in Parliament, however small maybe the minority in the country on which it is based, and however subservient to the executive it mostly is, has encouraged a form of government which is the most secretive in the Western world and, apart from France, the most centralised as well. And France is currently making strenuous efforts to decentralise itself. Neither of these characteristics produces notable feats of administrative efficiency, and certainly do not lead to the promotion of the individual's rights against or within the state.

Let me divert to consider the somewhat linked and undoubtedly important secrecy issue. To a greater degree than in any other democracy, secrecy is endemic in our government system. It affects the way we are governed in a variety of adverse ways:

1. Ordinary citizens, or interest groups working on their behalf, are often denied access to information on which Whitehall decisions have been based.
2. Public servants cannot be properly held to account.
3. Parliament itself is denied access to so-called secret information and therefore inevitably works less effectively on behalf of the electorate than it should.
4. Without full access to the facts, justice cannot be seen to be done.
5. Vested interests, particularly those who know how the system works, can, unseen by the public eye, apply secret pressure to obtain decisions beneficial to the interests which they represent.

But above all it produces the unacceptable hypocrisy of leaks from the top, accepted as part of the political game, and prosecution of those lower down in the bureaucratic hierarchy.

Secrecy extends beyond Whitehall. It has been endemic in the public utilities, whether nationalised or privatised. According to the Royal Commission on Environmental Pollution, it is a major block to the elimination of pollution in the United Kingdom. It is also a major block, as emerged in 1992, to making a true comparison between the relative costs of coal, gas and nuclear power for generating electricity. The nuclear energy industry is highly protected by secrecy: almost every detail about accidents, as well as about costs, has to be prised out rather than being published.

On the issues of secrecy and human rights alike successive governments of both governing parties have failed even to attempt to bring Britain into line with other civilised nations. There is a belief, founded on arrogance mixed with complacency, that, in spite of strong evidence to the contrary, all is well in the British constitutional condition. Every day now we have a couple of elaborate introductions into the House of Lords with ancient rites and semi-feudal formulas (mostly invented or re-invented in the nineteenth century, I suspect). Such traditions can be an agreeable icing on the cake, but not a substitute for constitutional arrangements which suit our needs today rather than those of static hierarchical nineteenth century Britain which, as the richest of countries and head of a world-wide empire, could afford eccentricities which are not now viable.

Note

1 The argument of this chapter was originally presented by Lord Jenkins at Glasgow University under the title 'Human rights: is the British empirical tradition enough?', 29.10.92.

References

Dicey, A. V. (1959) *An Introduction to the Study of the Law of the Constitution*, 10th edition, London: Macmillan

Home Office (1976) Green Paper, *Legislation on Human Rights with Particular Reference to the European Convention*, June, London: HMSO for Home Office.

CHAPTER THREE

Opinions: Public opposition to parliamentary sovereignty

WILLIAM L. MILLER, ANNIS MAY TIMPSON AND
MICHAEL LESSNOFF

Lord Jenkins makes a powerful case for a more formal, legal, constitutional framework for protecting human rights in Britain either by enacting a new British Bill of Rights or by incorporating the European Convention on Human Rights into British domestic law. He recognises four principal objections to such a legal framework:

1. There is no problem to be solved since there is greater respect for human rights in Britain than in most other countries in the world.
2. A legal, constitutional framework would conflict with the doctrine of parliamentary sovereignty.
3. It is better to rely on social and political rather than legal protections for human rights: the sense of fair play of ministers, the vigilance of backbench and Opposition MPs, the influence of a free press, and regular, free, secret, elections.
4. A constitutional framework merely shifts powers of discretion from elected, representative and accountable members of parliament to unelected, unrepresentative and unaccountable judges.

But he finds each of these arguments unconvincing.

For him there *is* a problem. He believes that public concern about the adequacy of existing safeguards for fundamental rights and freedoms has 'multiplied itself several times ... over the Thatcherite decade'. While he accepts that respect for human rights is stronger in Britain than in many countries, he argues that Britain's record is weak when compared with other countries that have a similar culture and a similar level of economic development.

He dismisses the doctrine of parliamentary sovereignty as 'the doctrine of unlimited power of a temporary majority in Parliament'. He recalls that some Scots have never accepted the English doctrine of parliamentary sovereignty and have always drawn a distinction between constitutional law such as the 1707 Act of Union and ordinary law such as the 1878 Dentists Act – even if Dicey did not.

He disposes of the third argument – that we can safely rely upon the 'sense of fair play of ministers' – by exposing the mentality of British Cabinet ministers, whose sense of fair play is conditioned as much by their instinct for order as their devotion to liberty. He could no doubt have expanded upon the many factors that curtail the vigilance of backbench MPs or restrict the freedom of the press.

Finally he admits that the recent behaviour of British judges does not inspire much confidence in their competence, let alone their impartiality or their commitment to human rights, though he hopes that recent changes in personnel may improve matters. He needs to be optimistic. Radicals and reformers, as well as revolutionaries, have had good reasons to view British courts and judges with suspicion. Far too often they have given way to hysteria and acted as instruments of repression. The Labour Party Manifesto for the 1910 election attacked the Osborne Judgement as 'only the latest example of Judge-made Law, from which you have already suffered so much'. Under a doctrine of sovereignty, whether monarchical or parliamentary, the law is bound to be an instrument of state power rather than a bulwark against it, if only because the state has absolute power to change the law. But times are changing. Perhaps we are now ready to be governed by an American-style 'government of laws not of men'. And European ideas, derived from recent experience of a new supra-national Europe, rather than the traditional culture of old European nation states, may also have had an impact on British political culture.

Let us see whether the public now believe there is a problem of human rights in Britain, whether they accept the doctrine of parliamentary sovereignty, whether they support the entrenchment of a constitutional Bill of Rights and whether they have sufficient confidence in judges and courts to back them against our elected parliament.

Is there a problem of human rights in Britain?

The proper international comparison, according to Lord Jenkins, is not with the Third World but with other economically advanced Western democracies. In our public opinion survey we asked whether 'on the whole, the rights and liberties enjoyed by British citizens are [greater/less] than those enjoyed by people who live in [America/West European countries like France and Germany/Scandinavian countries like Norway, Denmark or Sweden]?'. This question came in six different forms depending first, upon whether it used the word *greater* or *less*, and second, upon which of the three different international comparisons it used.[1] The six different forms were assigned randomly to interviews and each respondent was asked simply to agree or disagree with the proposition as put to them.

We were able to gauge popular perceptions of Britain's relative respect for human rights by averaging the percentage who agreed that rights were *greater* in Britain than elsewhere with the percentage who disagreed that they were *less* than in other countries. Our

Table 3.1   **International comparisons**

	General public	Local politicians
% agree rights are greater in Britain (or disagree that they are less) than in:		
America	60	58
Western Europe	55	49
Scandinavia	38	34

Table 3.2   **Perceived trends**

	General public	Local politicians
% agree British governments are reducing citizens' rights	61	63
% agree British governments are increasing citizens' rights	57	41

results suggest that while Britain compares well, in the public imagination, with America, it comes out badly in comparison with Scandinavia and just about as well as Western Europe. It seems therefore that the British public have a more complex, and perhaps a little more favourable, view of Britain's record than Lord Jenkins, though our sample of local politicians was slightly more critical than the general public. Interestingly, our results suggest that Britons may include perceptions of a country's welfare system in their assessment of its record on human rights.

Lord Jenkins claimed that British rights and liberties had been diminished 'during the Thatcherite decade'. We asked whether 'on balance, British governments have been [reducing/increasing] the rights and liberties of British citizens in recent years?'. Again the two forms of the question were randomly assigned to interviews, and each respondent was asked merely to agree or disagree with the statement as put to them. This proved an unusually difficult question for the general public: a majority agreed with the proposition whichever way it was put: 61 per cent agreed that British governments had been *reducing* rights and 57 per cent agreed they had been *increasing* them. This pattern suggests that the general public's perception of trends was unclear, weakly held, and at the mercy of their natural wish to be agreeable to our interviewers.

Politicians, however, had clear views: 63 per cent agreed that British governments were reducing citizens' rights and only 41 per cent agreed that they were increasing citizens' rights. So Lord Jenkins' perception was shared by local political leaders. Since the question explicitly mentioned government behaviour as well as human rights it naturally evoked a partisan response which was especially marked amongst the politicians. Labour, Liberal and

Scottish Nationalist group leaders were even more critical than their voters of the government's track record on human rights while Conservative group leaders applauded their government's record even more than Conservative voters. But partisanship was not everything: even amongst Conservatives a fifth of their group leaders and a third of their voters were critical of their own government's record.

Our survey suggests that public criticism of Britain's record on citizens' rights is not solely aimed at government. We found a more general and widespread feeling that too little had been done to ensure equal rights in Britain. We asked whether 'we have [gone too far/not gone far enough] in pushing equal rights in this country?'. Let us take agreement with 'not gone far enough' or disagreement with 'gone too far' as an index of support for more equal rights. On that basis three-quarters felt we should push further for equal rights in Britain. For them, there was a problem.

The perception is significant, not least because as Lord Jenkins notes, 'the make up of the nation has changed' considerably since the Second World War and as a result both new and recently mobilised groups of citizens have become more conscious of discrimination in their daily lives. We tested consciousness of discrimination directly by asking whether people had personal experience of being 'discriminated against in some important matter on grounds of sex, race, ethnic background, religion, age, disability or political beliefs'. The question was designed to exclude the minor irritations of social life and focus upon significant discrimination. Just over a quarter of the general public alleged discrimination.

Those who had felt discrimination were asked to identify the main grounds for that discrimination and the main culprit. Obviously that question format prevents any discussion of multiple discrimination – either on multiple grounds (e.g. race and gender) or by multiple culprits (e.g. police and employers). But it has the advantage of identifying the grounds and the culprit who seemed most significant to the victim. Few blamed government or its agents: most blamed employers or just 'other people' with whom they came into contact. Substantial numbers alleged discrimination on grounds of age and gender and, within Scotland, religion. Much to our surprise, political leaders claimed to have suffered more discrimination than the public at large, mainly because so many of them claimed to have suffered political discrimination and the politicians, unlike the public, did blame government officials as well as employers and others.

Different sections of the public complained of particular forms of discrimination: women complained particularly of gender discrimination, the young and old complained particularly of age discrimination, Roman Catholics particularly of religious discrimination, though to a large extent one complaint substituted for

Table 3.3 **Discrimination**

	General public	Local politicians
% agree we have not gone far enough (or disagree we have gone too far) in pushing equal rights in this country	73	73
% personally felt discrimination	28	41
Discrimination was by:		
employer	58	48
police	6	2
local or national government official	8	20
other people	28	30

Table 3.4 **Helpful government**

	General public	Local politicians
% found local councillor helpful	71	92
% found council offices helpful	66	95
% found MP helpful	74	82
% found government department helpful	70	72

Note:
% of those who had made contact and expressed a view about helpfulness.

another. Thus women complained very much more than men about gender discrimination but much less than men about racial, religious and political discrimination.

Although our results indicate that there is a degree of concern about the limited protection of citizens' rights in Britain, we did not find that this amounted to a crisis in the relationship between citizens and the state. There was general concern about rights and some, though very much less, personal experience of discrimination. But, politicians apart, government itself was not regarded as the main culprit. Indeed, when people came into personal contact with government or its agents they usually found both its elected and unelected officials helpful.

We asked whether people had ever personally contacted a local councillor, council offices, a Member of Parliament, or an office of a central government department and whether 'on balance you found them helpful or unhelpful?'. On average 70 per cent of the general public found such contacts helpful. Not surprisingly, over 92 per cent of senior local government politicians found contacts with other people in local government helpful, though they found central government offices no more helpful than did the general public and MPs only a little more so. Undoubtedly governors, at

Table 3.5   **Health services and police**

	General public	Local politicians
% satisfied with NHS treatment	89	94
% found police courteous	81	86
% found police helpful	68	81
% agree police protect rather than harm liberties (or disagree police do more to harm than protect)	75	82

whatever level, find their own government machine particularly helpful. Nonetheless the important point is that between two-thirds and three-quarters of the general public also found a variety of personal contacts with government helpful.

We examined the relationship between citizens and the state further by asking people about their experiences of dealing with the National Health Service and the police. In the first case we inquired of respondents whether 'in the last few years you, or anyone in your household received treatment at an NHS hospital' and, if so, whether they were 'satisfied or dissatisfied' with the service provided. In this case, the response was very positive: almost nine-tenths of our respondents were satisfied with their NHS treatment.

Although their relationship with the police was not as positive, our survey showed that the majority found any contact they had with the police to be satisfactory. We asked whether people had 'personally been stopped and interviewed by the police about a traffic violation or anything else' and, if so, whether on balance the police had behaved 'courteously or rudely'; whether they had 'personally ever been the victim of a crime such as having your house broken into, your car stolen, or being assaulted' and, if so, whether on balance the police had been 'helpful or unhelpful'. Over two-thirds of the public had found the police helpful and four-fifths had found them courteous. The figures were even higher amongst politicians. Of course, it is also true that one-fifth of the public found the police rude and some of that fifth may have found police conduct much worse than rude. Personal contact with agents of government proves helpful to the majority of the public but certainly not to everyone.

As with equal rights and personal experience of discrimination, these questions about direct personal experience were complemented with a broader question about the extent to which people felt the police either protected or harmed their liberties. We asked whether: 'On the whole, the police [do more to harm our liberties than to protect them/protect our liberties more than they harm them]?'. As usual, each form of words was used in a randomly selected half of the sample. In this case, the wording made little difference: roughly three-quarters of the public disagreed with the first version and agreed with the second, that is, three-quarters felt the police did more to protect than to harm our liberties. Amongst politicians, over four-fifths felt so. General perceptions therefore mirrored personal experience: something less than complete satisfaction but certainly not a crisis of relations between citizen and state.

The doctrine of parliamentary sovereignty

Lord Jenkins dismissed the doctrine of parliamentary sovereignty as just another name for what Lord Hailsham has christened an 'elective dictatorship'. We found strong support for his position. Throughout Britain there was almost universal agreement with the proposition that 'constitutional checks and balances are important to make sure that a government doesn't become too dictatorial and ignore other viewpoints': 96 per cent of the general public and 98 per cent of the politicians we surveyed agreed with this statement.

Lord Jenkins noted that some Scots, perhaps many, had never accepted what is a distinctively English, rather than British, doctrine. Few Scots, of course, have a sound grasp of constitutional law or even of Scottish history. The few who do make the headlines and make the nation appear more distinctive than it is, but the distinctive are not necessarily the typical. We found nothing distinctive about Scottish public opinion on the need for constitutional checks and balances. On the other hand, checks and balances are an American rather than an English notion, fundamentally at odds with any notion of unlimited sovereignty. The surprise is not that the Scots failed to reject the notion of parliamentary sovereignty (they did reject it) but that the English also rejected it.

However when we put the proposition the other way round we found a large majority apparently willing to support the principle of government prerogative and discretion: 79 per cent of the British public (and only slightly less in Scotland) agreed that 'it is important for a government to be able to take decisive action without looking over its shoulder all the time'. Nonetheless, there was much less than universal support for this principle, and evidence that some of that support was conditional. No one has much difficulty accepting decisive government when it acts in a way that they approve. The issue only becomes acute when government does something of which they disapprove. So we asked: 'suppose Parliament passed a law you considered unjust, immoral or cruel. Would you still be morally bound to obey it?'. Those, like Dicey, who accept the unlimited sovereignty of Parliament would have to agree. Lord Jenkins described this doctrine of obedience to an unjust law as Dicey's 'second constitutional doctrine'. In practice many others might obey such a law under duress, fearful of the

Table 3.6 **Parliamentary sovereignty**

	General public	Local politicians
% agree importance of constitutional checks and balances	96	98
% agree importance of decisive government	79	72
% feel morally bound to obey unjust law passed by Parliament	51	66
% who feel important issues should be decided by referendum rather than by Parliament	64	33

penalties of disobedience, but compliance under coercion does not signify acceptance of sovereignty.

Half, but only half, the general public agreed they would be morally bound to obey such a law. Politicians were more liberal than the public on most aspects of citizens' rights, but not on their moral duty to obey Parliament: two-thirds felt morally bound to obey unjust laws. Realistically, much might depend upon the particular nature of a law. There are degrees of injustice and immorality. No doubt the percentages who feel a moral duty to obey an unjust law would vary with their perception of the degree of injustice. As Lord Jenkins noted, Dicey himself did not adhere to his own doctrine of obedience when faced with the Irish issue. Nonetheless there seems to be a large body of public opinion, though significantly less in political circles, which simply does not accept the principle of Parliament's sovereign right to pass whatever legislation it thinks fit. Support for decisive government is not support for unlimited government and the principle of constitutional checks is so universal as to be part of our common culture.

Indeed public opposition to parliamentary prerogative goes further: two-thirds of the public – though only one-third of politicians – believe that important issues should be decided by the people themselves, by referendums, rather than by Parliament. We asked whether: '[Important political issues are too complex to be decided by everyone voting in a referendum and should be left to Parliament to decide / It would be better to let the people decide important political issues by everyone voting in a referendum rather than leaving them to Parliament as at present]?'. Irrespective of which way the proposition was put, the public came down decisively in favour of referendums and the politicians equally decisively against. Perhaps local politicians have a deeper understanding of the nature of political issues. Perhaps they have a degree of empathy for their parliamentary counterparts. But this result certainly reveals a lack of deference amongst the general public towards the wisdom and authority of Parliament.

Table 3.7 **Trust in politicians**

	General public	Local politicians
% trust most people	90	97
% trust politicians	33	58

Alternative checks and balances

While the American Revolutionaries devised a complex system of legal and constitutional checks and balances to put restraints on arbitrary government, English traditionalists like Dicey preferred to rely upon purely informal and political mechanisms: the government's sense of fair play, the vigilance of backbench MPs, routine elections and the influence of a free press.

But unlike Dicey, the public does not trust politicians. We asked whether: 'most politicians can be trusted to do what they think is best for the country?'. It was a one-sided question. If that produced any bias it should have *inflated* the degree of trust in politicians. The question was rather kind therefore – indeed perhaps too kind – to politicians. Elsewhere in the interview we inserted another question, designed to calibrate this first one. We asked: 'generally speaking, would you say that most people you come into contact with are trustworthy or untrustworthy?'.

Although 90 per cent of the general public felt that most people they met were trustworthy, only 33 per cent felt they could trust politicians. Politicians had a rosier view of human nature, or perhaps more fortunate personal experiences: 97 per cent felt that most people they met were trustworthy but only 58 per cent felt they could trust (other) politicians. So even politicians were ambivalent about the trustworthiness of other politicians, and a large majority of the public simply distrusted them. Dicey's view is not representative of the electorate today if, indeed, it ever was.

We can also measure the extent of public confidence in some of the other informal checks upon which Dicey relied. We asked respondents to give a 'mark out of 10 for how much you feel citizens' rights and liberties are protected by' 17 different potential safeguards for citizens' liberties. These included a proposed 'Bill of Rights, passed by Parliament, and enforced by the courts', 'backbench MPs in Parliament', and three elements of the press – 'tabloid newspapers like the [Sun/Daily Mirror]', 'quality newspapers like the [Guardian/Telegraph]', and 'television'. The list also included 'local government councils' which ought to have won high marks from *local* politicians at least.

Among both public and politicians a constitutional Bill of Rights scored significantly higher than either backbench MPs or the press.

Table 3.8   **Public evaluations of alternative protectors of rights**

	General public	Local politicians
% *who give 6 or more marks out of 10 for protecting citizens' rights to:*		
a Bill of Rights	73	81
backbench MPs	54	72
television	64	69
the quality press	66	74
the tabloid press	24	23
local government councils	52	76

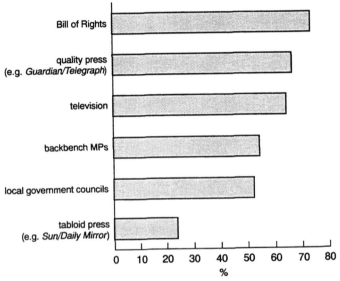

Figure 3.1   Effective protectors of citizens' rights (% of public giving clear pass)

Let us focus on the percentage who awarded an item more than a bare pass, that is, at least 6 marks out of 10. Among the public, a Bill of Rights got a clear pass mark from 73 per cent, backbench MPs from only 54 per cent, and local government councils from only 52 per cent. Local politicians naturally had a good opinion of their own councils, but they had an even better opinion of a Bill of Rights: 83 per cent gave a clear pass to a Bill of Rights, 76 per cent to local government councils and only 72 per cent to backbench MPs. No one placed much reliance on the tabloid press to defend citizens' rights and liberties. Politicians rated television and the quality press about as effective as backbenchers and local councils while the public rated them more highly. But even television and the quality press got about 10 per cent less than a Bill of Rights. A

Table 3.9   **Public perceptions of courts and judges**

	General public	Local politicians
% who give 6 or more marks out of 10 for protecting citizens' rights to:		
British courts	70	70
European courts	65	73
% who give 6 or more marks out of 10 for fairness and impartiality to British judges	60	68

century ago, Dicey may have felt that political checks were more effective than constitutional ones, but neither public nor politicians feel that now.

Unelected, unrepresentative and unaccountable

The final argument against a formal, legal, constitutional framework for the protection of rights is that it would only shift power from elected, representative and accountable politicians to unelected, unrepresentative and unaccountable judges. Consequently some people may support the idea of constitutional checks and balances in the abstract, but refuse to accept it in practice because they do not trust the courts.

Despite long-standing suspicions, reinforced by a series of recent miscarriages of justice, public confidence in British courts and judges was surprisingly high: 70 per cent gave British courts a clear pass mark (6 or more out of ten) for 'protecting citizens' rights and liberties' – far less than 100 per cent certainly, but still a comparatively good score. Rather fewer, particularly among the general public, gave judges a clear pass for 'fairness and impartiality', which seems to indicate more public confidence in juries than judges. The right of a jury to acquit, whatever the weight of evidence in favour of the Crown, was established in a series of celebrated English 'free speech' cases during the seventeenth and eighteenth century (Hurwitt and Thornton 1989: 30), and juries have recently reaffirmed their role as defenders of the citizen against the state in, for example, the 1985 Ponting case (Ewing and Gearty 1990: 143–47). European courts were rated about the same as British courts and higher than British judges.

But such generalised perceptions of courts and judges are not quite the issue. The critical question is whether Parliament or a court should have the final say in a dispute over citizens' rights. We asked about both British and European courts. First we asked: 'Suppose we had a Constitutional Bill of Rights, as some other countries do. If Parliament passed a law but the courts said it was

Table 3.10   **Should Parliament have the final say?**

	General public	Local politicians
% who say the court should overrule Parliament when the court is:		
a British court enforcing a Bill of Rights	48	36
European Court of Human Rights	55	59

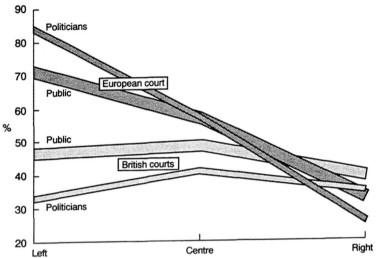

Figure 3.2 *Ideology and parliamentary sovereignty* (% *who back court against Parliament*)

unconstitutional, who should have the final say, Parliament or the courts?'. Although the text was not explicit, the position of this question in the interview and the implication of the wording invited comparison between Parliament and specifically British courts. Then we went on to ask: 'Suppose someone in Britain objects to a law passed by Parliament and takes the case to the European Court of Human Rights. Who should have the final say, the European Court or the British Parliament?'.

A slender majority of the public would give the final say to Parliament rather than British courts, but to the European Court rather than Parliament. Politicians distinguished much more sharply between British and European courts: only 36 per cent would let a British court overrule Parliament, but 59 per cent would let the European Court do so. On that evidence, incorporation of the European Convention on Human Rights into British domestic law as advocated by Lord Jenkins would only be acceptable if the possibility of appeal to courts outside Britain were retained.

Table 3.11 **Ideology and parliamentary sovereignty**

	General public	Local politicians
% who would let a British court overrule Parliament among those who place themselves:		
on the left	47	33
in the centre	49	41
on the right	40	35
% who would let the European Court overrule Parliament among those who place themselves:		
on the left	71	84
in the centre	57	57
on the right	33	26

Support for British courts overruling Parliament was greatest among those who described themselves as being 'in the centre' politically and lower amongst those who placed themselves on the right or on the left – especially amongst left-wing politicians, who clearly remained suspicious of British courts. Ideological differences were not great, however.

By contrast there were very sharp ideological differences in support for the European Court. Among the public, the European Court was backed by over twice as many on the left as on the right; among politicians, it was backed by over three times as many on the left as on the right. Of course the survey took place when a right-wing government had been in power for a decade, which was bound to incline those on the left towards any system of restraint, but the left only gave strong backing to the European Court, not to British courts.

The addition of a supra-national layer to government strikes at the very principle of parliamentary sovereignty. Opposition voters, and more especially opposition politicians, remain suspicious of British courts but are more willing to accept an external, supra-national court, a court which is above, as well as beyond, domestic politics. It is possible, as Lord Jenkins surmises, that if a British Constitutional Court were set up, public opinion would distinguish between that court and other domestic courts. But we suspect a new name, a new remit, and even new personnel would not by themselves be enough to lift such a court above domestic politics. The new Constitutional Court would need to establish a track record for upholding the rights of British citizens against the British government, as the European Court has already done, before public opinion – especially opposition opinion – would accept it as anything more than a creature of British government.

While Lord Jenkins' main concern is to redress the inadequacies of the British constitutional tradition through the introduction of a People's Bill of Rights, it is clear that he also wants to see a more open and accountable style of government in Britain. At the end of his chapter, he notes how the British style of 'muddling through' is expensive, undemocratic and reinforced by the 'secrecy that is endemic to our government system' which 'extends beyond White-hall'. Do the British public share his views on the issue of freedom of information as they appear to do on parliamentary sovereignty? We shall answer this question in Chapter 5. But before we consider what local politicians and the general public feel about access to government information, let us consider the case for being 'economical with the truth'.

Note

1 We shall standardise on the use of square brackets and slashes, [/], to indicate variants of question wording randomly assigned to sub-samples. See Chapter 1 for a full description of our randomised-wording technique.

References

Ewing K. D. and Gearty, C. A. (1990) *Freedom under Thatcher: Civil Liberties in Modern Britain*, Oxford: Oxford University Press.

Hurwitt, M. and Thornton, P. (1989) *Civil Liberty: The Liberty/NCCL Guide*, London: Penguin.

PART TWO

Freedom versus the National Interest

CHAPTER 4

Argument: The case for confidentiality in government [1]

LORD ARMSTRONG OF ILMINSTER

At the start of a chapter on open government, it is clearly appropriate for the writer to declare his credentials and his starting point. What I have to say is based on nearly 40 years in government service, 13 or so at or near the very centre of the government, in 10 Downing Street and in the Cabinet Office, under administrations of both the main political parties: one of the goldfish swimming around in the goldfish-bowl of government. But I am today an elderly superannuated bureaucratic carp, out of that bowl for over five years now, peering into it from outside, gratefully and affectionately but not nostalgically; and my reflections will be tempered by my view of what the bowl now looks like from outside.

The subject of open government and freedom of information has been on the political agenda as a live issue at least since the setting up of the Committee under Lord Franks to review the working of Section 2 of the 1911 Official Secrets Act. The Franks Committee reported in 1972, though legislative action to reform Section 2 had to wait until the late 1980s, after I had retired from the public service, so that I was able to make my maiden speech in the House of Lords in July 1988 in a debate on the White Paper outlining the then government's proposals for replacing Section 2 of the 1911 Act.

That Act was passed by Parliament in a hurry in 1911. The atmosphere at the time when the legislation was introduced is well caught in John Buchan's novel *The Thirty-Nine Steps*. Its main purpose was to extend the protection of the criminal law over information and establishments concerned with military matters and national security which were vulnerable to the threats of espionage from potential enemies. That indeed was the express object of Section 1 of the Act, which still remains in force. But there was another section, Section 2, which had the effect of making *any* unauthorised disclosure of information from inside the government a criminal offence, however serious or trivial the information disclosed.

There was some protection against the abuse of this provision by the authorities: for instance, a prosecution could be brought only with the agreement of the Attorney General, and it could be assumed that the Attorney General would give this agreement only when there was a seriously damaging unauthorised disclosure of information of significant importance and sensitivity. Nonetheless, Section 2 was incorporated in a declaration which all civil servants (but not ministers, though they were and are no less subject to the law of the land) and many people outside the civil service who had access to sensitive government information were required to sign.

Section 2's blanket coverage of all information came to be widely seen as inherently unreasonable and excessively oppressive. Its existence was thought to inhibit people from disclosing information which could be disclosed without causing any damage, and by its very comprehensiveness and lack of specificity to create a general climate of uncertainty about what could or could not be said. More generally, it was seen as a manifestation of an endemic and deplorable attitude of secrecy – or perhaps it would be more accurate to say secretiveness – in government.

Of course it is difficult to defend a statutory provision which in theory at any rate makes it a criminal offence to tell an outsider what is on the menu in the office staff canteen. The reason for making a provision in that form, in an Act of Parliament which was introduced and passed into law in a hurry, was no doubt that it avoided the need to formulate statutory definitions of the types and categories of information to which the sanctions of the criminal law were to be applied, and left as much scope as possible for the exercise of discretion and judgement by reasonable and sensible people in the application of the section in particular cases.

If that was the reason, I must admit to having some sympathy with it. We have seen, since the publication of the Franks Report in 1972, the difficulty of drafting statutory definitions of types and categories of information which will be at once precise and clear enough to stand the strain of scrutiny and argument in courts of law and be generally acceptable to those affected. There were newspaper editors who, privately at any rate, objected to almost any reform of Section 2 on the grounds that their exercise of editorial responsibility and discretion would be fettered by more precisely targeted and therefore more effective legislation: if they were in any doubt whether a particular piece of information was covered by the new provision, they would have to spend time and money on getting legal advice before deciding whether to publish it.

In 1911 it might have seemed more acceptable than it may seem today to rely upon the good sense and reasonableness of those who would be called upon to decide whether to invoke the full apparatus of the criminal law in particular cases. It was, I think, very much in the British tradition of not trying to prescribe precise and detailed statutory rules and definitions but allowing for the development of case law 'broadening down from precedent to precedent'. In this respect the spirit of the times seems to be changing: we appear in this as in other matters to be moving towards a world in which statutory rules and definitions are laid down as precisely and strictly as possible and as comprehensively as is thought necessary, and it is then for the courts of justice in the last analysis to rule on their application in particular cases. No doubt it is all good business for the lawyers.

I have also to say that, however logically indefensible the 'catch-all' nature of the old Section 2 may have been, looking back on the way in which it actually worked, I think that its ill effects were greatly exaggerated. I have honestly to say that I cannot remember any occasion on which I myself felt in practice inhibited by Section 2, or by the Official Secrets Act declaration which I had signed when I became a civil servant, or by the fear of prosecution under Section 2 for prosecutions under Section 2 were extremely rare. If I was inhibited by anything, and no doubt I was, it was not by that. Nor can I say that I detected any significant sense of inhibition on account of Section 2 among the ministers whom I served – of whatever party – or among my fellow civil servants.

There was much force in the analogy by which Section 2 was often characterised: that of the blunderbuss, an elderly, old-fashioned weapon which makes a lot of noise and scatters its shot unpredictably and often ineffectively over a wide field of fire, and is almost as likely to blow up in the shooter's face as to hit the target. It was a museum piece, to which everyone – politicians, civil servants, editors and journalists alike – had become used. However lethal it looked on the shelf, in practice it did not frighten or inhibit any one very much. When the first attempts were made to replace the blunderbuss with an Armalite rifle – a legislative provision which greatly limited but specifically defined the areas of information to be protected and the legal obligations of the various people concerned – it was quickly realised that the new provision was likely to be a great deal more difficult to live with, certainly for the media, than the old.

Moreover, though the replacement of Section 2 has decriminalised disclosure of most government information, save in a few closely defined areas, I do not detect that that has greatly diminished the level of complaints about attitudes of secretiveness in government. That is partly, no doubt, because Section 2 was a symptom rather than a cause of any tendency to secretiveness. But perhaps it is also for what might be called a philosophical reason. Official secrets legislation is not concerned with defining what information should or may be disclosed. It is not even concerned with defining what information should not be disclosed without authority. It is concerned only with defining what information is so important and so sensitive that its protection requires the sanctions of the criminal law. And it is much easier to be specific in that narrow area than in the other wider matters which official secrets legislation does not address.

Even in relation to types of information not covered by the new official secrets legislation, there remain, as it seems to me, large areas where information ought not to be disclosed without authority. This is not to say that all of such information is information that ought not to be disclosed at all. Much of it may well be information that could and should be available to Parliament, to the media and to the public. The rub lies in disclosure *without authority*.

In government, as in many other walks of life, people acquire a great deal of information by virtue of their occupation that they would not otherwise acquire. They have a duty of confidence in relation to that information. It may well be that much of the information can be disclosed without damage or disadvantage to any one. However, there will be some information which employers consider to be sensitive for whatever reason and which they are entitled to identify by means of confidentiality marks of one kind or another, and in such cases there must surely be a duty not to disclose it to any one not entitled to receive it without the agreement of those who have placed a condition of confidentiality upon it.

A breach of confidence of this kind is not as such a criminal offence, but it may provide the basis of an action for tort under the civil law. It was a civil action for breach of confidence that the British government undertook against Mr Peter Wright and his publishers in the Australian courts in the attempt to stop publication of his book *Spycatcher*. There is no doubt – indeed Peter Wright acknowledged as much – that if he had been resident in this country and *Spycatcher* had been published in this country he would have been liable to criminal charges under the Official Secrets Acts. But he lived in Australia, outside the jurisdiction of the English criminal law, and the British government could proceed against him in Australia only by action for breach of confidence under civil law.

The Australian High Court eventually decided in effect that it should look behind the British government's civil proceedings in the Australian courts and should regard them as an attempt to enforce the sanctions of the Official Secrets Acts in Australia, which ought to be dismissed as outside the jurisdiction of the Australian courts. The issue of principle was thus never brought to a decision in Australia. It was, however, pursued in the English courts, in the form of injunctions taken out against newspapers which published parts of *Spycatcher*, and was resolved, so far as domestic law was concerned, by a judgement of the House of Lords in November 1988. Their Lordships did not try to shut the stable door after the horse had escaped, but they were strongly critical of Peter Wright's actions, and they reaffirmed the duty of confidence which someone in his position owes. Their judgement thus upheld the principle which the British government had sought to establish, and stands as an authoritative judicial statement of the domestic law on breach of confidence in relation to such matters.

The case against Peter Wright became a political *cause célèbre* in this country, for a whole variety of reasons which I do not propose to itemise here: there are times when a certain 'economy with the truth' is no more than a merciful dispensation to one's readers. Even with the benefit of hindsight, however, it seems to me that the British government could hardly have done otherwise than to pursue the case. Admittedly the proceedings gave a not very good and in many respects inaccurate and misleading book a degree of notoriety and a volume of sales worldwide which it would hardly have achieved on its merits. But the book did disclose secret matters of which Peter Wright had become aware as a result of his employment in the Security Service, which Peter Wright had no business to disclose, and the publication of at least some of which was potentially damaging.

Moreover, if the government had done nothing to try to prevent its publication, there would have been many other people with stories to tell – including some who would have liked to publish books which they believed would give the lie to Peter Wright – who would have felt that they had the green light to go ahead. Whether or not the action against Peter Wright would be successful in preventing publication of his book – and from the outset it was recognised that it might not be – it was arguably justified, not just in relation to Wright himself but also, and as importantly, *pour décourager les autres*.

To linger on 'old, unhappy, far-off things, and battles long ago' is something of a self-indulgence, particularly as there is another dimension to this matter – the matter of disclosure without authority – which is not a matter of law but of trust.

It is crucial to the relationship between ministers and civil servants that ministers should be able to trust their civil servants:

1. Not to withhold any information available which is relevant to a decision to be taken;
2. To give dispassionate and honest advice: as Queen Elizabeth said of Sir William Cecil: 'This judgement I have of you . . . that without respect of my private will you will give me that counsel that you think best';
3. To keep the confidences entrusted to them.

Developments which occurred during my time as Head of the Home Civil Service suggested to me that the time had come when it would be useful and salutary to restate these truths as publicly and formally as possible. In February 1985, after consultation with my fellow Permanent Secretaries and with their full agreement, I issued a memorandum on the duties and responsibilities of civil servants in relation to ministers. This memorandum was the subject of considerable parliamentary and public scrutiny and discussion during the ensuing couple of years, following which I re-issued it in December 1987, in a slightly revised form. In that form it still stands today.

It is perhaps worth quoting in this context what I had to say in that memorandum about the importance of trust and confidence in the relationship between ministers and civil servants and about the implications of that for the conduct of the civil servant:

Para 6. The British Civil Service is a non-political and professional career service subject to a code of rules and discipline. Civil servants are required to serve the duly constituted government of the day, of whatever political complexion. It is of the first importance that civil servants should conduct themselves in such a way as to deserve and retain the confidence of Ministers, and to be able to establish the same relationship with those whom they may be required to serve in some future administration. That confidence is the indispensable foundation of a good relationship between Ministers and civil servants. The conduct of civil servants should at all times be such that Ministers and potential future Ministers can be sure that that confidence can be freely given, and that the Civil Service will at all times conscientiously fulfil its duties and obligations to, and impartially assist, advise and carry out the policies of, the duly constituted government of the day.

Para 7. The determination of policy is the responsibility of the Minister (within the convention of collective responsibility of the whole government for the decisions and actions of every member of it). In the determination of policy the civil servant has no constitutional responsibility or role distinct from that of the Minister. Subject to the conventions limiting the access of Ministers to papers of previous administrations, it is the duty of the civil servant to make available to the Minister all the information and experience at his or her disposal which may have a bearing on the policy decisions to which the Minister is committed or which he is preparing to make, and to give to the Minister honest and impartial advice, without fear or favour, and whether the advice accords with the Minister's view or not. Civil servants are in breach of their duty, and damage their integrity as servants of the Crown, if they deliberately withhold relevant information from their Minister, or if they give their Minister other advice than the best they believe they can give, or if they seek to obstruct or delay a decision simply because they do not agree with it. When, having been given all the relevant information and advice, the Minister has taken a decision, it is the duty of civil servants loyally to carry out that decision with precisely the same energy and good will, whether they agree with it or not.

Para 8. Civil servants are under an obligation to keep the confidences to which they become privy in the course of their work; not only the maintenance of the trust between Ministers and civil servants but also the efficiency of government depend on their doing so. There is and must be a general duty upon every civil servant, serving or retired, not without authority to make disclosures which breach that obligation. This duty applies to any document or information or knowledge of the course of business, which has come to a civil servant in confidence in the course of his duty. Any such unauthorised disclosures, whether for political or personal motives, or for pecuniary gain, and quite apart from liability to prosecution under the Official Secrets Acts, result in the civil servant concerned forfeiting the trust that is put in him or her as an employee and making him or her liable to disciplinary action including the possibility of dismissal, or to civil law proceedings. He or she also undermines the confidence that ought to subsist between Ministers and civil servants and thus damages colleagues and the Service as well as him or herself.

(Hansard, O. R. 2 Dec. 1987, W.A. cols. 572–5)

Leaving aside the operation of the law and of codes of discipline in the civil service, the reality is that civil servants who breach a confidence undermine the trust put in them and make it difficult or impossible for ministers or indeed their colleagues to trust them to keep confidences in future. This was, I believe, demonstrated in the case of Clive Ponting a few years ago. As a fairly senior civil servant in the Ministry of Defence, he sent a confidential Ministry of Defence document to a Member of Parliament. He did so without authority, indeed without consulting any one else in the Ministry of Defence, minister or civil servant. He was acquitted by a jury of an offence under the Official Secrets Act. But, whatever reason he may have had for what he did, and whatever the reason for the jury's verdict, about which of course we can only speculate, that is in a sense beside the point.

Ponting had been a good civil servant, and had won much respect and a public honour for the work he had done, particularly on the improvement of efficiency in the Ministry of Defence. But by his action in this case he forfeited the trust of ministers and of his colleagues: it would never have been possible to be sure that what he had done once he would never do again, and it would therefore have been difficult or impossible to trust him in a position in which he had regular access to sensitive material. Ponting himself in effect recognised this by his decision to resign from the Civil Service afterwards, despite his acquittal.

And I should again emphasise the point that civil servants who thus breach the trust placed in them undermine more than their own personal position. They also damage the general reputation for trustworthiness on which their civil service colleagues depend if they are to be able to discharge their duties effectively.

As far as I am concerned, it was these considerations of trust, to a very much greater extent than fear of the sanctions of the then still unreconstructed Official Secrets Act or of the penalties of the civil law, that most inhibited me, and would still inhibit me, in dealing with information that came to me in the course of my duties as a civil servant. It was important to me – indeed essential, if I was to be able to do my job effectively – that both the ministers whom I served and the colleagues with whom I worked should be able to rely on my ability and willingness to keep the confidences entrusted to me. It is, or should be, a matter of trust, and only when the relationship of trust breaks down should it become necessary to resort to the costs and toils of the law or to disciplinary sanctions.

So far I have been discussing restraints on disclosure. Let me now turn to the more positive aspect of the matter: the matter of what should be disclosed.

I have some doubt whether we do much service to serious discussion of the subject when we use simple slogans like 'open government' and 'freedom of information'. It sometimes seems to me that their use constitutes a kind of emotional or political blackmail: nobody would like to say that he or she was not in favour of such patently desirable good things. Perhaps the more serious point is that 'open government' cannot be an absolute. The pursuit of 'open government' conflicts, or can conflict, with the pursuit of other desirable things, such as the right of individual privacy, or – dare I say it – the preservation of national security. Even the most ardent advocates of 'open government' accept that government cannot be completely open, that it is not practicable or even desirable that all government information should be freely and unconditionally available outside government. It is a question of reconciling irreconcilables and striking balances.

So, when I am asked whether I am in favour of 'open government' or 'freedom of information', my reply usually begins with some variant of the old response: 'it depends what you mean by it'.

Nor do I think that it illuminates counsel to talk about a 'right to know'. Certainly I have not found that it assisted me in trying to form my own judgements and conclusions on the subject. Once again this seems to me to be a loaded slogan. I do not believe that it would be recognised by any of the great political philosophers of the past as a fundamental human right. And, once again, even if one were to accept its implications, it would not be an absolute: there are conflicting interests and considerations. It is with some of these conflicts, and with how they might be reconciled, that I should now like to concern myself.

One of the problems in all this seems to me to be that we are engaged on a secular process of trying to graft on to the institutions and structures of representative parliamentary democracy the concepts and practices of public accountability. In our system, ministers in government are formally accountable to Parliament, and particularly to the House of Commons. Parliament has itself been intensifying its scrutiny of government through the institution, in 1980, of the new departmental select committees which shadow and monitor the activities of the various departments of the government. And in these days the scrutiny of the policies, decisions and actions of government extends well beyond Parliament not only to the press and the electronic media but also to many other organisations and people outside Parliament, including a whole host of special interest groups and not a few academics. I would not have it otherwise: as a general rule, accountable government is likely to be better government.

The concept of public accountability clearly requires that the auditors should have access to as much as possible of the information available to those who are being held accountable. So I start from the position that the government should be prepared in principle to make its information available outside, either at its own initiative or on request, save where there are good reasons for withholding it.

There is of course some information available to the government which it would be generally accepted that it cannot release. The categories of information to which this would apply include defence and national security; information obtained in confidence from overseas governments and international organisations; information supplied to the government in commercial confidence, and the publication of which could prejudice the interests of an industrial or commercial company; and information about the financial and other private affairs of individual citizens.

Nonetheless, the fact is that the British government today makes public a torrent – a veritable Niagara – of information in one way and another; through statements and answers to questions in Parliament, speeches in parliamentary debates, written and oral evidence to parliamentary select committees, government replies to reports of such committees, Command papers presented to Parliament – White Papers, Green Papers, Blue Books, annual estimates, reports and accounts of government departments, quangos and other public boards and bodies, and so on.

The publication of information, however it is done, is not without cost. While the provision of information required by Parliament in order to discharge its functions is legitimately a cost to the taxpayer, there may even here be limits to what it is justifiable to ask the taxpayer to bear. For instance, successive governments have set a limit on the maximum cost to be incurred in answering a parliamentary question, and, if the cost of extracting the information requested would exceed that limit, the minister may decline to answer the question on grounds of cost, even if the information is of a kind that would, once extracted, not need to be regarded as confidential. When a body or person outside government or Parliament asks the government for information which the government is not extracting for its own purposes, it would seem to me not unreasonable that the body or person concerned should be asked to reimburse the cost of providing the information: I do not see why that cost should fall upon the taxpayer.

But, however much information the government publishes in the various ways I have described – and it is a great deal – it seems that it is never enough. Parliament and others outside government feel the need to know, not just what the government does or decides to do, and the information which was available to it when a decision was being considered or action taken: they feel the need also to know *how* and *why* a particular decision or action was taken. That is not just a matter of knowing what facts and figures were available to the decision-makers; it is a matter of knowing what facts and figures were actually taken into account in the decision-making process. Moreover, decisions are informed by factors and considerations which cannot be readily reduced to facts and statistics; and in any process of decision-making there is a kind of hierarchy, not only of facts and figures but also of factors and considerations, so that some loom larger and have greater influence than others on the outcome of the deliberations.

So the objective is to be able to scrutinise not only the decisions taken by government, and the reasons for those decisions, but also the process by which the decisions, are reached: to see the working papers of government open to public inspection not just 50 or 30 or 10 years after the event but *at the time*, even while the matter is under consideration, so that the debate within government can be informed by public comment and contribution as it proceeds. And some would like to see the government obliged by law to produce this information, in so far as it falls outside the categories of information which by general consent ought not to be made available.

It seems to me that there is a good case for saying that, in order that the government can be sensibly called to account for its decisions, it should be expected to give as comprehensive an account as is reasonably possible of the facts, figures, factors and considerations that were taken into account during the process of making a decision and of the relative weight given to them in arriving at the outcome. It also seems to me that there is a good case for saying that the present arrangements by no means invariably deliver that result.

Because of the supremacy of Parliament in our system of government, and because ministers are accountable to Parliament, there is a convention that all major and many minor decisions of government are promulgated in the first instance to Parliament (when Parliament is sitting), and only secondarily to the media. As things are at present, governments provide Parliament with explanations of decisions at the time those decisions are announced, in the form of oral statements or written answers to arranged parliamentary questions, or sometimes in the form of a Command paper presented to Parliament.

But Parliamentary time is at a premium: the House of Commons is apt to be resentful if a ministerial statement and the subsequent period of question and answer cut too deeply into the time available for whatever main debate is scheduled for the business of the day. There are therefore scheduling pressures to keep statements as short as possible. And, since ministers who make a statement are expected to answer questions on the subject after the statement, it is no more than political human nature that they should seek in their statement to put the best face possible on the decision that they are announcing.

Nor is a ministerial speech in a parliamentary debate, save perhaps for a great set piece like the annual Budget speech of the Chancellor of the Exchequer, an ideal vehicle for a comprehensive explanation for a major decision. Such speeches have other functions besides the conveying of information; and the kind of comprehensive and systematic explanation of facts, figures, factors and other considerations which would be required simply does not lend itself to oral exposition in the course of a speech in a parliamentary debate which may take place in an atmosphere of some political tension and be subject to interventions and interruptions as it proceeds.

These considerations make it inevitable that ministerial announcements in Parliament are likely to be less than completely comprehensive accounts of the basis for the decisions they are announcing. I almost said that they impose on ministerial statements in Parliament an inevitable degree of 'economy with the truth'. If I thus recycle a phrase with which my name is now inextricably associated – even though I claim no originality or copyright for it – it is in order to emphasise that, in this as in other instances, 'economy with the truth' is not a euphemism for telling lies. It means the truth, and nothing but the truth, but (for whatever reason) not the whole truth.

In *Emma* Jane Austen creates in Jane Fairfax a character who is forced by circumstances to practise economy with the truth. At one point she has to explain to her aunt why she did not go with her friends the Campbells to visit their daughter in Ireland, without being able to disclose the main reason. Jane Austen writes of this: 'With regard to her not accompanying them to Ireland, her account to her aunt contained nothing but the truth, though there might be some truths not told.' Angela Carter says of a character in one of her novels: 'Mrs Chance was sometimes stingy with the truth, but never lied.' Even more to the point, Edmund Burke wrote in one of his *Letters on a Regicide Peace* (1796): 'Falsehood and delusion are allowed in no case whatever; but, as in the exercise of all virtues, there is an economy of truth. It is a sort of temperance, by which a man speaks truth with measure, that he may speak it the longer.'

I sometimes permit myself a wry smile when I see the phrase 'economy with the truth' brought out yet another time in critical comment upon others by representatives of the media who are themselves among the most consistent and assiduous practitioners of this particular variety of temperance.

So what can and should be done to provide Parliament and the public with more comprehensive analyses of the basis on which government decisions and actions are taken? There are some who argue that only legislation on freedom of information which required the disclosure of the working papers leading up to a government decision or action would strip off the veil of secrecy, flush out the deceits and malpractices with which they believe that governments are endemically rife, deny governments the opportunity to manipulate the processes of decision-making to their own political advantage, and enable those outside government properly to scrutinise the real basis upon which a decision or action is taken.

There may well be a case for introducing legislation to ensure that people who are personally and directly affected by a government decision – by a decision to build a road across their garden, for instance, or to give planning permission for some development by which they will be directly and adversely affected – have access to all the information on which the decision was based and all the papers leading up to the decision, except in so far as considerations of personal privacy or commercial confidence inhibit complete disclosure. There may be a case for legislation to ensure that individuals have access to information about themselves and their personal and financial affairs held in government files, so as to be able to satisfy themselves that it is correct. There may be a case for legislation to enshrine the right of privacy, and to protect individuals from the disclosure, whether by government or by any one else, to others of personal and financial information relating to themselves.

There may also be a case for reducing the length of time before public records are opened to the public to something less than 30 years – say, 15 years – though of this I am not so sure: there are arguments both ways.

But I do not believe that there is a good case for legislation which would require the disclosure of the working papers of government either while a decision is under consideration or even shortly after it has been taken and announced. On the contrary, I believe that any attempt to make such disclosure a statutory requirement would be ineffective and damaging: it would fail to bring out the information which it was supposed to produce, and would in the process damage the integrity and effectiveness of decision-making in government.

The effectiveness and coherence of Cabinet government depends upon the maintenance of collective responsibility. That in turn depends upon the maintenance of an administrative process within government that ensures that relevant information and material is as freely available as possible to those concerned within government, and which enables those who share and are expected to accept collective responsibility to take part as fully as possible in the process of collective discussion and decision-making. And an important element in the effectiveness of this process is what Lord Jenkins of Hillhead once described as the essence of collective responsibility: 'the right to change one's mind in private'.

Such a process of collective discussion and decision-taking depends, in a modern organisation of government, on a high degree of formalisation into a system of collegiate and conciliar discussion and on the availability of working papers which expose to those concerned not only the relevant facts and figures but also the various arguments pro and con.

So effective and coherent government depends upon a high degree of frankness and openness within the processes of discussion and decision-making in government. That frankness and openness would be severely inhibited if the whole of those processes were open to public inspection as they occurred, or very soon thereafter. Civil servants and other advisers would in some circumstances be reluctant to give the full information and dispassionate advice which it is their duty to give, if it was going to be exposed immediately to the public gaze. Ministers would fear that the advice being given to them was being coloured by the knowledge that it was likely to become public knowledge very shortly. They would be even more vulnerable to the activities of pressure groups who were seeking to prevent, or protest against, a particular course of action. And they would in some circumstances be reluctant to commit themselves to positions, or to change or adjust positions once taken, for fear of the possible consequences of their being publicly known to be doing so.

The result would be that, particularly on issues of great sensitivity (just those in which political opponents and outside commentators would be most interested), the exchange of information and the real processes of discussion and decision would be diverted into channels that escaped the statutory requirements of disclosure. Papers would be written with a view to disclosure rather than to advancing serious consideration and discussion, or written in forms that avoided the statutory requirements of disclosure, or not written at all. Discussions would take place in informal meetings, or 'non-meetings', without any minutes or records, save for such records as were sufficiently uninformative not to give rise to problems and embarrassments when disclosed.

Thus any papers disclosed to satisfy the statutory requirements would be brief, bland, correct and deeply uninformative: such as not to reflect either the extent of the information and arguments considered or the reality of the discussion that had taken place. This would contribute nothing to the objectives of openness and accountability.

And the processes of decision-making would tend to be driven underground, into holes and corners, to non-meetings that never took place and were never recorded, to whispers in corridors, to scraps of paper and backs of envelopes. This would be to substitute an atmosphere of conspiracy and mistrust for the trust and openness-in-confidence on which good government depends and would be the reverse of effective, coherent and accountable government.

At first sight it sounds like a splendid idea to make government a goldfish bowl. On closer examination it is one of those utopian notions that would be impracticable in real life and disastrous if attempted.

The reality is, surely, that governments, just as much as

companies or newspapers, are entitled to make up their minds in private, and so to conduct their affairs as to be able to do so. Not for the first nor for the last time Edmund Burke put his finger on the point when he wrote, in another passage in the letter from which I have already quoted:

> I admit that reasons of state will not, in many circumstances, permit the disclosure of the true ground of a public proceeding. In that case silence is manly, and it is wise. I take the distinction to be this: the ground of a particular measure making part of a plan it is rarely proper to divulge; all the broader grounds of policy, on which the general plan is to be adopted, ought as rarely to be concealed.

Is there, then, a course of action available and practicable, which lies between the two extremes of the present arrangements, admittedly unsatisfactory in some respects, and the goldfish bowl, which would improve the accountability of government without undermining its effectiveness? I believe that there is.

I suggest that there should be established a new convention of government that, in every case where an important decision of policy is announced or a significant action decided upon and put into effect, the minister responsible for the decision or action should, at the same time as making an announcement in Parliament or in a speech or press notice, publish as a separate explanatory memorandum a comprehensive account of the facts and statistics, the factors and considerations, taken into consideration in arriving at the decision, and of the weight given to them in reaching the eventual decision.

Details of the format and content of such explanatory memoranda could be prescribed in general terms in a Code of Practice, rather like the Highway Code for road users, which ministers and their civil servants would be expected to observe and follow. Such a Code would not itself be a statutory document, and its provisions would not be statutory requirements, any more than those of the Highway Code are; but failure to comply with it properly would expose a minister to the censure of Parliament. The Code could define the types and categories of information which explanatory memoranda were expected to include, and those which could justifiably be excluded: for instance, information about the personal or financial affairs of individual citizens, information obtained in confidence from foreign governments and international institutions, information obtained in commercial confidence from companies and information whose publication would be damaging to national security.

The form of publication in which such explanatory memoranda were issued would depend upon the importance of the subject matter and the decision and upon the extent of public interest and concern. It might sometimes be appropriate, in the case of a major decision of policy, to publish the accompanying explanatory memorandum as a Command paper. In less important cases it might be sufficient to make copies of the explanatory memorandum available on request in duplicated form. There are various other possibilities between these two. However it was done, copies of explanatory memoranda would be sent to the appropriate parliamentary select committees, and would be available to Members of Parliament in the Vote Office. They could also be made available to the media, to non-governmental organisations and to members of the public, if need be on payment of an amount estimated to cover the cost of production: being an old Treasury hand, I am well aware of the importance of defusing Treasury objections in advance.

Compliance with the Code would not be a statutory requirement, and explanatory memoranda would not be subject to judicial review, though of course the decisions themselves would be no less subject to judicial review than at present, and explanatory memoranda could be called in evidence in the course of the process. If it were thought necessary to police the operation of the Code, so as to ensure that ministers and departments did not keep back information which should properly be included, it would be possible to give Members of Parliament the right to refer an explanatory memorandum to the Parliamentary Commissioner for Administration, or to some other watchdog specially appointed for the purpose, who would be empowered to inspect the working papers and to advise on whether the provisions of the Code had been complied with. But I am not convinced that that would be necessary. We have a good many watchdogs already, without creating another; and even without such an arrangement there would be strong pressures upon ministers and departments to do the job properly – not least the fear of exposure and censure in case of wilful failure to comply.

Explanatory memoranda of this kind would go a very long way to satisfying the appetite of Parliament, the media and interested members of the public for the supply of material on which thorough scrutiny of the decisions and actions of government could be based. They would thus improve the accountability of government. And the knowledge that an explanatory memorandum was going to have to be produced would, I believe, improve rather than prejudice the process of decision-making in government. It would be a salutary discipline upon those engaged in the process. No doubt it would become customary to start preparing an explanatory memorandum very early in the decision-making process, so that the work of preparing it would inform the conduct of the process, and make it more systematic and comprehensive. Thus I believe that the institution of explanatory memoranda on these lines would make for more orderly and responsible decision-making in government.

Some of those who favour the idea of the transparent goldfish bowl might argue that the publication of an explanatory memorandum after a decision had been taken would be too late to enable subsequent parliamentary and public discussion to influence the outcome. I have already described the objections that I see to the transparent goldfish bowl. And I think that those who argue in this way take too little account of the fact that relatively few decisions of government take immediate effect. Many, if not most of them, cannot take effect until the appropriate primary or secondary legislation has been passed. Even where there is no requirement for legislation, there is usually some time before a decision takes effect, during which it is possible for there to be second thoughts, if the government can be persuaded that the decision should be varied or recalled.

Advocates of legislation for freedom of information may say that nothing short of legislation will achieve the degree of openness which they regard as desirable. No government, it is argued, can be relied upon to come clean unless it is constrained to do so by legislation.

In the past I have certainly detected that the attitude of many politicians to freedom of information has tended to depend to a considerable extent upon whether they are in government or in opposition. On this subject 'the native hue of resolution' apparent in opposition has tended, once office is assumed, to become 'sicklied o'er with the pale cast' of responsible and diplomatic caution, and 'enterprises of great pith and moment with this regard their currents turn awry and lose the name of action'. It is only fair to record that this charge cannot be laid at the door of the government led by Mr Major, which has demonstrated in a variety of ways its determination to act upon its commitment to greater openness in government.

But I have already indicated why I believe that legislation would be ineffective and damaging. If I am right – as I am modestly but realistically sure that I am – in thinking that legislation would simply drive the processes of decision-making in government into channels which escaped the clutches of the law, then it is essentially a matter of political will. If the political will exists, *really* exists, for greater openness, it needs no legislation to bring it about. If on the other hand the protestations of the politicians who claim to espouse open government are mere lip-service and the political will does not really exist, no legislation can compel it.

It is clear that the political tide is running in the direction of greater openness in government, as a means of achieving greater accountability of government to Parliament and to the people, and that to that extent there does exist a diffused and general political will for greater openness, which any government will ignore at its peril. If I am right in this, then the scheme which I am suggesting offers a way of expressing and giving effect to this trend towards greater openness and accountability in a manner which is consistent with our system of parliamentary democracy and should go far to satisfy the wishes of those who seek to bring the government to strict account for its decisions and actions as well as the need to maintain an effective and coherent administration of government.

In the end it comes back, I believe, to a matter of trust. Benjamin Disraeli wrote in his political novel *Vivian Grey*: 'I repeat that all power is a trust, that we are accountable for its exercise, that from the people, and for the people, all springs, and all must exist.' But trust is a two-way traffic. As government is accountable for the exercise of the power that is entrusted to it, so that trust must embrace reciprocally trusting Parliament and the people with as much as possible of the information upon which the decisions and actions for which government is accountable are based. And I believe that in this matter virtue will bring its own reward: it is by extending and enlarging that trust to Parliament and through Parliament to the people that government can best earn and deserve the trust of the people, not just in its decisions as to what information cannot be disclosed, but also in its ability and will to govern in the best interests of the country and of its people. In this matter of open government, trust is a better foundation than coercion for relations between government and people in a mature democracy.

Note

1 The argument of this chapter was originally presented by Lord Armstrong at Glasgow University under the title 'Open government: a view from the goldfish bowl', 12.5.92.

References

Burke, E. (1796) *Letters on a Regicide Peace* in Burke, E. (1834) *The Works of Edmund Burke,* vol.2, London: Holdsworth and Bell.
Hansard (1987) *Memorandum on the Duties and Responsibilities of Civil Servants in Relation to Ministers,* London: HMSO.

CHAPTER 5

Opinions: Public support for secrecy

WILLIAM L. MILLER, ANNIS MAY TIMPSON AND
MICHAEL LESSNOFF

Despite a lifetime of discreet public service dealing with a myriad of issues over the years, Lord Armstrong is best known to the general public for recalling a phrase of Edmund Burke's. A British government letter, he told the Supreme Court of New South Wales in November 1986 'contains a misleading impression, not a lie. It was being economical with the truth.' That phrase won him his only entry in the *Oxford Dictionary of Modern Quotations* (1991: 10). To many a horrified liberal or left-wing journalist it was a revealing indiscretion but, as he makes clear in the previous chapter, not to Lord Armstrong. He denounces what he calls the 'simple slogans' of 'open government', 'freedom of information' or the public's 'right to know' as 'emotional blackmail' and adds: 'the more serious point is that open government cannot be an absolute. The pursuit of open government conflicts, or can conflict, with the pursuit of other desirable things, such as the right to individual privacy or the preservation . . . of national security.' In short, the fundamental issue for Lord Armstrong, is one of 'reconciling irreconcilables and striking balances'.

Our survey set out to measure support for what Lord Armstrong calls the 'simple slogans' of open government and freedom of information. We would prefer to call them 'abstract principles'. But it also set out to measure support for other, conflicting, abstract principles such as respect for authority. We can use these measures to see how the public and politicians 'reconciled irreconcilables and struck balances'. As will become clear, public opinion actually does take the kind of complex and sophisticated attitude towards the free flow of information that Lord Armstrong advocates. The sophistication of public opinion should not be underestimated.

Abstract principles

At least three general principles are involved in public attitudes towards censorship: principles of *free expression*, freedom of information (the *'right to know'*), and *respect for authority*. On the one hand there is respect for authority, for good order, and for the powers that apply censorship. But on the other, there are two, not one, conflicting principles – the right of the journalist to free expression, and the right of the public to information. In concrete

Table 5.1 **Free expression**

	General public	Local politicians
Average marks out of 10 for importance of guaranteeing everyone the right to free speech	9.2	9.4
% who give 10 out of 10 for the importance of guaranteeing everyone the right to free speech	67	74
% who disagree that free speech is just not worth it if it means we have to put up with the danger to society from extremist views	64	88

situations, we find, these three principles combine in different ways. Respect for authority almost always has a strong effect towards increasing support for censorship while the 'free expression /freedom to publish' principle has a similar, though generally weaker, effect towards decreasing support for censorship. However the influence of the third principle, the public's 'right to know', is more varied: it has a particularly strong influence upon attitudes towards censoring political information but much less on attitudes towards censorship of other kinds.

As Lord Armstrong surmised, most people in Britain accept the 'simple slogans' or abstract principles of free speech and freedom of information. We asked people to give marks out of 10 for the importance of 'guaranteeing everyone the right of free speech'. Both public and politicians gave marks that averaged over 9 out of 10. Indeed, two-thirds of the public and three-quarters of politicians opted for the maximum 10 out of 10. In principle at least there seems almost universal belief in the sanctity of free speech. This finding should not be dismissed too lightly. Universal principles are the stuff of a common culture. They may not be much help to the analyst trying to predict how particular individuals will behave in particular circumstances – because, by definition, universal principles do not discriminate well between individuals – but these principles nonetheless underlie collective moods and influence every individual. They are the background against which less pervasive, more discriminating and contingent factors exert their varying influences.

We also made our respondents confront a tougher question about free expression which is more useful for discriminating analysis. We asked them whether: 'Free speech is just not worth it, if it means we have to put up with the danger to society from extremist views?'. The question was deliberately framed to encourage people to admit any misgivings or reservations they might have about the principle of free expression. To record a commitment to free expression they had to disagree with this proposition. Even so, a majority did disagree, and thereby indicated support for free

Table 5.2   **The public's right to know**

	General public	*Local politicians*
% who give unqualified support to a public 'right to know' about:		
information on themselves	93	94
government plans	83	83
dangerous business activities	93	94
all of the above	77	79
Average marks out of 10 for a Freedom of Information Act as a protector of citizens' rights and liberties	7.8	8.2

expression despite a question deliberately loaded against it. Even by this fairly stringent measure, 64 per cent of the public and 88 per cent of politicians were committed to the principle of free expression.

Support for a general right to know was also nearly universal though, once again, we were able to identify a substantial minority who had reservations. We asked: 'Should people have a general right to know the facts about each of the following:

1. Information about themselves, for example their own medical records and credit ratings?
2. The government's plans?
3. Private business activities that might affect the health of people who live near the company's factory?'

Over 97 per cent felt people should have a right to know information about themselves and about threatening business activities. Though rather less, around 92 per cent, felt they should have the right to know about the government's plans, that figure still reflects overwhelming public support for the principle of access to information.

However, a number of our respondents qualified their comments about access to government information. Although we did nothing to stimulate or encourage such reservations, we noted any that were expressed spontaneously. Reservations were expressed particularly frequently on the right to know about government plans. Only 83 per cent gave *unqualified* support to the citizen's right to know about government plans, and only 77 per cent gave unqualified support to a right to know about all three kinds of information taken together. In most people's minds therefore, freedom of information remained a well-respected principle, even when these reservations were taken into account, but nonetheless one with less than universal support.

This was confirmed by answers to our battery of questions about the contribution of various institutions and policies towards the

Table 5.3 **Respect for authority**

	General public	Local politicians
Average marks out of 10 for importance of respect for authority	8.2	7.5
% who give 10 out of 10 for importance of respect for authority	40	28

protection of citizens' rights and liberties. We included in this a question about the value of 'a Freedom of Information Act, giving more legal access to government information'. Out of 17 institutions and policies currently in existence or proposed by reformers, a Freedom of Information Act got the top score from both public and politicians – averaging slightly under 8 out of 10 marks from the public and slightly over 8 out of 10 from politicians. Indeed, comparison with the other 'protectors of liberty' discussed in Chapter 3, shows how much more effective a Freedom of Information Act was seen to be. This lends support to Lord Armstrong's observation that 'the political tide is running in the direction of greater openness in government'.

Nonetheless Lord Armstrong makes a powerful case for secrecy in government based, in part, on the need to protect the authority of ministers and their civil servants. And while our study showed that people supported both free expression and the right to know, it also revealed that they held less libertarian principles as well. We asked for a mark out of 10 to indicate the importance people attached to 'respect for authority'. Among the public, respect for authority scored just over 8 out of 10, and not far less among politicians – though it is significant that those who themselves exercised political authority put less importance on respect for it than did the general public. Fully 40 per cent of the public though only 28 per cent of politicians gave respect for authority the maximum 10 out of 10.

Liberty, authority and government secrets

People interviewed in our survey could not get away with 'empty political slogans' because their support for abstract principles expressed at the start of the interview was later tested against a range of specific scenarios. One of these concerned publication of government secrets. We asked whether: 'Newspapers which get hold of confidential government documents about [defence/economic/ health service] plans should not be allowed to publish them?'. As before, a randomly selected third of interviews asked about defence plans, another third about economic plans, and a final third about

Table 5.4   **Support for a ban in publishing government secrets**

	General public	Local politicians
In full samples (% for ban)	58	46
Among those whose commitment to free expression is:		
high	53	43
low	66	65
Effect	− 13	− 22
Among those whose commitment to a citizens' right to know is:		
high	54	40
low	69	69
Effect	− 15	− 29
Among those whose commitment to authority is:		
high	68	71
medium	58	55
low	43	24
Effect	+ 25	+ 47

health service plans. Obviously these wording variations had an influence on the answers, but let us ignore that for the moment. Taking all the interviews together, 58 per cent of the public but only 46 per cent of politicians would ban publication of government secrets.

This particular example allows us to explore the effect that values and principles have upon people's opinions about specific situations. Our data allow us to categorise people into those with a high commitment to free expression (defined as those who disagreed with the proposition that 'free speech is just not worth it if it means we have to put up with the danger to society from extremist views') and those with a low commitment. Similarly, we can categorise people into those with a high commitment to freedom of information (defined as those who gave unqualified assent to all three of our 'right to know' questions) and those with a low commitment. Finally we can categorise people into those who put a high (10 out of 10), medium (8 or 9 out of 10) or low (7 or less out of 10) stress upon respect for authority. (Remember that the average score on respect for authority was over 8 out of 10.)

If we use these criteria, we can see how a commitment to the principle of free expression reduced support for a ban on publishing government secrets by 13 per cent among the public and by 22 per cent among politicians. Similarly, a commitment to freedom of information reduced support for a ban by 15 per cent among the public and by 29 per cent among politicians. By contrast, high respect for authority raised support for a ban by 25 per cent

Table 5.5 **Combined effect of respect for authority and commitment to freedom of
information on support for ban on publishing government secrets**

	General public		Local politicians	
Commitment to freedom of information (right to know) =	Low	High	Low	High
Respect for authority is:				
low	52	41	49	19
medium	71	53	71	49
high	76	65	80	66

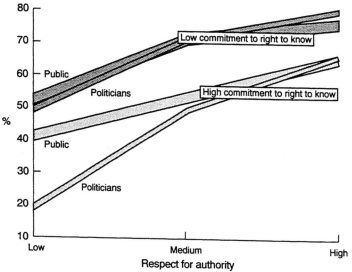

Figure 5.1 **Support for censorship of government secrets**

among the public and by a massive 47 per cent among politicians.
So abstract principles clearly do matter; they do influence reactions
to specific scenarios. They seem to be particularly influential among
politicians; but they also influence the general public quite
strongly.

Our data also allow us to explore the influence of conflicting
principles on public attitudes to specific situations. For example,
we can examine how attitudes towards authority and the right to
know combine to affect support for a ban on publishing government secrets. If we contrast (a) those with a low respect for
authority and a high commitment to freedom of information
against (b) those with a high respect for authority and a low
commitment to freedom of information, we find a 35 per cent
difference among the public in their support for a ban, and a
difference of 61 per cent among politicians. Indeed, while only

19 per cent of politicians with the first combination of values would ban publication of government secrets, 80 per cent of those with the second combination would do so.

Policy areas and the national interest

One of the main reasons advanced by Lord Armstrong for restricting publication of government information is that it could damage the collective national interest. However, we found that the legitimacy of his claim varied from one issue to another. Both public and politicians were strongly influenced by the policy area involved: roughly 30 per cent more would ban publication of defence plans than of health service plans.

But we also tested public sensitivity to the national interest more directly by randomly adding the phrase 'because publication might damage our national interests' to our question in half the interviews. This overt appeal to the national interest increased public support for censorship by 11 per cent on average, though politicians were more resistant to it than the public.

The interaction of policy areas and appeals to the national interest is particularly revealing. Among the public, overt appeals to the national interest produced a moderate increase in support for a ban on publication of economic plans and a small increase in support for a ban on publishing either defence or health plans. Among politicians however, overt appeals to the national interest really only worked at all in the economic policy area; it had very little effect on their willingness to ban publication of defence plans and was actually slightly counter-productive when advanced as a (spurious) reason for banning publication of health plans. The relevance of the national interest to health plans is difficult to establish, while its relevance to defence plans is difficult to overlook. Hence the effectiveness of an overt appeal to the national interest in the 'grey area' of economic plans.

Overall, therefore, we have found a great deal of evidence for Lord Armstrong's hope that when people are forming their attitudes to censorship and freedom of information they will weigh conflicting values and respond to detailed circumstances. We have found little evidence for his fear that the public as a whole is overinfluenced in practice by what he calls 'simple slogans' and 'emotional blackmail'.

Ideology and secrets

As might be expected, those who placed themselves on the left were much less willing to ban publication of government secrets than those on the right. Among the general public, the difference between

Table 5.6   *Effects of policy areas and overt appeals to national interests*

	General public	Local politicians
% *willing to ban publication of confidential government documents:*		
in all interviews	58	46
without appeal to national interests	53	43
with appeal to national interests	64	49
on defence plans	75	62
on economic plans	51	45
on health plans	47	32

Table 5.7   *Effect of appeals to national interests in different policy areas*

	General public	Local politicians
% *willing to ban publication of secret:*		
defence plans		
without appeal to national interests	72	60
with appeal to national interests	80	63
Effect	+ 8	+ 3
economic plans		
without appeal to national interests	42	36
with appeal to national interests	60	53
Effect	+ 18	+ 17
health plans		
without appeal to national interests	42	33
with appeal to national interests	51	30
Effect	+ 9	− 3

left and right was 35 per cent, among politicians 56 per cent. These left/right differences remained almost constant across policy areas, from defence through economic plans to health plans. The left is traditionally suspicious of secret government and doubly so when the government in office is right-wing. As we shall see in later chapters however, the left is not so libertarian on other aspects of censorship.

The Opposition mentality

One final point concerns the 'opposition mentality'. Although he excepted Prime Minister John Major from the charge, Lord Armstrong suggested that national politicians tended to support the concept of open government more fervently in opposition than in office. We can explore the possibility further by considering

Table 5.8 **Ideology and attitude to government secrets**

	General public	Local politicians
% *willing to ban publication of government secrets*		
among those who place themselves:		
on the left	40	17
in the centre	57	55
on the right	75	73
Right/left effect	+ 35	+ 56

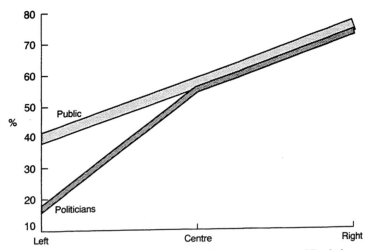

Figure 5.2 **Ideology and government secrets (% who would censor publication)**

whether holding office in local government produces a 'governing perspective' on secrecy.

For local politicians the concept of being in government or opposition is ambiguous. As party politicians they are intensely aware whether 'their party' is in government or opposition at Westminster; and as local councillors they are aware, more than most, of the power of British central government (Stoker 1991; Byrne 1992; Judge 1993). In that perspective, every Conservative-voting group leader (which includes many leaders of Independent groups as well as leaders of Conservative groups on local councils) may have felt a special sympathy with government, while every local group leader who did not vote Conservative may have sympathised with the opposition.

We certainly found substantial differences between Conservative-voting local politicians and the rest. Non-Conservatives were 5 per cent more committed to free expression, 27 per cent more committed to freedom of information, and 29 per cent less respectful of authority. They gave a Freedom of Information Act

Table 5.9 **Effect of being in control rather than in opposition locally**

	Among Conservative politicians	Among Labour politicians	Among Lib-Democrat politicians
% with high commitment to a citizens' right to know:			
if in office locally	60	90	86
if in opposition locally	69	93	93
Effect of office	− 9	− 3	− 7
% willing to ban publication of government secrets:			
if in office locally	91	40	67
if in opposition locally	92	25	41
Effect of office	− 1	+ 15	+ 26

a score of 9 out of 10 compared to the Conservatives' 7 out of 10. On every topic except racial incitement (which is dealt with in Chapter 7) non-Conservatives were less favourable to censorship – usually much less – than Conservatives. For example, while only 27 per cent of non-Conservative politicians would ban publication of government secrets, 75 per cent of Conservative-voting local politicians would do so, a difference of 48 per cent.

But differences between Conservatives and non-Conservatives reflect ideology as well as a government-versus-opposition perspective. In or out of office, left-wingers may be more opposed to censorship. At a local level however, Conservative-voting local politicians could be in or out of control – as could Labour, Liberal Democrat, or Scottish Nationalist-voting politicians. We asked all group leaders whether they regarded themselves as 'on the side of the parties or groups which control your council, or in opposition to the parties or groups which control your council, or neither?'. Thus, at a local level, some Conservative politicians were in office while others were in opposition. Contrasting those in office and those in opposition *within the same party* largely eliminates the influence of ideology and reveals the influence, if any, of direct personal experience of office.

Within each party, those in office were only slightly less committed in principle to freedom of information than those in opposition, but when it came to banning publication of government secrets, particularly on defence, Labour and Liberal politicians in office were much more favourable to censorship than their colleagues in opposition. To a limited extent then, even local government office seemed to strengthen their 'governing perspective'.

This chapter has unravelled some of the complexities inherent in public attitudes to censorship and freedom of information. While the British public favour the development of legislation to promote freedom of information, their attitudes to the publication of government papers are by no means straightforward. They are shaped by ideological orientations and by the nature of the information itself. As we shall see in the next four chapters however, questions about freedom of information and censorship do not relate to government documents alone. They also raise important issues about the responsibility and independence of the press, to which we now turn.

References

Byrne, T. (1992) *Local Government in Britain*, London: Penguin.

Judge, D. (1993) *The Parliamentory State*, London: Sage.

Oxford Dictionary of Modern Quotations (1991), Oxford: Oxford University Press.

Stoker, G. (1991) *The Politics of Local Government*, London: Macmillan.

PART THREE

Freedom versus Responsibility

CHAPTER 6

Witness: The dangers of press 'power without responsibility'[1]

FEDOR BURLATSKY

The fall of Mikhail Gorbachev in December 1991 had greater political repercussions than the removal of Khrushchev or the assassination of President Kennedy. His resignation was accompanied by the disintegration of the Soviet Union into 15 new states. He proved to be the first and the last President of the Soviet Union. Tempting though it is however, I will not dwell upon all the ups and downs of the political struggle that took place during Gorbachev's last years as President. I will limit myself, in this chapter, to the role played by the press in these events.

For me, that is at once an easy and a difficult task. On the one hand it is easy, because I worked in the press throughout the years of *perestroika*, initially as a political commentator and later as editor-in-chief of the Soviet political weekly innocuously titled *Literaturnaya gazeta* ('Literary Gazette'). Moreover, in my capacity as Chairman of the Subcommittee on Humanitarian Cooperation and Human Rights in the USSR Supreme Soviet, I was actively involved in drafting the new law on the Press and Mass Media and making every effort to ensure its implementation. At the same time I find it difficult to comment on the role of the press, because my perspective is that of mainstream liberal democracy which makes it difficult for me to undertake a dispassionate analysis of other sections of the Soviet – and now post-Soviet – press, the right-wing communist press, the nationalist press, and the left-wing radical press. All the same, I shall do my best to rise above the emotions and loyalties that consumed us all during the stormy transition that took place at the end of 1991 and the beginning of 1992.

Under *perestroika*, the mass media became an independent power in the land for the first time in Soviet or Russian history, a genuine 'third estate' – though that new status may now be under threat. Most of the decisions taken during *glasnost* and *perestroika* were encouraged by the media and the fall of Gorbachev himself was prepared by the press. Gorbachev could say that he gave the press its freedom and it repaid him by pushing him out of office and encouraging the collapse of the Soviet Union which he tried so hard to preserve, reform and renew.

For the press, the period of *perestroika* and after can be divided into a number of periods. From 1985 to August 1990 the forces of *glasnost* were born and began to acquire strength. Although the media remained formally under the control of the Communist

Party, the state, the trade unions or other public organisations and the system of censorship was still in existence, some of the informal pre-conditions for a free press were being created. During this period the press actively supported *perestroika* and Gorbachev, in person, as its author.

The second period lasted from August 1990 until August 1991. It was during this period that the new *Law on the Press and Other Means of Mass Communication* was prepared and adopted. A legal basis was established for freedom of speech, censorship was abolished, a genuine pluralism of mass communications began to develop, and the first independent publications appeared. 1990 was the high point of Gorbachev's power; his successes in foreign policy were particularly striking. The press, with very few exceptions, supported the policies he was pursuing and continued to support Gorbachev personally. But during the autumn of 1990 and spring of 1991, Gorbachev began to move to the right, seeking to establish a centre-right block in an attempt to preserve and renew the Soviet Union. The radical left-wing press transferred its support to Boris Yeltsin, and in the union republics outside Russia proper the press began to support local republican or nationalist leaders. The tone of newspaper articles became increasingly hostile towards Gorbachev. At the same time the right-wing conservative communist press stepped up its attack on him. He had to navigate between Scylla and Charybdis and ended up shipwrecked.

The third period began with the short-lived vaudeville coup of August 1991. By September power had begun to move from Gorbachev into the hands of Yeltsin in Russia, and in December he was effectively removed from power and obliged to resign. The press during this period divided into several different sections, not one of which supported Gorbachev. Only television, and then somewhat diffidently, continued to provide information on what the President was doing.

After the fall of Gorbachev a new period began in the work of the mass media. The Soviet Union collapsed. The press in each of the now independent republics began to seek its own place in the sun, and information on the affairs of the former republics became increasingly one-sided.

Let me now dwell in a little more detail on the evolution of the mass media during the years of *perestroika* and especially in the period after the short-lived coup of August 1991.

In the first stage (1985–90), the progressive press concentrated on exposing the crimes of Stalinism. A particularly important role was played by journals like *Ogonek* ('Little Spark'), *Literaturnaya gazeta*, *Moskovskii novosti* ('Moscow News'), and also by *Znamya* ('Banner') and *Novyi mir* ('New World') which published the previously (and still formally) banned works of Alexander Solzhenitsyn: *The Gulag Archipelago* and *Cancer Ward*. But criticism of Stalinism was not combined with attacks on the communist system as such, nor with doubts about Lenin. The October 1917 revolution was still portrayed as a necessary part of the social development of the USSR, though some voices already criticised the enormous price paid for its victory. For the first time information began to appear about the number of victims of the Stalin years (at least 15–20 million people), and about the number who had died during the civil war (between three and five million). These figures were later confirmed in more detail in the press and anything up to a sixth of the population of the country were now seen as direct or indirect victims of Stalinism.

During this period the press also supported moves towards a new relationship with the United States and Western Europe and backed the Soviet withdrawal from Afghanistan. All this was in keeping with Gorbachev's policy, but it drove him further than he intended. The programme of disarmament and gradual elimination of nuclear weapons by the year 2000, put forward by Gorbachev in 1986, reflected the view of the more liberal section of the press that the military budget should be drastically reduced, that SS-20 rockets should be destroyed, that the arms race should be reduced and that chemical weapons should be prohibited.

Press treatment of relations between the USSR and Eastern Europe was of particular significance. These countries were increasingly treated as an example of political and economic reform for the Soviet Union itself, and liberals within the Soviet Union began to connect their hopes for structural reform within their own country with the reconstruction of Eastern Europe. Yet not a single article at this time gave any hint of what was to come – the collapse of the Warsaw Pact, the end of the Council for Mutual Economic Assistance (Comecon), the series of anti-communist revolutions and the reunification of Germany. The most radical articles at this time limited themselves to the 'Finlandisation' of Eastern Europe, though even this idea was rejected by Gorbachev himself. During his triumphal journeys through Eastern Europe he counted upon the appearance in those countries of 'mini-Gorbachevs' who would help him in his struggle against conservatives inside the CPSU Politburo. But neither in his speeches, nor in any part of the Soviet press, was there any suggestion of a complete break between these countries and the theory and practice of communism, nor of an evolution towards the West.

The press undoubtedly performed a service for *perestroika* and Gorbachev with its determined attack on the Brezhnev doctrine of limited sovereignty, and its reconsideration of the Hungarian Revolution of 1956 and the Prague Spring of 1968. I was able myself, as early as 1988, to publish an article in *Sovetskaya kul'tura* ('Soviet Culture') in this spirit.

The press was also particularly critical of the war in Afghanistan. In many newspapers and journals, not only left-wing publications but also more centrist ones like *Izvestiya* ('News', the paper of the

Soviet Government) and *Trud* ('Labour', the paper of the official trade unions), there was a series of articles about the losses of the Soviet army in Afghanistan, about the bereavement of tens of thousands of families and about the hopelessness and immorality of the war itself.

Another movement of opinion which originated in this period was concerned with the restoration of freedom of conscience and of religious belief. On matters of this kind there was very little difference between the right-wing, centrist and left-wing press. In effect, all these publications 'opened the floodgates' to the full rehabilitation of, above all, Russian Orthodoxy, and then of other confessions. The press, particularly *Ogonek* and *Literaturnaya gazeta*, published sensational articles on the repression of religious leaders from the 1920s up to the 1980s and on the persecution of members of Christian beliefs other than the Orthodox Church, such as Roman Catholics in the Baltic, Uniates in the western Ukraine, Baptists and Mormons. In the republics of Central Asia and in Azerbaijan more and more articles dealt sympathetically with Islam.

Towards the end of this period, in 1989 and 1990, the press began to promote Western values more and more openly. 'New thinking', which had its roots in the USSR as far back as the 1970s, was raised to the level of an official foreign policy doctrine by Gorbachev himself. But it was the press which channelled that 'new thinking' into domestic politics, arguing for profound reforms of domestic social and political systems with demands for Western-style parliamentarianism, open government, human rights, and the return of the Soviet Union to world society.

Let me refer to my own experience at this point, not because it was in any way unique but because it is most familiar to me. After the meeting between Gorbachev and Reagan in Geneva, I was able to put on a play called *Black Saturday* in one of the Moscow theatres. The play dealt with the Cuban missile crisis and the outstanding role of Jack Kennedy and Nikita Khrushchev in preventing the escalation towards nuclear war. From 1985 onwards, I published a series of articles arguing for democratic reform within the USSR itself and for an end to the Cold War outside. In 1988 my book called *New Thinking* was published, and a play was presented on television called *Two Views from the Same Study* which dealt with the origins of the political struggle inside the CPSU. The main figures represented Gorbachev and Ligachev, and in a later play Boris Yeltsin. I published the first article for 20 years about Khrushchev, and sought to give him proper credit for his struggle against Stalin's cult of personality. I wrote another about Brezhnev, as the embodiment of the command-administrative system. At the end of this period, I published an article in *Literaturnaya gazeta*, entitled 'On Soviet Parliamentarianism', in which I advocated a directly and popularly elected Parliament and

President, a Declaration of the Rights of Man and the Citizen, and a Constitutional Court to secure those rights.

Unfortunately, at this time, Gorbachev was not yet ready to agree with proposals of this kind. Instead he accepted a plan put forward by his then deputy, Anatolii Luk'yanov which sought to reactivate the system of soviets which had existed during Lenin's days and which had been formalised in the 1924 Constitution. These rather different proposals were very damaging to the development of more democratic norms because the Soviet system had never embraced the separation of powers, and the principle of the sovereignty of soviets at every level was interpreted as absolute sovereignty. This led directly to a struggle for power between soviets at different levels (particularly between the all-Union Supreme Soviet and the republican Supreme Soviets) which became known as the 'war of laws'. And Gorbachev himself missed a historic opportunity to become a president directly elected by the whole people at a time when he could still have defeated any possible opponent.

Throughout 1989 and 1990 the press became actively involved in the reconstruction of the political system. A vigorous struggle developed between different tendencies within the Communist Party, as well as outside it, which led to the formation of several different political groupings and the press also split more clearly into opposed groups. The journal *Ogonek* and the newspapers *Moskovskii novosti* and *Literaturnaya gazeta* were opposed by the right-wing press, represented above all by *Sovetskaya Rossiya* ('Soviet Russia') and *Pravda* ('Truth', the paper of the Soviet Communist Party), although *Pravda* at this time generally took the same centrist line as Gorbachev himself.

One of the most striking examples of this clash of political positions was the struggle that took place in connection with the article by Nina Andreeva, 'I cannot sacrifice my principles', which appeared in *Sovetskaya Rossiya*, and gained the personal support of Yegor Ligachev. In *Literaturnaya gazeta*, I gave a critical reply to Andreeva's article, under the title 'What kind of socialism do the people need?'. *Pravda* published an editorial, partly written by Alexander Yakovlev, which also criticised Andreeva.

At the end of 1990 the press responded to increasing activity by nationalist movements: the left-wing press by advocating national freedom in the Baltic countries for example, and the right-wing press by carrying primitive propaganda for Russian chauvinism. The first of these positions was represented in the pages of *Literaturnaya gazeta*, *Ogonek* and *Moskovskie Novosti*, the second in the pages of *Sovetskaya Rossiya*, the journal *Sovremennik* ('Contemporary') and various other publications. Russian chauvinism in turn stimulated nationalist tendencies in the local republican press within Ukraine, Georgia, Azerbaijan, Moldova, and the Central Asian republics. Nationalism of one kind or another soon brought together communists and anti-communists in the republics and became the main alternative to the still-dominant Soviet system.

Meanwhile a number of periodicals including *Literary Gazette, Znamya* and *Izvestiya* began to advocate Westernism. They rejected communism as a system, on the grounds that it had shown itself to be not only cruel but also ineffective, and advocated parliamentarianism, individual liberty, and market economics. Views of this kind were reflected in the publications of such leading writers as Nikolai Shmelev, Yuri Afanas'ev, Tatiana Zaslavskaya, Abel Aganbegyan, and many others. After I had become its editor-in-chief, *Literaturnaya gazeta* was the first to proclaim itself independent of the USSR Writers' Union which up to this point had been its sponsoring institution, and became instead the paper of all those who worked in the journal itself. Many other publications adopted this model, including even *Pravda* and *Izvestiya* eventually.

Gorbachev was not ready to support such Westernising views at this point. He was determined to defend 'socialism', although he later referred to it in more moderate terms as a 'socialist orientation'. He defended the collective ownership of land, and a reformed federal USSR.

At the same time, Westernising opinion had a significant influence upon the political process. As Chairman of the Commission on International Cooperation in Humanitarian Problems and Human Rights of the USSR Supreme Soviet, I took part in the preparation of a whole series of basic laws in the area of human rights – laws on the freedom of the press, on freedom of conscience and religious belief, on the freedom of social and political organisations, and on the right of free movement. The struggle which took place around the law on the freedom of the press was a particularly notable one. The draft law was presented in the name of the CPSU Central Committee to a commission of the USSR Supreme Soviet. We organised a wide-ranging discussion of this draft and managed to have it rejected, because it was entirely based upon the preservation of party control over the press. It also maintained the state and public character of the mass media, and denied any possibility of newspapers, journals or television being owned by private individuals. We prepared a very different draft, which was the basis of the version that was finally approved on 12 June 1990.

The approval of this law after a lengthy struggle, a whole series of discussions in committees and commissions, and finally a debate in the USSR Supreme Soviet itself, was a landmark in the history of the development of the mass media in the USSR. According to a 1918 decree from Lenin's time, publications which did not support the new regime were 'temporarily prohibited' and it was only our new press law of 1992 which put a formal end to complete state control of freedom of speech and expression in the Soviet Union.

The first article of the law under the heading 'freedom of the press' was of particular significance. It stated:

The press and other news media are free. Freedom of speech and freedom of the press, guaranteed to citizens by the USSR Constitution, signify the right to express opinions and beliefs, and to seek, select, obtain and disseminate information and ideas in any form, including the press and other news media. Censorship of the mass media is not permitted.

This was the most impressive victory that liberal opinion had won in the whole history of *perestroika*. At the same time, many other articles in the law were the result of vigorous struggle and were often compromises. Article 7, on the right to establish an organ of mass communication, is a good example. We were able to assert the principle of private ownership and personal initiative in the establishment of an organ of mass communication. We managed to include a reference to the right of all citizens of the USSR to establish an organ of this kind. This right, however, was included at the very end of the article, after a lengthy listing of the 'main' founders of organs of mass communication – state bodies, political parties, public organisations, and other groups.

Article 5, which was concerned with the abuse of freedom of expression, included a rather obscure reference to 'divulging information that constitutes a state secret'. There is still no definition of what this information might be. A whole series of articles refer to the right of journalists to receive information from state bodies, but no means were indicated by which they might be able to implement this right.

On my own insistence, a very important article (Article 33) was included providing for the right of citizens to have access to information from foreign sources, including 'direct television transmission, radio broadcasts and the press'. But the law said nothing about the rights of foreign news agencies and of foreign journalists within the USSR, indicating only that this question would be resolved in the future by special legislation. No legislation of that kind has yet been adopted.

But with all these ambiguities and inadequacies, this law of August 1990 represented a real revolution. Publications that were already in existence began to breathe more freely and began to liberate themselves from party and state control. And very soon, like mushrooms after the rain, all kinds of new publications began to appear. These included newspapers like *Kuranty* ('Chime'), *Kommersant* ('Merchant'), *Nezavisimaya gazeta* ('Independent') and *Megapolis Express*, together with Christian, Jewish and Muslim newspapers, legal and medical publications, journals like the monthly *Delovye lyudi* ('Businessman'), and hundreds of local publications in Moscow, Leningrad, Kiev and the other republican capitals. The circulation of newspapers reached a peak at this time: the weekly paper *Argumenty i fakty* ('Arguments and Facts'), for example, sold more than 20 million copies, *Komsol'skaya pravda* (newspaper of the Young Communist League, Komsomol) sold 18 million, and *Literaturnaya gazeta* sold 4.5 million.

Gorbachev's reluctance to give up his plans for a 'socialist alternative' and fully embrace Western notions of freedom and democracy attracted sharp criticisms in the liberal press at the beginning of 1991. A letter in *Moskovskie Novosti* from a group of writers and other cultural figures demanding his resignation was the first. But their demand was soon taken up by right-wing groups and that in turn was one of the reasons for Gorbachev's movement towards conservative forces within the party in his last year as a great reformer. He came into increasing conflict with a powerful opposition movement. While overt criticism of Gorbachev had earlier been limited to Boris Yeltsin's Inter-Regional Group within the Congress of USSR People's Deputies, now it came from conservatives and right-wingers within the Communist Party and beyond.

At the 4th Congress of People's Deputies, which met at the end of 1990, Gorbachev moved decisively towards the conservatives in the CPSU, armed forces and military-industrial complex, partly because events in Nagorno-Karabakh and in Central Asia made him fear that the Union was disintegrating but partly because he was under increasing pressure from the right and had been stung by criticisms in the left-wing press. Shevardnadze warned against the threat of dictatorship and later resigned. I spoke next and on behalf of 300 deputies announced some support for Shevardnadze and appealed to Gorbachev to form a left-centrist block. Gorbachev, however, took no notice of our views and proposed Gennadii Yanaev as vice-president, the same Yanaev who was subsequently to head the coup of August 1991.

The whole of 1991 was marked by an increasingly bitter struggle between different sections of the press. *Sovetskaya Rossiya*, to a significant extent *Pravda*, and many other papers controlled by the Communist Party attacked both the domestic and foreign policies associated with *perestroika*. Their attacks were not always directed at Gorbachev personally but these were his policies and it was easy to guess their real target. By implication at least, he was held to blame for the loss of Eastern Europe, especially the German Democratic Republic, for the collapse of the Warsaw Pact, and for the collapse into chaos which had already begun within the USSR itself. At the same time the left-radical press started to support leaders, primarily Boris Yeltsin, who advocated national sovereignty and the formation of independent states to replace the USSR.

Under my direction, *Literaturnaya gazeta* came out in support of the liberal democrats, warning of the danger of civil war, and calling for an alliance of radical and more moderate left-wing opinion, together with Gorbachev and Yeltsin personally. We saw this as the only possible means to prevent either a right-wing or a left-wing dictatorship. At the same time, we became increasingly critical of Gorbachev's shift towards the right. In January 1991, together with Stanislav Shatalin and Sergei Alekseev, I published an article titled 'Alternative' in which we criticised Gorbachev for his rapprochement with conservative forces in the party and society, and we put forward the programme of a Movement of Democratic Forces. In an article called 'The Kremlin and the White House on the Embankment', published the same month, I discussed the possibility of a coup and specifically predicted that the White House, home of the Russian republican Parliament, would be surrounded by tanks. At the same time, the article expressed certainty that the coup would end in a farce, since neither the events of 1956 in Hungary nor those of 1968 in Czechoslovakia could be repeated in Russia, where public opinion, social movements and the press had now become a powerful democratic force.

The press played an enormous role in the victory of Boris Yeltsin at the presidential elections in June 1991. Indeed, he owed his victory to the press. Yeltsin won 57 per cent of the vote, despite the opposition of the Communist Party and of those means of mass communication that were still under its control, including Central Television. What was decisive in this election was not so much the direct support that the press offered Yeltsin, as its criticism of Gorbachev. Voters saw in Yeltsin an opportunity to reject Gorbachev's policies, particularly on economic matters, where conditions were becoming increasingly desperate. The main reason for this was the breakdown of economic links between the different regions of the country which had existed for many decades. Under these new conditions, leaders of republics or even of individual regions moved increasingly towards separatism to protect the population of their own area. They only succeeded in making a difficult situation worse. The breakdown of economic links between the regions led to a sharp fall in output (by about 15 per cent in 1991), irregular deliveries of foodstuffs, and a full-scale food crisis.

The major struggle in the press during the first half of 1991 concerned the Union Treaty, which was to replace the Treaty originally concluded in 1922. It was a confrontation between federalists and confederalists though the confederalists soon switched to advocating a set of sovereign independent states. The left-radical press denounced repressive policies in Tbilisi, Vilnius, Riga and other parts of the former USSR. Many publications increasingly supported national separatism. At *Literaturnaya gazeta* we supported the idea of an (Economic) Commonwealth of States with institutions similar to those of the European Community.

Despite our arguments Gorbachev would make no concessions. He decided to overcome all resistance with the help of a referendum on the continuation of the USSR, in which he won 70 per cent of the vote – an enormous majority for the federalists. With this popular support Gorbachev asked the republics to sign the new Union Treaty on 20 August 1991, but the Yanaev coup intervened on the 19th. The coup not only prevented signature of the Union Treaty, but led to the final destruction of the communist system and the Soviet state.

At the time, it produced a sharp differentiation within the press. *Pravda* and *Sovetskaya Rossiya* supported the coup while publication of the democratic press including *Literaturnaya gazeta*, *Moskovskie novosti* and *Nezavisimaya gazeta* was banned by the coup leaders' State Emergency Committee. At the time I was on vacation in the Crimea, not far from Gorbachev's dacha, but from there during the first hours of the coup I gave instructions by phone to publish an illegal edition of *Literaturnaya gazeta* with a clear rejection of the conspirators. Unfortunately my first deputy lacked the courage to carry out this instruction, which later led to a crisis inside the paper itself and as a result I eventually resigned and appointed one of my other deputies to the editorship.

After the collapse of the coup, a bitter power struggle developed between Yeltsin and Gorbachev. At the end of December 1991, Gorbachev was removed from power, and the Soviet Union dissolved. There followed an entirely new stage in the development of the country with important consequences for freedom of expression and of the press.

In the West, there are two mistaken views of the events of 19–21 August 1991 and of the reasons for the collapse of the USSR and of the Soviet system as a whole. The first was presented in the excellent BBC series *The Second Russian Revolution*. From a professional point of view the film was beyond reproach. But a mistaken interpretation was given of the August events in that they were represented as a second – democratic – Russian revolution. The democratic revolution in the USSR in fact began much earlier than this. It began with Khrushchev's report to the 20th Congress of the CPSU in 1956 on the crimes of Stalin. His 'secret speech' delivered a powerful blow to the whole structure of totalitarianism. Khrushchev began the process by which the USSR evolved from a totalitarian into an authoritarian regime, preserving the domination of a single party, but refraining from mass oppression. Persecution of dissidents continued during the Brezhnev years but the era of the Gulag receded further and further into the past.

August 1991 represented a *national* stage in the revolution in the USSR, and one that was by no means entirely connected with the development of *democracy*. So far there has been little evidence to suggest that a greater degree of freedom and more respect for human rights are likely to be established in the newly independent post-Soviet republics than in the post-Khrushchev USSR. In many of them there has been a clear move backwards towards authoritarianism. The democratic achievements of the period of *perestroika* in the old USSR nonetheless remain its most enduring achievement. I might also observe that the mistaken interpretation of the August events as a second democratic revolution has become the orthodox view in many of the organs of mass communication in Russia. Only from 1992 did we begin to judge these matters a little more soberly.

The second mistaken view was expressed by President Reagan, who announced that the collapse of communism was the result of American foreign policy and his own foreign policy in particular, insofar as the USSR could not sustain the arms race. This is also incorrect. The USSR did sustain the arms race and created a powerful system of armaments which was not inferior to that of the USA. But communism did not survive a different kind of competition with the West and with Japan – an economic and technological one. Living standards and the quality of life in the USSR became one of the lowest in the world, and it was an understanding of this fact, together with some hostility towards Stalinism and its repression of all human liberties, that led to the movement of the '1960ers' inside the party, those 'Khrushchevists' who went significantly further than Khrushchev himself. Liberalism began to erode the Soviet system from inside and our press played all but the decisive role in the subsequent emergence of *perestroika*. By way of example, let me quote my own articles and books which were directed against Stalinism in the 1960s to 1980s: articles and books on Mao Zedong, Hitler, Franco, on the critique of totalitarianism, predicting an 'interregnum' and a 'time of troubles' when one after another leaders would be replaced and an era of major structural reforms would begin. I could name many people who wrote in this sense, above all that great liberal Andrei Sakharov.

The August events gave rise to a powerful centrifugal movement. On the one hand, this was a great achievement for the peoples of the 14 republics which eventually became independent. On the other hand, the collapse of the former USSR led to a whole series of problems. Three new nuclear powers appeared – Ukraine, Belorussia, and Kazakhstan. The army and fleet were divided. The destiny of the Crimea and of Sevastopol came into question. The war between Armenia and Azerbaijan continued. Economic links between all areas began to break down. There were new humanitarian problems: 75 million former Soviet citizens now live outside their 'own' republics, including 25 million Russians, a third of all Ukrainians, and two-thirds of all Tatars. The problem of refugees and the resettlement of whole peoples became still more acute. National minorities, Russian speakers especially, began to require assistance. Foreign states, among them Iran, Turkey and Romania, began to interfere in the domestic affairs of the newly independent states. Currencies began to compete with each other. The food crisis, and many other problems, became much more difficult.

In the press, as in political life as a whole, several competing groups clearly emerged. The national-democratic tendency was the dominant one, represented in Russia by state television and by the newspapers *Komsomol'skaya pravda*, *Izvestiya*, *Rossiiskaya gazeta*

('Russian Gazette'), *Moskovskii novosti* and many others. A different tendency was the national-communist, represented by *Pravda*, *Sovetskaya Rossiya* ('Soviet Russia'), *Literaturnaya Rossiya* ('Literary Russia'), and the newspaper *Den* ('Day'). Yet a third tendency was the Westernising one, represented by *Nezavisimaya gazeta*, *Kuranty*, *Delovye lyudi* and others. Liberal-democratic journals were in decline. After I left *Literaturnaya gazeta* it began to lose its role as a proponent of the freedom of the individual, of economic liberty, of the rights of private property and an open society. Associating itself with none of the existing tendencies, it increasingly lost influence and its circulation fell to 350,000, at the same time as the circulation of *Nezavisimaya gazeta* rose to over a million. Even the nationalist paper *Den*, in a relatively short period, managed to achieve a circulation of 200,000. But all publications were placed in some difficulty by a general fall in circulation levels.

In 1992 prospects for a genuinely free and independent press worsened considerably. First, there was a 10 to 20-fold rise in the price of newsprint and printing. No paper could survive that, and every paper became financially dependent on state subsidies. The Russian government declared it would give financial support only to 'properly oriented' papers – by which they meant loyal papers. The press gradually began to lose its freedom. Television changed completely; so that both the former USSR service based in Ostankino and Russian television only publicised official propaganda. Only a few papers, *Nezavisimaya gazeta* (literally, of course, 'Independent') for example, remained able to present an impartial viewpoint.

At the same time, the newly independent states, particularly Ukraine, Moldova, Azerbaijan, and Armenia, became increasingly dissatisfied with the central press. So the idea of maintaining a television and newspaper service which could serve the whole Community of Independent States received little support outside Russia itself.

On the whole the press reacted fairly calmly to the fall of Gorbachev. But the struggle between different publications did not abate; it became more intense. It focused on issues like the division of the army and fleet, price rises, the position of national minorities, and inter-ethnic conflicts.

What distinguished the post-Soviet most clearly from the Soviet press was its critique of Lenin and rejection of Communism both as a practical system and as an ideology. But the post-Soviet press had very few constructive ideas, and was prone to outbursts of intemperate abuse and intolerance: it still had a general tendency to denounce. The transition from a totalitarian to a free democratic press was still in its very earliest stages. The fall of Gorbachev, a basically liberal leader, did nothing to enhance the freedom of the press. The struggle for that still lay ahead.

Note

1 This chapter was originally presented by Fedor Burlatsky at Glasgow University under the title 'The fall of Gorbachev and the role of the Soviet press', 20.5.92. The quotation in the editor's title is from Prime Minister Stanley Baldwin's celebrated attack on the British press, when it tried to undermine his authority.

CHAPTER 7

Opinions: Public support for press censorship

WILLIAM L. MILLER, ANNIS MAY TIMPSON AND
MICHAEL LESSNOFF

Fedor Burlatsky has given an eyewitness account of the role of the
Soviet media during the Gorbachev years: initially leading the fight
for freedom by publishing officially banned material, exposing the
oppressions of the past, putting the case for liberal-democratic
institutions and helping to create a whole culture of freedom; then
fanning the flames of national and ethnic antagonisms; then sliding
back towards becoming, once more, the tool of government. While
Lord Armstrong raised the issue of government secrets, Fedor
Burlatsky raises the issue of an irresponsible press publishing
material that is not so much secret as *offensive* – offensive either to
intellectual norms of truth or to the targets of its abuse. He accuses
the Soviet press of irresponsibly undermining the authority of
President Gorbachev, as Prime Minister Baldwin accused the British press of undermining *his* authority, of exercising what Baldwin
called 'power without responsibility, the prerogative of the harlot
throughout the ages'. Current British governments seem little more
pleased with the press than was Stanley Baldwin. Although Fedor
Burlatsky's analysis is based upon the role of the Soviet press, the
issues he raises of press freedom, press responsibility and press
censorship are as acute in Britain as in the new democracies of
Eastern Europe.

Public support for censorship highlights two related but distinct
dimensions of freedom: freedom of information and freedom of
expression. In Chapter 5 we discussed the publication of government secrets, a scenario that was more closely linked to the issues
of freedom of information and open government raised by Lord
Armstrong, than to the issues of freedom of expression and the
right to be irresponsible raised by Fedor Burlatsky. Our focus
changes from consumers to producers, from readers and viewers to
journalists and programme makers, from the government's desire
to censor publication of its secrets to the public's desire to censor
what it finds irresponsible or disagreeable, from freedom of information to freedom of expression.

Secrecy and acceptability

In our survey, respondents were presented with nine different censorship scenarios, each of which came in two or more variants. In Chapter 5 we discussed the scenario variants concerned with the publication of government secrets. In this chapter we turn to those that throw more direct light on the question of press responsibility. Both situations involve attitudes to authority and both involve principles of freedom but not the same principles of freedom to the same degree. If we compare, for example, our respondents' attitudes towards censoring publication of government secrets with their attitudes towards banning abusive attacks on religion, it is clear that these involve two different kinds of freedom: freedom to hear, and freedom to speak.

In Chapter 5 we showed how respondents' commitment to freedom of information reduced their support for a ban on publishing government secrets by more than their commitment to freedom of expression. By contrast, when we asked respondents about banning publication of abusive attacks on religion, we found that their commitment to freedom of expression reduced their support for such censorship by more than their commitment to freedom of information.

The contrast was particularly marked amongst politicians whose support for censorship usually reflected their abstract principles more closely in any case. Amongst politicians, commitment to freedom of information reduced support for a ban on publishing government secrets by 29 per cent, while commitment to free expression reduced it by only 22 per cent. By contrast, politicians' commitment to freedom of information reduced support for a ban on publishing religious abuse by a negligible amount (a mere 1 per cent) while their commitment to free expression reduced it by 16 per cent.

Mapping the boundaries to acceptable press freedom

Beyond general principles of openness, freedom of speech and respect for authority there are many other concerns that come into play when considering particular censorship scenarios. Our nine censorship scenarios were designed to make people weigh their support for free expression and freedom of information not only against their general respect for authority but also against their specific antipathy towards terrorism and violence, their religious feelings, their sympathy for minorities, and their commitments to privacy, the national interest, fairness and truth – a wide range of competing values and principles. By considering these together we may hope to map some of the boundaries of acceptable publication or, what is the same thing differently expressed, the boundaries of

Table 7.1   **Effect of abstract principles: censorship of government secrets and religious attacks**

	General public	Local politicians
Average % support for ban on publication of confidential government documents among:		
those whose commitment to freedom of information is:		
high	54	40
low	69	69
Effect	− 15	− 29
those whose commitment to freedom of expression is:		
high	53	43
low	66	65
Effect	− 13	− 22
Average % support for ban on publication of attacks upon religions among:		
those whose commitment to freedom of information is:		
high	37	35
low	43	36
Effect	− 6	− 1
those whose commitment to freedom of expression is:		
high	34	34
low	43	50
Effect	− 9	− 16

Note:
Average percents' because there were six variants of the government secrets question and two variants of the religious abuse question.

desirable censorship. Mallory Wober has explored the limits to public acceptance of violence, sexuality and coverage of the Royal Family on British television (Wober 1989; 1990; 1991; 1992). Our focus here is somewhat different, but our objective is fundamentally the same: to map at least a sector of the boundaries of public acceptability.

We began with a battery of five questions. We asked:

Some people think there should be no restrictions on what can be published in books and newspapers or screened on television, but others disagree. For each of the following please say whether you think it should be [*allowed* on television without any restrictions, or *restricted* for example to late night viewing, or *banned* from television altogether / *allowed* in newspapers without any restrictions, or *restricted* for example to books, or *banned* from publication altogether].

A randomly selected half of the interviews asked about television and the other half about newspapers. This introduction was followed by a list of five items that might be allowed, restricted, or banned, three of which used variable wording. Each interview covered all five items, though only one variant of each question. The list was:

1. Pictures of extreme violence;
2. Abusive attacks on [the Christian religion/minority religions such as the Muslim or Hindu religion];
3. Interviews with supporters of [IRA terrorists/Protestant terrorists in Northern Ireland];
4. Stories that intrude into [ordinary people's/leading politicians'] private lives;
5. Lies and distortions of the truth.

On average neither public nor politicians made much distinction between television and the print press. Support for censorship varied sharply with news-*topic* but not with news-*medium*. So we shall combine answers to questions about television and newspapers and refer to them, generically, as questions about 'the press'.

In his essay 'On Liberty' John Stuart Mill put the views that we should tolerate the publication even of what we take to be lies and distortions of the truth because we may be wrong; that the best defence against the publication of lies is uncensored publication of truth, not censorship of lies; and that, in the end, truth will drive out lies. Neither public nor politicians agree: three-quarters supported an outright ban on publication of lies and distortions of the truth.

They were only a little more tolerant of intrusions into the private lives of ordinary people: 64 per cent of the public and 55 per cent of politicians would ban these. But they were very much more tolerant of intrusions into even the *private* lives of leading politicians: only 43 per cent of the public and 34 per cent of local politicians would ban them.

In October 1988 the then Home Secretary, Douglas Hurd, issued an order to the BBC and IBA (Independent Broadcasting Authority) under the 1981 Broadcasting Act, banning both networks from broadcasting any words spoken by a person 'representing or purporting to represent' organisations which included the illegal IRA and UVF (Ulster Volunteer Force) and the (then) legal Sinn Fein and UDA (Ulster Defence Association), except where those words were spoken in Parliament or during an election campaign.[1] Just under half the public and one third of politicians – though only a minority in each case – supported that type of ban. Neither public nor politicians drew much distinction between IRA and Protestant terrorists.

But the public and, more especially, politicians drew a distinction between the abuse of Christianity and of minority religions. Among the public 32 per cent would ban abusive attacks on Christianity, but 44 per cent on minority religions. Politicians were even more willing than the public to tolerate abuse of Christianity (only 22 per cent would ban it) but even less willing to tolerate abuse of minority religions (49 per cent would ban it). Across the whole range of questions asked in our survey, including questions about

Table 7.2 **Support for ban on publication of five items** (*percentages*)

	General public	Local politicians
lies and distortions	77	75
Intrusions into the private lives:		
of ordinary people	64	55
of leading politicians	43	34
Interviews with supporters of:		
IRA terrorists	50	38
Protestant terrorists	45	37
Abusive attacks upon:		
the Christian religion	32	22
minority religions	44	49
pictures of extreme violence	32	33

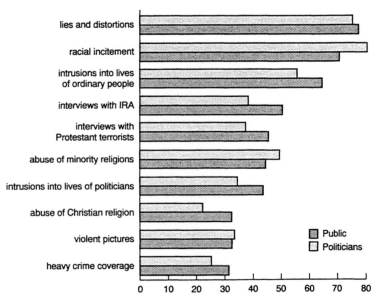

Figure 7.1 **Boundaries of public tolerance for press** (*% who would ban*)

censorship, political leaders were usually more tolerant, more libertarian, and less restrictive than the public, except where tolerance
might disadvantage religious and racial minorities. But it is still
significant that both public and politicians were more tolerant of
abuse of the majority religion than of the minority. Racial and
religious prejudice can sometimes be favourable to minorities. And
it is important to remember that no interview asked about banning the abuse of both Christianity and minority religions; so no

Table 7.3 **Effect of general principles on support for censorship of five items**

	General public	Local politicians
Effect of commitment to free expression upon willingness to ban:		
interviews with terrorist supporters	− 19	− 24
intrusions into private lives	− 12	− 15
attacks on religion	− 9	− 16
pictures of extreme violence	− 7	− 18
lies and distortions	+ 4	− 11
Effect of commitment to freedom of information upon willingness to ban:		
interviews with terrorist supporters	− 10	− 21
intrusions into private lives	− 9	− 10
attacks on religion	− 6	− 2
pictures of extreme violence	− 2	− 7
lies and distortions	0	− 3
Effect of respect for authority upon willingness to ban:		
interviews with terrorist supporters	+ 30	+ 46
intrusions into private lives	+ 19	+ 23
attacks on religion	+ 14	+ 18
pictures of extreme violence	+ 9	+ 15
lies and distortions	+ 8	+ 17

Notes:
1 'Effect' defined as % support for censorship among those whose commitment to the principle is high, minus % support for censorship among those whose commitment to the principle is low.
2 High and low support for these principles defined as in Chapter 5.
3 For simplicity, in this table both versions of the questions on intrusions into private lives, attacks on religions, and interviews with terrorists have been combined.

respondent was under any conscious pressure to appear more sympathetic to minorities than to the Established faith.

Finally, just a third would ban pictures of extreme violence. While we did not distinguish between news and entertainment, the context of the interview probably focused respondents' imaginations towards violent news rather than violent entertainment.

This variability of opinion implies that some principles other than a general commitment to free speech, openness and respect for authority come into play when people consider banning particular kinds of publication. People value a right to privacy, though more for ordinary people than for leading politicians, and they have a very practical sympathy towards minorities and/or a fear of exacerbating racial and religious tensions. Above all they have a strong commitment to the undistorted truth and an abhorrence of lies.

In addition to these more specific principles however, general commitments to freedom of expression and information, together with a general respect for authority still influenced attitudes towards censorship across this range of questions. Taken separately, all three general principles had least effect upon support for a ban on lies and distortions and most upon support for a ban on interviews with apologists for terrorism. Among the public, commitment to free expression reduced support for a ban on interviews with apologists for terrorism by 19 per cent, commitment to freedom of information reduced it by 10 per cent, and respect for authority increased it by 30 per cent. Among politicians the fit between principles and practice was even closer: commitment to free expression reduced support for a ban by 24 per cent, commitment to freedom of information reduced it by 21 per cent, and respect for authority increased it by 46 per cent.

The power of argument

We also put three further questions about censorship of sensational crime stories and stories that might intentionally or unintentionally incite racial hatred. These questions also tap support for a truly open society, open to the things that well-meaning liberals dislike as well as the things they do like. More important, they allow us to assess the power of explicit arguments presented either before or after the expression of opinion.

We asked whether: 'Heavy television and press coverage of dramatic crimes like murders or terrorist incidents should be banned?'. In one third of the interviews, randomly chosen, we gave no justification for a ban; in one third, we added the phrase 'because it may encourage others to commit more crimes'; and in the remaining third we added 'because, later on, it may prevent an accused person getting a fair trial'.

Politicians were significantly less willing to ban heavy crime coverage (32 per cent compared to 44 per cent among the public) and also less easily influenced by arguments. Without an argument for censorship, 31 per cent of the public supported a ban, rising to 47 per cent and 53 per cent when we put the 'encourage more crime' and 'fair trial' arguments respectively. Among politicians, 25 per cent favoured a ban without an argument, rising only to 27 per cent and 44 per cent respectively when we put the two arguments for a ban. So politicians were almost totally uninfluenced by the fear of 'encouraging more crime' and only influenced by their desire for a 'fair trial'.

Similarly we asked whether newspapers 'should be banned from publishing research showing very high rates of crime among blacks'. In half the interviews, we gave no justification; and in half we added 'because this may encourage prejudice against them'. Public support for a ban was twice as high as among politicians (40 per cent compared to 23 per cent). Once again argument had an

Table 7.4 *Effect of arguments for censorship of crime coverage and racial/religious incitement*

	General public	Local politicians
% willing to ban heavy coverage of dramatic crimes:		
without argument	31	25
with 'more crime' argument	47	27
with 'fair trial' argument	53	44
% willing to ban publication of crime rates among blacks:		
without argument	35	19
with 'prejudice' argument	46	26
% willing to ban racial/religious incitement:		
racial incitement	70	80
religious incitement	58	69
% willing to reconsider among:		
pro-censorship people challenged by 'free speech' argument	50	45
anti-censorship people challenged by 'prejudice' argument	48	34

influence, though a more modest one. Among politicians support for a ban ran at 19 per cent without reference to prejudice rising to only 26 per cent with it; among the public the figure was 35 per cent rising to 46 per cent.

We did not consider racially sensitive expression solely in the context of a publishing scenario. We also asked our respondents a more general question: 'Do you think it should be against the law to write or speak in a way that promotes [racial/religious] hatred?'. In half the interviews (randomly chosen) we used the word 'racial', in the other half 'religious'. The offence of racial incitement was introduced in 1965 and extended in the 1986 Public Order Act. It is now an offence to publish or broadcast, except on BBC and IBA programmes, anything likely to stir up race hatred *whether or not that is intended*; and it is an offence *even to possess* such material unless ignorant of its contents – though prosecutions have been rare (Hurwitt and Thornton 1989: 40–1). Of all our questions about censorship this was the only one apart from the question about 'abusive attacks on minority religions' where politicians were more in favour of censorship than the general public. Two-thirds of the public and three-quarters of politicians would ban racial or religious incitement.

Once again however, we found that opinion was fluid and open to argument. After people had answered the question, we put a counter-argument to them. If they approved a ban on publishing racial/religious incitement we asked: 'If this results in less freedom of speech about important public issues, would you feel differently about it being against the law?'. Half now said they would feel differently. On the other hand, if people had opposed censorship of

*Table 7.5   **Effect of general principles: censorship of government secrets, crime coverage and racial incitement***

	General public	Local politicians
Effect of commitment to free expression upon willingness to ban publication of:		
confidential government documents	− 13	− 22
black crime rates	− 17	− 20
heavy coverage of dramatic crimes	− 18	− 28
racial incitement	0	− 4
Effect of commitment to freedom of information upon willingness to ban publication of:		
confidential government documents	− 15	− 29
black crime rates	− 6	− 9
heavy coverage of dramaic crimes	− 6	− 15
racial incitement	0	+ 1
Effect of respect for authority upon willingness to ban publication of:		
confidential government documents	+ 26	+ 47
black crime rates	+ 24	+ 23
heavy coverage of dramatic crimes	+ 25	+ 32
racial incitement	− 2	0

Note:
'Racial incitement' does not include 'religious incitement' in this table.

racial/religious incitement we asked: 'If this results in more racial/religious prejudice, would you feel differently about its not being against the law?'. Almost half the public and one third of politicians now agreed that they would reconsider their opposition to a ban. We used this technique of counter-arguments on other topics besides censorship. Neither public nor politicians always proved so ready to reconsider their initial opinions. On capital punishment for example we found much more rigidly held views on both sides. So our finding on censorship of racial incitement indicates flexibility on that specific question, and deep concern for both free expression and racial prejudice, rather than a general willingness to retreat in the face of any counter-argument on any subject whatsoever.

General principles of free expression, openness and respect for authority influenced attitudes on these three questions about censorship of crime and race stories. But comparison between the effects of general principles on support for censoring these three different stories, and comparision with support for censorship of government secrets, is revealing. Respect for authority greatly increased support for censorship of government secrets, black crime statistics and heavy crime coverage, but fractionally *reduced* support for a ban on racial incitement: it was libertarians, not authoritarians, who were the most willing to impose censorship on racial abuse.

Table 7.6 **Ideology and limits to public toleration of press freedom** (% **willing to ban various items**)

Among those who place themselves on/in	General public			Local politicians		
	Left	Centre	Right	Left	Centre	Right
Large left/right differences						
confidential government documents	40	57	75	17	55	73
interviews with terrorist supporters	35	48	55	17	43	57
Small left/right differences						
sensational crime coverage	35	45	48	22	40	35
intrusions into private lives	51	53	55	37	51	46
lies and distortions	77	75	80	71	79	76
Left/right difference reversed						
incitement to racial hatred	75	71	62	87	79	73

Conversely, commitment to free expression produced a significant decrease in support for censorship of government secrets, heavy crime coverage, even publication of black crime rates, but hardly any decrease in support for censorship of racial incitement. Commitment to freedom of information sharply reduced support for censorship of government secrets and marginally reduced support for censorship of crime reporting but, like commitment to free expression, did nothing to reduce support for censorship of racial incitement.

Ideology and acceptable press freedom

We found in Chapter 5 that people who placed themselves on the left were far less willing to ban publication of government secrets than those on the right. Those on the left were also much less willing to ban interviews with apologists for terrorists – whether the IRA or their Protestant counterparts. But left/right differences on censorship of sensational crime stories, press intrusions into private lives, or publication of lies and distortions were small. Indeed, among politicians, it was those who placed themselves in the *centre* of the political spectrum who were most willing to ban such publications – not those on the right. And it was those on the *left*, not in the centre and still less those on the right, who were most keen to ban racial incitement. So each part of the political spectrum had its own 'hit-list' for censorship. Nonetheless, the only issues which sharply divided left and right put right-wingers in favour of censorship and left-wingers against. Overlaid on top of each ideological camp's tendency to draw up a private hit-list there is evidence that the left were generally less comfortable with censorship.

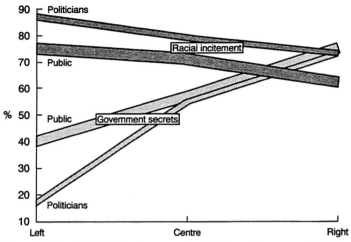

*Figure 7.2 **Ideological hit-lists for censorship (% who would censor publication)***

How much public support is there for censorship?

Our results show that public support for censorship is highly
variable. It varies first of all, according to the nature of the
offending material. Although less than one-third of our respondents
would ban attacks on the Christian religion or pictures of extreme
violence, up to three-quarters of them would ban publication of
lies, distortions of the truth and (as we saw in Chapter 5) secret
defence plans.

Attitudes to censorship are also affected by the context in which
this option is considered and, in particular, by the arguments made
in favour of censorship of particular items. Thus we found that
public support for censorship increased by up to 22 per cent if we
mentioned the need to avoid encouraging crime, or to take account
of national interests, or to ensure a fair trial. And many people,
about half in one of the tests we carried out, are willing to
reconsider their attitude to censorship even when challenged by
arguments produced *after* they have already expressed a view
about it.

Politicians, however, are generally less willing to support censorship, and less easily influenced by implicit or explicit arguments,
but they make an exception where censorship is designed to protect
racial minorities.

None of that variability and malleability of opinion means that
people do not have real feelings about censorship. Quite the contrary. While people have general principles that dispose them to be
more (or less) favourable to censorship under any and all circumstances, many people – perhaps most – are sufficiently flexible and
sophisticated to take into account the particular circumstances of

the case, specific principles uniquely relevant to that case, and the arguments advanced by other people, as well as their own more general principles and predispositions.

Note

1 See Ewing and Gearty (1990: 243). The UDA was legally banned later.

References

Ewing, H. D. and Gearty, C. A. (1990) *Freedom under Thatcher*, Oxford: Oxford University Press.

Hurwitt, M. and Thornton, P. (1989) *Civil Liberty: The Liberty/NCCL Guide*, 4th edition, London: Penguin.

Wober, M. (1989) *Lives and Liberties: Attitudes to Religion, Ethics and Innovation on Television*, London: IBA.

Wober, M. (1990) *The Role of Television in the Wake of the Satanic Verses*, London: IBA.

Wober, M. (1991) *Rules and Regulations: Attitudes to 'Drawing the Line' on Television*, London: ITC.

Wober, M. (1992) *No Menace to Monarchism: Stable Attitudes after Discussion of a Widely Publicised Book*, London: ITC.

Mill, J. S. (1962) 'On Liberty' in *Utilitarianism*, London: Fontana.

PART FOUR

Freedom versus Accountability

CHAPTER 8

Witness: A media war of independence[1]

ELEMER HANKISS

It is better to have a war of words and political strategies around the media than to have a war fought with tanks and guns in the fields. And it is better to have a public television fighting for its independence than to have one which has accepted, and is resigned to, its dependence. In this light, the Hungarian media's war of independence may be considered as a sign of relative peace and maturity. At the same time, it is the exception that does not make the rule. And it is not quite normal.

One has to be careful, though, with the use of the word 'normal' in the East Central European context. The region has such a long history of absurdities and abnormalities that one is frequently at a loss to know what the words 'normal' and 'abnormal' really mean. For two hundred years most of the social and economic problems of the region have been left unsolved. State boundaries have been arbitrarily drawn and redrawn by various peace treaties – the Congress of Berlin, the Treaty of Versailles, the Yalta Conference and the post-Second World War treaties. And 45 years of communism has further deepened the social and economic backwardness and crisis of the region. So present-day events and developments are questions of life and death for each individual, family, group and class in these societies. Current events are deciding who will be the winners and who will be the losers in the next decades; who will profit from, and who will lose by, the transition to a new social and economic model; whose children will be poor and whose will be rich; who will belong to the propertied classes and who will be the have-nots.

If we consider all these facts then we may be inclined to think, at least for a fleeting moment, however cynical it may sound, that the Yugoslav situation is normal and the relatively peaceful development in the Czech Republic, Slovakia, Poland, and Hungary is abnormal. It is fascinating to see the discipline and moral strength of people walking in the streets of Budapest, Warsaw, or Prague. They live in a world of unbearable tensions, uncertainties and conflicts. Why do they not fly at one another's throats? Why do they not scream from stress and pain? How can they smile and sit around and sip their undrinkably strong espresso coffees? Is this not abnormal?

The gentle revolution brought to East Central Europe the long expected freedom of the (print) press but, at the same time, in most of the countries it has not liberated the electronic media, public television and radio, from the control of those in power. There has been, of course, a substantial change in the character and intensity of control, but the fact remains that in most of these countries public television is government television or presidential television according to the political system in the countries in question. Changes in government have been routinely followed by changes in the leadership of public television. In most cases, one of the first steps of new prime ministers and presidents has been to replace the old television leadership and news staff by new leaders and new staffs with new loyalties. That seems to be the norm in present-day East Central Europe.

But for more than two years Hungary was a happy or unhappy exception, in many ways. Hungary entered the process of transformation with a different and better legacy than most of its neighbours. A couple of other East Central European countries also began to experiment with economic and political reforms in the late 1950s or 1960s. But this process was halted, and even reversed, in Czechoslovakia in August 1968 and was interrupted in Poland in 1981. In Hungary it went on, with only temporary setbacks, throughout the 1970s and 1980s. Czechoslovakia was frozen in its hardened communist regime until the moment of revolution in November 1989. In Poland, a major confrontation developed between the Communist Party and Solidarity in the late 1980s and this political confrontation absorbed most of the energies of the country until mid-1989. But in Hungary, on the contrary, important economic reforms were implemented in the early 1980s (opening the field, for instance, to small group enterprises) and in the late 1980s, well before the revolution, some basic institutions of the market economy were established by the still hundred per cent communist Parliament (a double-level banking system, a Company Law and a Transformation Law allowing the transformation of state enterprises into joint stock companies, etc.).

In addition, the disintegration and inner pluralisation of the Communist Party went farther in Hungary than in any other East Central European country. It was there that the younger and more dynamic generations of the communist oligarchy discovered, earlier than anybody else in the region, the possibility and the need to 'convert' their political power into economic assets and to prepare themselves for their new roles in the emerging market economy. Having discovered this escape-route, they were able to open up politically, engage in a dialogue with the opposition groups, and manage the smoothest transition to democracy in the region.

In 1989–90, the situation in Hungary was therefore more favourable for the development of a pluralistic version of democracy than in neighbouring countries. In Czechoslovakia, the rule of a monolithic communist oligarchy was replaced, after the first free elections, by the new Parliament dominated by one major party, the

Civic Forum (and its Slovak counterpart) and the real political articulation and pluralisation of the political forces surfaced in Parliament only after the 1992 elections. In Poland, the overwhelming influence of Solidarity, KOR, and Walesa slowed down the healthy process of political pluralisation within the parliamentary system. So much so that when it emerged, after the election in late 1991, it led to an absurd proliferation of small parties and the dangerous fragmentation of the political field.

Hungary, with its deeply divided Communist Party and well-articulated opposition forces had a better chance in 1989 and 1990 to establish a pluralistic, multi-party parliamentary system. It was a further advantage that at the general elections in March and April 1990, none of the parties gained a decisive majority and that even the governing coalition won only a slight majority in Parliament. All these factors together contributed to setting in motion the multi-party parliamentary machinery in Hungary. This situation and, on the other hand, the slower than expected pluralisation of Hungarian polity and society in general, led to what is called in Hungary the 'media war'.

In those countries in which, after the collapse of the communist regime, a dominant party or a dominant personality came to power, public television and radio could not escape government or presidential control. This was, or has been, the case in Czechoslovakia, Poland, Rumania, Bulgaria, Serbia, Croatia, Slovenia. There were good and bad reasons for exercising control over the media. Among the good, or at least not entirely wrong ones, there is the argument that the extremely difficult process of transition to democracy and a market economy calls for common goals, national unity, the broad national support of government plans and policies. For the success of this strategy of national unity and mobilisation television and radio are indispensable. In several, if not most cases people appointed to top jobs in the television and radio companies sincerely believed – and some of them still believe – that their duty is to serve, or at least help, the government. But not in Hungary.

The background

The first free elections since 1947 were held in Hungary in March and April 1990. After the elections the MDF (Hungarian Democratic Forum), the main governing party, had only a slight majority and had to make a pact with the strongest opposition party. In particular they had to agree upon the main rules of the game. One of the first points in this pact was that they would pick two independent persons for the positions of presidents of Hungarian Television and Hungarian Radio. This was not an easy task since in the buoyant years of 1988–89, and in the heat of the 1990 electoral campaign, few people could resist the temptation to jump headlong into party politics. After 40 years of forced passivity, people had every reason to be impatient to do something for their country, let alone the fact that the position of a leading politician became almost overnight the most glamorous and attractive social role, which could bring not only power but also fame, prestige, and a new identity after so many years spent in anonymity if not in anomie.

It was in this situation that in June 1990, after the elections, the prime minister and the leader of the main opposition party came to us (Csaba Gombar and myself, both political scientists teaching at the University of Budapest) and offered us these jobs. They told us that we were proposed as two independent persons who were supposed to be able to keep a middle course between the governing parties and the opposition and ensure the impartiality of the two institutions. At that time, in the post-revolutionary euphoria, all the parties seriously believed in the sanctity of the *principle* of the freedom of the press. They did not know yet how annoying the *practice* of this freedom would soon become for many of them.

For several weeks we said no, no and no. Finally we gave in and told them that we would accept the nomination under the condition that the law regulating the appointment of the presidents was changed. In the communist regime, the Council of Ministers had the right to appoint the presidents of Hungarian Radio and Television (under the almost overt and imperative control of the Party Politburo). We made it clear that we would not accept appointment at the hands of the Prime Minister because we did not want to be dependent in any way on him or on the government. Our point was accepted and the law changed overnight. According to this new law, which became the foundation of the independence of the two institutions in the coming two years, the Prime Minister had only the right to nominate his candidates, who – after hearings in a parliamentary committee – would, or would not, be appointed by the President of the Republic. Even with this amendment, we accepted these positions only for six months, or more precisely until a new media law had been passed and our successors found. This was in July 1990. More than two years passed and there was still no media law in Hungary and our successors had not been found. We had a media war instead.

After our appointment in August 1990, the honeymoon (if there was any) with the governing parties came to an early end. They realised very soon that they had picked the wrong people. My friend at Hungarian Radio was a soft-spoken, gentle man, with a timid smile and an overdose of modesty. He is one of the best Hungarian political scientists but behaves as if he were a first-year student. He unwittingly misled the government politicians with his timid smile – if they had looked for somebody who could be used, influenced, intimidated – because behind his boyish appearance there is a strong and courageous character. As for myself, I may be less modest and less soft-spoken but happen to be rather sensitive to independence and allergic to people who want to tell me what to do.

But their biggest mistake lay somewhere else: they forgot or ignored the fact that we, too, suffered from a disease which was widespread among East European intellectuals in the four decades of communism. It was an uncomfortable giddiness, a feeling of lightness, of weightlessness, a feeling of uncertainty about ourselves. The fear that one day we could be called to give account of the seriousness of our ideas; called to prove that we had really meant what we said and wrote about for 40 years; that the ideas that we opposed to communism in our writings, discussions and books for four decades – the ideas of justice and democracy, civic courage and tolerance, truth and freedom – were more than mere words and intellectual frivolities; that, instead of only speaking about them, we could live up to them. In 1989, the moment of truth finally came. This was a happy and a slightly alarming surprise. We had to prove the integrity and consistency of our ideas and actions. On the one hand, this was an easy task since we were convinced that the freedom of the press and the independence of the public media from any political or governmental influence was one of the main imperatives of a democratic polity and we acted accordingly. On the other hand, the situation may have prompted us to embark on a potentially quixotic campaign.

For two and a half years Hungarian Television and Radio were the most independent public media not only in East Central Europe but also in Europe as a whole – East or West. This was not a pure blessing. Due to the new law regulating the election of the presidents and due also to the absence of a new media law, which would have created a good balance between the independence of these institutions and their social control, the two newly elected media presidents had practically absolute control over their institutions. One might almost say that if we had decided to transform our institutions into, say, shoe factories, it would have been quite difficult legally to stop us from doing so.

Actually, we set out in a less (or perhaps more) absurd direction: we made an attempt to transform these formerly party-controlled institutions into West European-type public television and radio companies, with a high level of public responsibility, impartial news and current affairs programs, and a wide range of educational, cultural and entertainment programs. We both did and did not succeed. We did, because by 1992 our programming could already stand its ground against most European public broadcasting despite a much weaker financial background. But, on the other hand, we failed because after more than two years of successful resistance, we were finally defeated by party politics. This was not a big surprise since almost all the power was on the other side throughout the media war. The governing parties and the government itself had all their legislative and executive powers of coercion.

But we too had some protection and some important allies. We could, first of all, rely on the letter and spirit of the law. Second, in the course of the media war, we got more and more support from the greater and, in my opinion, better part of the print press and from the parties in the opposition. Last, but not least, we had the power of being independent. Our adversaries as well as our friends knew that we were not personally interested in keeping our positions, that we did not want to accumulate power for ourselves, and that we would be happy to go back to our own profession as soon as possible. So we could not be blackmailed or intimidated into any bad compromise or conformism.

The facts

Let me begin with a *caveat*. Since I have been one of the actors in this conflict my report is necessarily and inevitably biased. I shall list the main steps in the conflict but I am sure that even these facts would be seen, or at least interpreted, in a different light and a different way by those who stood on the other side – I mean the government and the governing parties, and especially the populist-nationalist right-wings of these parties. They would certainly emphasise that they supported the principle of a free press at least as much as we did and they would claim that the government was forced, by various factors outside its control – including our misbehaviour – to curb the autonomy of Hungarian Television and Radio.

I have no reason to question the sincerity of the government, or at least that of the late Prime Minister, Mr Antall, when he spoke of his dedication to the freedom of the press. For 40 years, the freedom of the press was a Holy Grail to be attained for all of us who were in opposition to the communist regime. And it is beyond doubt that in the euphoric months around the first free elections in early 1990, most of the new politicians were, as a matter of course, for the freedom of the press, including the freedom of the electronic media. It would have been an anathema and an unacceptable absurdity on the part of any of the parties in the election campaign to propose the control of the media by the future government.

I have already mentioned that after the elections of early 1990 the major governing party and the strongest opposition party signed a pact. According to the third paragraph of this pact, the two parties agreed to pick two independent persons to become presidents of Hungarian Television and Hungarian Radio, respectively. There is no reason to believe that any of the signatories did not really believe that the independence of the two media was in the interest of the country (both parties believed, at least, that without this pact, the other would have a better chance to control these media).

The question of who is responsible for starting the media war is still a controversial issue. According to the government, the main responsibility lies upon the print press, which, sympathising with the opposition, launched a wholesale attack against the government and against anything it did or failed to do from its very first days in office. In this situation the governing parties were forced to find a solution. First they tried to establish a pro-government press, or at least some newspapers and weeklies sympathising with the government. After the failure of this attempt, they had to turn towards the two great electronic media and began to lobby, and later to press, for more and more support from them. Since these media were – according to the government – controlled by former socialists turned liberals, it was justified, even in the name of the freedom and the compulsory neutrality of the press, to extend a kind of government control over them and force them to achieve a better balance.

According to the opposition parties however, all this was unfounded accusation and empty rhetoric to cover the attempt by the government and governing parties to concentrate all power in their hands and to extend a direct political control over the electronic media; and to do so in order to be able to build up an authoritarian type of democracy, win the next elections, and establish themselves for ever as a coalition of dominant parties.

I personally think that, on the one hand, the liberal press was indeed biased against the government in the first months of the new regime and throughout 1990. After mid-1991, however, the best organs of the print press had become more and more neutral and impartial and by 1992 had reached a relatively high professional quality. As for Hungarian Television and Radio, I think they were less biased against the government than the written press, and their programmes had been well balanced between various political forces since early 1991 (in spite of the survival of some pro-government and pro-opposition programmes). It was the fault of the government and the governing coalition that, lacking the necessary skills and public relations expertise, they could not profit from the openness of these two institutions and blamed television and radio for their own weakness and failures. It was simply a cynical strategy to justify their attack against these two institutions by alleging pro-opposition bias.

Finally I know that the Hungarian government is not the only government in Europe, including the Western part of the continent, that has made successful or unsuccessful attempts to extend its control over public broadcasting and I have to admit that in the first two years of the conflict – during which the Hungarian government observed the legal regulations of the country and tried to win the media war by legal means – its strategy was more civilised and acceptable than the means used by some of its Western counterparts.

The fact, however, that in the last months of the conflict the government lost its patience and invaded public television and radio before a court could have ruled whether it had, or had not, the right to do so, was not the most serious offence it committed. The government did the real harm by destroying the autonomy of two important public institutions in a country, and in a region, which had been kept in a semi-colonial and backward state by centuries of authoritarian rule, bureaucracy and overcentralisation. By reinforcing this destructive East European tradition, instead of encouraging the development of a pluralistic democracy of interactive autonomous institutions it has, in my opinion, dangerously slowed down the post-1989 process of democratic transformation in Hungary.

So much for the *caveat*; now the facts. In July 1990 the two presidential candidates were proposed by the Prime Minister, unanimously approved by the Cultural Committee of the Parliament, and appointed by the President of the Republic. By December conflicts with the governing parties and the government had begun. Government politicians saw no 'guarantees' in the persons I had appointed to leading positions in Hungarian Television. They cut our budget subsidy by half. In the new year we began a radical reorganisation of Hungarian Television to transform it from a rigid bureaucratic state institution into a modern and flexible public broadcaster, like commercial television in its organisation and management but keeping its public values and duties intact. Right-wing groups and the governing parties began to attack us on various counts. They claimed, for example, that:

1. *We were 'commercialising' national television.* In fact we had to develop our commercial activities in great haste. We founded a joint company with one of the world's greatest media agencies and doubled our advertising income within a year, so that we could survive in spite of the government-inflicted budget cuts – much to the dismay of our governmental adversaries.
2. *We were 'Americanising' Hungarian national television.* In fact, although we began to screen episodes of *Dallas* and other American series, the proportion of Hungarian and European-made productions remained much higher in our programming than in most other European public televisions.
3. *We paid more to our stars than the salary of the Prime Minister of the country.* In fact our stars did earn more than the Prime Minister, as their counterparts do in all Western countries. But after having lived for a thousand years in highly hierarchical societies, it was difficult to understand and swallow the fact that the king earned less than the clown.
4. *Our journalists and programmes were too critical of, even biased*

against, the government. In fact, in the first month after the elections of 1990 this was at least partly true. By the first half of 1991, however, our overall programming was already well balanced, with some pro-government and pro-opposition programs still remaining.

5. *By reorganising the institution, we had ruined the old workshops and as a result jeopardised the dominance of Hungarian national cultural values in the programmes.* In fact we dismantled the big departments of the old institution and replaced them by a number of small producer-units which were to compete for the orders of the two television channels. The outcry came from those who had lost their departments and lost the power which they had under the communists but who had turned their coats in time and by 1990 were already sailing under nationalist and pro-government flags.

From April 1991 onwards, the Prime Minister, supposedly under pressure from the right-wing of his party, began to propose various persons as vice-presidents of Hungarian Television and Radio (with the less and less veiled intention of having someone reliable there through whom the government could exert its influence within these institutions). For almost a year, he failed to get his way.

In May, government experts excavated an old decree of 1974 from the then communist Council of Ministers, which gave the Council the right to 'supervise' Hungarian Television. The Prime Minister used this – to say the least, anachronistic – decree as one of his main weapons in the ensuing media war. In November, I started a new evening news programme to counter-balance the increasingly right-wing tendencies of the existing news programme. We were punished in December when the government cut practically all our remaining budget subsidy.

On 1 March 1992 the Prime Minister finally succeeded in forcing his own vice-presidents on the two broadcasting institutions. Two days later I suspended my vice-president from his position. This led to a long and passionate legal controversy between the Prime Minister and myself to which I shall return in a moment. Not being able to win the legal controversy, and presumably more and more pressured by his right-wing, the Prime Minister proposed to the President of the Republic in early summer that I and my colleague at Hungarian Radio be dismissed from our positions. After hearings in a parliamentary committee, the President turned down the proposal.

In August, Mr Csurka, vice-president of the governing Hungarian Democratic Forum, published his ill-famed pamphlet in which he drew the outlines of a vaguely populist and nationalist ideology and programme, with xenophobic and anti-modernist overtones. This made the nationalist-versus-European, conservative-versus-liberal controversies even more passionate and absurd. In Mr Csurka's mythology there was a Judaeo-Bolshevik-liberal-cosmopolitan conspiracy against the Hungarian nation. Csaba Gombar of Hungarian Radio and myself were depicted by him or some of his followers as the chief agents in this conspiracy. The craze went even further in September 1992 when nationalists staged hunger-strikes against us and right-wing groups organised demonstrations against the President of the Republic, my radio colleague and myself in the streets of Budapest. A crowd of about 15,000 men demanded my resignation in my favourite square in front of the Budapest Television building. A week later, a counter-demonstration by about 60,000 people protested against these attacks and affirmed their commitment to human rights and basic democratic values.

I dismissed the editor-in-chief of the main news programme (a former party secretary turned into the mouthpiece of nationalist and populist forces) and the editor-in-chief of our main foreign news magazine (a former member of the Communist Party presidium in Hungarian Television, who, after 1989, became the untouchable hero of nationalist forces in Hungary – apart from which he was a gifted journalist). Csaba Gombar had taken similar steps at Hungarian Radio a few weeks earlier. At the end of the year the Prime Minister retaliated by starting disciplinary proceedings against me and later suspended me. I immediately questioned his right to do so and began a legal action against the Office of the Prime Minister since, in my reading, he was not and could not be my employer. Such dependency would be against the law and would jeopardise the freedom of the press. The parliamentary majority passed a proposal to incorporate the budgets of Hungarian Television and Radio into the budget of the Prime Minister's Office as from 1 January 1993 but a comprehensive new media bill collapsed in Parliament.

Together with Mr Gombar, I submitted a letter to the President of the Republic asking him to relieve us of our office. By mid-1993 he had not yet accepted our request. According to the Prime Minister, with our 'resignation' we ceased to be the presidents of these two institutions. According to the President of the Republic we did not resign, or if we did, he had not yet accepted our resignation. We were now in the absurd and slightly comic situation of being, and yet not being, the presidents of these two institutions.

The present situation

Writing in mid-May 1993 I have to confess that I have no idea about who or what I am. I may be still the president of Hungarian Television, though I hope not. Perhaps *de jure* I am and *de facto* I am not. Or would it be more precise to say that according to one interpretation of Hungarian law I am, and according to another interpretation, I am not?

When Mr Gombar and I wrote our letter to the President of the Republic asking him to relieve us of our duties, we gave the following reasons. First, after the failure of the Media Bill in December 1992, and with no hope of a new bill before the general election in 1994, we felt ourselves exempt from our promise to stay until a media law had been passed. Second, losing their financial independence with the new Budget Law, our institutions lost their hard-won autonomy and reverted to the East European type of government-controlled state media. Their organisational transformation back into what they had been before 1989, in the bad old days, was well under way. Third, we did not want to lend assistance in the destruction of two of the most important autonomous institutions in our new democracy.

The Prime Minister eagerly jumped at the opportunity. In his letter of 20 January 1992 he wrote to us that he accepted our 'resignation' and entrusted the two vice-presidents with running the two institutions. Next day, the President issued a statement according to which (1) we did not resign, (2) it was his exclusive right to accept or reject our request to be dismissed, (3) the Prime Minister had the right to propose our dismissal, (4) but if that happened he, as President, would consider the proposal and make his decision in due time.

It would not be tragic, nor exceptional, for the Prime Minister and the President of a republic to disagree on an important matter and even to quarrel publicly. From France to the former Czechoslovakia and Poland there are numerous examples of such conflicts – though such conflicts are, of course, more dangerous in emerging, fledgling, fragile new democracies. Tragic it was not, but it was absurd, this situation in which Mr Gombar and myself were forced to decide whether the President or the Prime Minister was right. And it would have been nonsensical and cruel if each of our several thousand colleagues – managers, producers, cameracrew, editors, security guards, cleaners and others – had been forced to decide day by day whom to obey: us, or the new men installed by the government. We had no wish to involve our innocent colleagues in this ordeal or to get entangled in a hopelessly vicious and degrading squabble with the government's placemen who, in any case, had all the means and power in their hands. So we published an open letter in which we stated that we considered ourselves the lawful presidents of Hungarian Radio and Television but would not attempt to exercise our rights until the President, the Prime Minister, or the Parliament, or the Constitutional Court, or any Court (I have mentioned that I had brought a suit against the government) had cleared up the mess. That was, I hope, our final action in the media war.

The rules of the game

There were several episodes in the media war which may be of some interest for those who study the situation and the role of the media in the process of democratisation in East Central Europe or elsewhere. Among them were the parliamentary hearings of the two media presidents in mid-1992. When the Prime Minister saw that he could not win his case legally, he looked for direct political ways and means to bring me and my radio colleague to our knees. In May 1992 he asked the Cultural Committee of the Parliament to investigate our 'ability' to run these two institutions. Having a government majority in this Committee, it seemed he did not take too much risk.

Mr Gombar and myself chose different strategies. He went to the hearing and read a short statement saying that he did not accept the authority of the Committee because it was not a neutral body, and then walked out. Scandal! Next week I walked in with five experts and thousands of documents and announced that I was happy to be there and to be able to discuss important matters with distinguished politicians. Hilarity! 'But', I added, 'I shall force you to take these hearings seriously, since parliamentary hearings in a decent democracy should be taken seriously. I shall make your lives miserable in the coming days. I shall do my best to make it very difficult for you to pass judgement without considering the facts, figures and proofs which I shall submit to you.' The hearings lasted for 30 hours over three long days.

During the hearings, deputies from the governing parties first argued that I had not observed some rules and laws in the course of the transformation and management of Hungarian Television. When we proved that they were wrong, they tried to convince the public, and themselves, that Hungarian Television did not serve the interests of the Hungarian nation well enough, that it had become too international, Americanised, commercialised, 'anti-Magyar'. When we proved with figures, statistics, and analyses that the contrary was true, they finally lost their temper, swept all the documents, figures, proofs, and pieces of evidence off the table and retreated to the *ultima ratio* of party politicians: 'We, the governing parties, have lost confidence in you and this is a sufficient reason to propose your dismissal even without any further facts, proofs, or arguments.'

It was an interesting exercise in learning democracy. It was almost moving to see how governing party deputies, or at least some of them, struggled with their consciences; to see how they tried to squeeze their party interests (and their antipathies for this meddlesome television president) into the forms and strait-jacket of legal rules. By that time, almost the whole country was watching. And those who watched may have understood, for the first time in their lives, that democracy was not an abstract construct of a couple of sublime ideas but simply and very prosaically a well-defined set of rules of the game. They could understand that a democratic polity needs well-defined rules agreed upon by all the interested parties, and a willingness on the part of its citizens to observe these rules, even if their momentary interests would be better served by breaking these rules. Hundreds of people have admitted, and hundreds of thousands would certainly agree, that these hearings were an elevating and traumatic experience for them. It was a fascinating and shocking sight to see how the deputies of the governing parties first made enormous efforts to attain their goals within the framework of the democratic rules of the game, and tragic to see their final failure and self-humiliation.

Half a year later, in January 1993, the same ceremony was repeated but, by this time, without the respectable personal drama of some of the participants. By that time, after having been more than two years in office, government politicians seemed to have lost their former timidity. They seemed to have realised more and more that they were in power and had the power to have their own way. With the national congress of the MDF approaching, they had also increasingly lost their tempers and some among them went out of their way to prove their unrelenting patriotism to the forces of the right. In the disciplinary procedure he started against me, the Prime Minister appointed the Minister of Justice as commissioner and three other ministers as members of the disciplinary committee. After making, with lordly nonchalance, one legal and formal mistake after the other, they played the cynical comedy of a formal trial to the end. This was a real scandal, resounding in the country. The minutes of the trial were published (in a form and under circumstances reminiscent of the good old days of *samizdats*) and they became a best-seller overnight; in one of the theatres of Budapest actors read passages of it with the audience roaring with laughter and indignation; the media war had turned into a kind of tragi-comedy.

Some journalists went so far as to label the procedure the 'first show trial' since the free elections of 1990. This was, of course, a metaphor which stretched similarities far too far. It is true that the whole process was motivated by the political will to get rid of the presidents of Hungarian Television and Radio. It is true that the whole case was prefabricated and the judgement had been passed before the trial. It is true that the disciplinary committee passed judgement without considering the hundreds of facts and pieces of evidence that proved the innocence of the defendant, and so on. But everything else was different. All this took place in the democracy of 1993, and not the dictatorship of 1953. The stakes were much lower. Instead of the hangman, cheering crowds and sympathising journalists greeted the condemned who appealed the verdict and announced that he would go to Strasbourg, to the Court of Human Rights, if necessary.

Public hysteria

Outside the former Yugoslavia, gunfire and the rattle of tanks have not accompanied the process of transition in East Central Europe.[2] Thank God. But outbursts of passions and prejudices, hatred and animosities, paranoic and hysterical reactions have indicated the underlying enormous tensions, the torturing uncertainties, the exorbitant price most of the people have had to pay, yet again, 'for a better future'. The media war was not an exception to this rule – quite the contrary. It functioned almost as a collecting lens of emotionality and irrationality.

There was nothing surprising in this. People's relationship with their television screen is extremely personal and emotional in normal times as well. They project their hopes and fears to the world of pictures moving on the screen. Freud might add, in a more professional style, that the struggle between our egos, ids and superegos is enacted in a symbolic way, on the screen. Or he could point out analogies between the 'dream world' of our subconscious and the transformation of the real world that takes place on, or behind, the screen. It could be described also as a Platonic play of shadows (in colour now in its modern version), which is the reflection of the word of ideas, of the essence of life and being, which we are unable to discover in real life. Sociologists would describe the screen as the only or most important *agora* of late twentieth century life, where conflicts are fought out and social consciousness is formed. The television screen is not a door but at least a window, the only window, for most of the people, opening onto public life, the only means of participation in politics, the only companion, the only real source of values, beliefs, and identities, the only *arbiter elegantiarum*, the highest moral authority. It is natural and inevitable that people react with extreme sensitivity to everything that happens on and around the screen.

The high stakes and tensions of the post-1989 world have, as a matter of course, worsened this condition and led to some of those episodes which seem absurd and incomprehensible to outside observers. I think for instance of the hunger strikes. In June 1992, Bishop Tokes, who had played an important role in triggering the Rumanian revolution (if it was a revolution) staged a short hunger strike to protest against the acquittal by a Rumanian court of those responsible for a bloodbath in Transylvania. He set a contagious example. A couple of weeks later a parliamentary deputy of the governing party in Hungary started a hunger strike with a much less glorious objective. He demanded the immediate resignation of Mr Gombar and myself. Following this, an editor at Hungarian Radio went on hunger strike, also demanding the immediate resignation of Mr Gombar. In response, two female pop singers announced that they would start a hunger strike in our support; they had some weight in surplus and had planned to go on a slimming cure anyway. Luckily, these various hunger strikers stopped their acts of protest before this epidemic of hunger strikes developed into a tragi-comedy and a destructive political chain reaction.

At the time I thought I had the privilege of being the first television president against whom a parliamentary deputy had staged a hunger strike. I was mistaken. A few weeks later I was told by my British colleagues that some years earlier a Welsh Member of Parliament (Gwynfor Evans) had gone on hunger strike to demand Welsh-language broadcasting by the BBC. He got it. His Hungarian counterpart was less successful; he got nothing beyond warm hugs from Mr Csurka and company.

The public demonstrations also had an aura of absurdity. As far as I know, it is not usual to have mass demonstrations in the streets of Rome or Los Angeles against television programmes and companies. This happened, however, in October 1992 in the streets of Budapest. But the real absurdity lay in the nature of the Budapest demonstrations, not the simple fact of their occurrence. I like colourful demonstrations and am not upset by the Hungarian tricolour as some of my more liberal friends are. But this demonstration involved a strange contradiction. On the one hand:

1. The demonstration was organised by the association of those who had suffered prison sentences after 1956.
2. They demonstrated against the communists, and against me.
3. They supported and acclaimed two of my colleagues in Hungarian Television.

But on the other hand:

1. I, too, went to jail after 1956 with the very same men who now protested against me.
2. I have never had anything to do with the Communist Party except that it put me in jail after 1956 and did everything to harass me in the following decades.
3. Of my two colleagues whom the demonstrators supported against me, one had been a Communist Party secretary and the other a member of the Communist Party presidium in Hungarian Television. The excuse proffered by Tamas Katona, the Cabinet Secretary, was that even democratic governments need good 'mercenaries'. According to reliable (or non-reliable) sources Mr Csurka succinctly added to this the verdict that: 'It is I who decide who is a good ex-communist.' (Fortunately this is still less than *'L'état c'est moi'*.)

Hunger strikes and street demonstrations came and went without exerting too much impact on the course of events. But they raised an important issue and called attention to a dangerous weakness of emerging democracies. Extra-parliamentary and extra-institutional phenomena (social conflicts, unprocessed group interests, new ideas and aspirations, demonstrations, strikes, acts of civic disobedience, hunger strikes, citizens' initiatives, social movements, etc.) are present and keep arising in all sorts of societies. One of the major functions of parliamentary systems, and existing institutions within them, is to absorb, process, integrate, 'institutionalise' these phenomena as soon and as completely as possible. In emerging democracies, however, institutions may not be strong and mature enough to achieve this task fast and well enough. As a consequence the extra-institutional sphere may overexpand and obstruct the functioning of the already existing institutions and dangerously jeopardise the further development of the whole institutional field.

In a way, this is a vicious circle. In societies in transition, where the old institutions have already collapsed and the new ones are still in formation, the rich upsurge of problems, conflicts, ideas, aspirations, group interests, and social action is natural, inevitable, and at least partly useful. But if it overflows the emerging institutions, it may threaten the development of the institutional system and ultimately undermine the democratic regime. The breakdown of the institutional system in former Yugoslavia under the pressure of far too strong and emotionalised conflicts of interest is only one of the examples at hand.

The process of institution building in Bohemia, Poland or Hungary, on the contrary, may become an example of a successful balancing of the institutional and extra-institutional field, though the new political elites, anxious to stabilise their countries, may have overplayed their role. Prompted perhaps by a feeling of uncertainty and *horror vacui* they have convulsively endeavoured to strengthen the new institutions and – instead of trying to integrate the rich variety of informal and spontaneous social aspirations and initiatives – have made serious efforts to ignore or suppress them. In the short run, they may have thus contained the extra-institutional forces but, in the long run, they may have prepared a dangerous explosion of these forces.

Lessons learnt

The Hungarian media war has done much harm. It has become a stupefying case of public hysteria and paranoia; a public ritual of hatred and prejudice; a tragi-comic and mythical war of nationalist and anti-nationalist passions and rhetoric. It has been an issue that has absorbed far too much political and social energy; that has delayed the legislative work of Parliament; that has generated hatred between the political parties and has reduced their ability and willingness to soberly negotiate and compromise.

But it has yielded at least some profit too. I have already referred to the lesson taught by the parliamentary hearing in June about the importance of the rules of the game in a democracy. And we, liberals and conservatives, politicians and media people, people in government and people in the street also learned a lot from other episodes of this conflict. It is too early to judge the social impact of the media war but it may have been quite substantial since this conflict became a major political confrontation in the second half of 1991 and remained one of the most publicised political issues throughout 1992 and early 1993. In their stubborn fight for autonomy, Hungarian Television and Radio became major actors in a society protesting against the centralising and authoritarian efforts of the government. The country was watching, with fear and hope, the ups and downs of this conflict between the Davids of television and radio and the governmental Goliath. It was, I think, an exciting show, full of important lessons for those who watched and who wanted to understand. Let me mention some of the lessons that may have been learnt.

Don't fear conflicts

After having lived for several decades in the artificial peace and lukewarm compromise of Kádárism, from which conflicts were paranoically and hermetically excluded, the media war was among those events which taught us that conflicts – if they are kept within bounds – play an indispensable and useful role in democratic societies. Don't fear them and don't seek them. But use them as an important political instrument. You may even generate conflicts if in the given situation they may give momentum to public and political life; if they bring to the surface latent and lingering antagonisms; if you think they may help locate and reveal problems which may have been ignored or swept under the carpet; if they help crystallise, handle and mediate social interests. The record of the media war in this respect is mixed. It helped both to reveal and disguise underlying, real social conflicts.

Mr Prime Minister, I think you are mistaken

After centuries of various forms and degrees of serfdom, the media war helped people realise that in a democracy even the highest power holder is not an almighty monarch; he or she has some rights and does not have some other rights. This must have been a pleasant and liberating surprise. People could witness with a shiver that a simple citizen can stand up and say in public that: 'Mr Prime Minister, I have to tell you, with all due respect, that you are mistaken.' And nothing happens. No hooting police cars coming, no martial courts convening, no jail doors slamming. Nothing.

The power of law

People could experience also, most of them for the first time in their lives, how powerful law may be in a democratic society. They could see that two fragile public institutions, which could rely only on the letter and spirit of the law, had been able to protect their newly won autonomy against extremely strong pressures and attacks coming from the side of the government and the governing parties for two years. It must have been a bewildering and fascinating experience for them that even the powerful, who could have obtained their goals by force, nonetheless did observe the law though it curbed their intentions and interests. Let me make this point very clear. Hungary had, of course, a well-established, European type legal system from the eleventh century, which was reinstated and further developed after the centuries of Turkish and Habsburg occupation. But the rule of law meant for its citizens first and foremost the rule of the law of the powerful. It may have protected them against their neighbours but it did not protect them, in most cases, against their lords and masters. The media war may have provided them with the first example in their lives of the law binding the hands of the powerful and protecting the powerless. A middle-aged woman stopped me in the street on a misty December morning. 'Now I know that we need not fear any more. Now I know that the communists are gone. Thank you.'

Responsibility

After 1989 it came as an uneasy surprise how difficult it is to be a democrat – especially in a democracy. This was a real surprise since it had been comparatively easy to be a would-be democrat in a dictatorship. After 1989 we have had to learn that democracy cannot be imported, it cannot be bought off the peg, and it is not brought about and established overnight by a first and single free election. It may be generated only in the course of a long and tedious learning process in which everybody has to take part and has to take up his or her responsibilities. The fact that we have a government responsible to Parliament does not mean that everybody else is relieved of all responsibilities or that we can go on living in the Heaven and Hell of childish irresponsibility which we enjoyed, and suffered from, in the four decades of communism when it was easy and legitimate to blame the communists for everything miserable in our lives. The media war may have shown to many that there is no democracy without citizens acting with responsibility and, if necessary, civil courage.

Two models of democracy

People may have understood also why the existence of autonomous institutions was a *sine qua non* of modern democracies. At one point, the media war triggered off a heated controversy over the best political model for the country. The Prime Minister, a historian of nineteenth century British parliamentarism, believed in the superiority of the Westminster-type, majoritarian democracy in which the party, or party coalition, which wins a majority in Parliament has practically absolute power while its government is in office. According to an alternative model, that of twentieth century pluralistic democracy, the interests of a complex contemporary society can best be mediated and integrated by the interaction of a wide range of autonomous institutions, among which the government is only one of the most important ones. Other independent institutions – Parliament, local governments, the judiciary, the Constitutional Court (if there is any), the Central Bank, the National Accounting Office, the media, the various institutions and bodies of interest intermediation – also play an indispensable and not subordinate role. This decentralised and interactive model may be especially important for a country like Hungary, the social and political development of which has been retarded and distorted by centuries of highly centralised authoritarian regimes, even if between 1867 and 1948 this was a democracy of the authoritarian kind.

I have tried to show that, in spite of all the negative effects, Hungarian society has also profited from the media war. Let me add that the very existence of a media war proves the relative strength of the emerging democratic polity in this country. The fact that two fragile public institutions, which could rely only on the letter and spirit of the law, were able to protect their newly won autonomy against extremely strong pressures from government and the governing parties, proves that all the main political actors, at least until the last act in the conflict, observed the rule of law and accepted the basic rules of the democratic game. A 'war' that proves the strength of democracy: that is another of those absurdities which characterise the region called East Central Europe. It is one of those absurdities from which people living in less absurd societies may also learn a few lessons.

Notes

1 This chapter was originally presented by Elemer Hankiss at Glasgow University under the title 'The Hungarian media's war of independence', 17.11.92, revised and updated in May 1993.
2 This was written before the storming of the Russian White House in October 1993.

CHAPTER 9

Opinions: Public opposition to government control of the media

WILLIAM L. MILLER, ANNIS MAY TIMPSON AND
MICHAEL LESSNOFF

Elemer Hankiss has described Hungarian Radio and Television's 'war of independence': his attempt to run Hungarian state television along the lines of an idealised BBC, providing informative but unbiased, or at least balanced, broadcasting. The concept of balance on the BBC itself was established in circumstances similar to those in Hungary. Throughout the 1930s the Labour Party had felt very badly treated by the BBC and a new commitment to political balance was one of Labour's conditions for participation in the wartime coalition government. Balance on the BBC therefore owed as much to a political deal between rival parties that needed each other in a national crisis as to any abstract conception of justice or fair play (Seaton and Pimlott 1987) – not unlike the circumstances that, according to Elemer Hankiss, led to the new democratic regime's short-lived commitment to balance on Hungarian radio and television.

There are other, less happy, parallels between Hungary and Britain. From a distance the freedom and independence of the British press and broadcasting may seem more evident than the practical restrictions put upon them. To those who live in Britain, however, their independence is less obvious. In the middle of a cold night in January 1987, seven Special Branch officers arrived to search the headquarters of BBC Scotland. A few days later 10 officers of the Strathclyde police returned, backed up this time by members of the Metropolitan police. They loaded 200 containers of film and video into police vans, including the complete BBC-Scotland documentary series entitled *The Secret Society*. No criminal charges were filed. Two years, and one General election later the BBC was able to screen the series in full.[1] That was hardly consistent with Elemer Hankiss's view of BBC independence. British realities shock East European idealism.

On the other hand, British public attitudes are not so far away from idealised East European conceptions. Despite widespread public support for banning publication of particular items of news and comment which we discovered in Chapters 5 and 7, the British public remains strongly opposed to the idea that government should control the media.

Table 9.1 **Protectors of liberty**

	General public	Local politicians
Marks out of 10 for protecting citizens' rights and liberties:		
Freedom of Information Act	7.8	8.2
quality papers like the *Guardian*	6.4	7.0
television	6.3	6.5
quality papers like the *Telegraph*	6.2	6.4
backbench MPs in Parliament	5.7	6.6
tabloid papers like the *Mirror*	4.4	4.4
tabloid papers like the *Sun*	3.3	2.9

Government control of the press and television

To say that publication of certain things 'should be banned' is not to say who should do the banning. Indeed it may be more of a moral than a legal demand. Logically of course, where the state claims sovereignty, it cannot escape ultimate responsibility for all forms of censorship whether these are direct, carried out through quasi-autonomous buffer agencies, realised through the misnamed process of 'self-censorship' under fear of future retribution, or facilitated by a legal framework which encourages well-funded private citizens to take legal action against the press. Censorship, whether before or after the event, whether realised through the criminal or the civil law, is ultimately the responsibility of Parliament and government.

In logic, Parliament cannot pass laws against libel or invasion of privacy and then disclaim responsibility for their consequences. But in politics it can. The difference between direct and indirect control of the press may be only a matter of detail rather than principle, but detail can have an enormous effect upon public acceptability. The public combine an acceptance of censorship with a distaste for government control; and they combine a low opinion of some sections of the press with a low opinion of Parliament, government and politicians.

We asked people to use marks out of 10 to indicate how important various institutions, existing or proposed, were for 'protecting citizens' rights and liberties'. In a battery of 17 possible protectors of liberty (19 if we distinguish between the *Sun* and *Mirror*, and between the *Guardian* and *Telegraph*) we included various sections of the press, a proposed Freedom of Information Act, and backbench MPs in Parliament. We did not include the government itself but it seems reasonable to suppose that government would score less, not more, than backbench MPs.

A Freedom of Information Act topped the whole list of 19 institutions with a score of almost 8 out of 10. Television and quality daily papers such as the *Guardian* and the *Telegraph* scored over 6 out of 10, and the tabloid press around 3 or 4 out of 10. Public opinion certainly did not rate the tabloid press well as a

Table 9.2   Opposition to government control of the media

	General public	Local politicians
% agree media should be more independent of government control	76	73
% disagree that there should be more government control of media	74	85

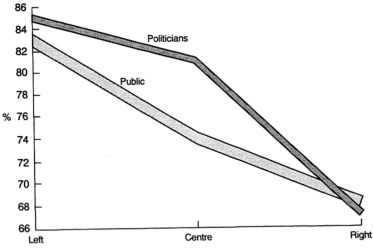

Figure 9.1   Ideology and opposition to government control of the media

defender of their liberties. But they rated television and the quality press above Members of Parliament and a Freedom of Information Act far above everything. So it would not be surprising if they backed the media against Parliament.

And so they did. We asked whether: '[Television and the press should be more independent of government control / There should be more government control of television and the press?]'. As usual, a randomly selected half of our interviews used each form of words. Irrespective of which way round we put the question the division of opinion was very clear. Three-quarters of both public and politicians agreed that the press should be more independent of government; and the same proportion disagreed with the suggestion that there should be more government control of the media.

Ideology

Public support for the media and opposition to government control cut right across ideological and party lines. Those on the left were

Table 9.3 **Ideology and opposition to government control of media**

	General public	Local politicians
% *agree to more independence (or disagree to more control) among those who place themselves:*		
on left	83	85
in centre	74	81
on right	68	67

most enthusiastically in favour of greater independence for the media and those on the right least so; but even on the right the balance of opinion was two to one in favour of more media independence and against more government control.

Principles

Commitment to free speech and freedom of information reduced support for government control while respect for authority increased it – but only by modest amounts. Even among those with the highest respect for authority two-thirds rejected more government control of the press. This seems to contradict the very high levels of support for censorship which we detected on some (though not all) topics in Chapters 5 and 7. Perhaps bans on publication conjured up images of the tabloid press for which people had scant respect while government control conjured up an image of political attacks on the BBC for which they had a high regard. But even if so, that is the nature of the problem that faces any government which moves to tighten censorship. It is difficult for government to single out only the most unpopular elements of the media for special restrictions. Indeed it is far easier, and far more frequent, for government to move against the highly respected quasi-monopolies in broadcasting than the widely criticised free-market tabloids.

Censorship and government

Above all, what is important is the simple message that public support for censorship did not translate into public support for an extension of government control over the media. Of course, those who were more willing to censor the press were usually less opposed to government control but still, on balance, they opposed it. If we take willingness to ban:

1. Interviews with terrorists;
2. Intrusions into private lives;

3. Heavy coverage of crime;
4. Publication of confidential government documents on economic or health (but not defence) plans;

and count the number of items out of these four which people are willing to ban we can construct an index of hard-line censorship attitudes.

*Table 9.4   **Opposition to government control despite support for censorship***

	General public	Local politicians
% agree to more independence [or disagree to more control] among those who would ban:		
none	88	84
one	80	85
two	74	76
three	73	75
all four	53	65
of the items listed in the note below.		

Note:
The four items were:
1 Interviews with terrorists;
2 Intrusions into private lives;
3 Heavy coverage of dramatic crimes;
4 Publication of confidential government documents on economic or health plans. Publication of confidential government defence plans was excluded from this list because there was such wide agreement that they should be banned. Consequently a willingness to ban publication of defence plans did not imply much support for government control of the media.

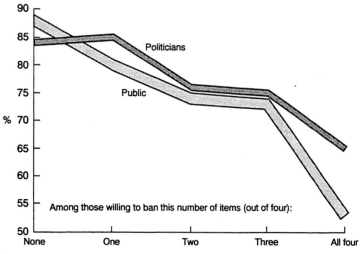

*Figure 9.2   **Opposition to government control despite support for censorship***

Among the public, 88 per cent of those who would not ban any of these four opposed government control of the media compared to only 53 per cent of those who would ban all four – a difference of 35 per cent. Clearly there was a marked relationship between support for censorship and support for government control. But even in the most extreme category, those who wished to ban all four items, the balance of support was still tipped towards media independence rather than government control. Even in that extreme category less than half the public and only a third of politicians favoured government control. Moreover, very few people fell into that extreme category: very few actually did want to ban all four items – less than 14 per cent of the general public and less than 10 per cent of politicians.

Our index of hard-line support for censorship consisted of a carefully chosen list of four censorship items, chosen to best predict support for government control of the media. On other censorship items, such as a ban on lies and distortions, a ban on racial incitement, or a ban on abuse of minority religions those who favoured censorship opposed government control of television and the press slightly *more* (not less) than those who did not.

So while many individual members of the public dislike particular things that appear in the press or on television and would willingly ban these particular items, they do not trust government to do the banning. Heavy-handed government intervention is fundamentally at odds with British public opinion. Through all the subtleties and complexities of public opinion that we have uncovered there still shines a clear public commitment to more freedom of information, fewer lies and distortions, and less government control of press and television.

Note

1 Ewing and Gearty 1990: 147–52; for a list of broadcasts suppressed by direct and indirect government pressure see Curtis 1984.

References

Curtis, L. (1984) *Ireland: The Propaganda War*, London: Pluto.
Ewing K. D. and Gearty, C. A. (1990) *Freedom under Thatcher: Civil Liberties in Modern Britain*, Oxford: Oxford University Press.
Seaton, J. and Pimlott, B. (1987) 'The struggle for balance' in J. Seaton and B. Pimlott (eds) *The Media in British Politics*, Aldershot: Avebury.

PART FIVE

Freedom versus Equality

CHAPTER 10

Argument: Through equality to liberty [1]

ROY HATTERSLEY

Enthusiasm for freedom is a comparatively modern emotion. Until the second half of the nineteenth century, order, with which freedom was thought to conflict, was regarded as a superior aspiration. Then in the years which separated the American and Soviet Revolutions, the idea of democracies as unions of free men and women was accepted with an accelerating enthusiasm which left the politicians, who spoke so eloquently of freedom, no time to pause and think what freedom was.

I shall offer the only definition which, to me at least, has any meaning and go on to describe how governments can best protect and promote it. I shall argue that the state must fulfil three clear duties.

1. To refrain from any action which reduces the sum of freedom within its boundaries, unless that reduction is necessary to protect the state itself from aggression or its members from the unlawful behaviour of others.
2. To remove the obstacles which society itself, and the vested interests within it, erect in order to restrict the freedoms of the generality of its members.
3. To increase the sum of freedom by creating the economic and social conditions in which the greatest number of men and women are able to make the choices (that is to say enjoy the freedoms) which exist when the state is not intrusive and private power is restrained.

Before I describe those duties in detail, three definitions are necessary.

First, we are concerned with personal freedom, not national sovereignty. The two conditions may coincide. But that is not always the case. Yeats wrote that Parnell came down the road and said to a cheering man: 'Ireland shall get her freedom and you will still break stone.' We examine not the freedom to which Ireland aspired but the freedom that might be enjoyed by the cheering man, the stone breaker and the average citizen.

Second, we shall regard 'liberty' and 'freedom' as descriptions of identical conditions. Isaiah Berlin did the same in his inaugural lecture at Oxford. If it was good enough for him, it is good enough for me.

The third definition is freedom – or liberty – itself. That may take a little time.

Professor Ted Honderich, after observing that 'every major political tradition . . . lays claim to being the tradition of freedom' (1991: 82), went on to write that 'one section of the New Right, sometimes called the neo-liberal section, has been pretty well unable to write a sentence of self-description that does not remind us of its mission of liberation. It has been sent by Friedrich Hayek and other Austrians to save us' (p. 82). Impatience with that claim is wholly justified. But it should not blind us to the fact that the persistence with which the neo-liberals laid claim to the title of freedom's champions had the predictable effect of making people believe that they were entitled to that description.

To Hayek, freedom is essentially the absence of restraint – a definition which boasts illustrious origins. 'A free man,' wrote Hobbes, 'is he who is not hindered to do what he has the will to do.'[2] Helvetius argued that 'the free man is the man who is not in irons, not imprisoned in gaol, not terrorised like a slave'[3] – leaving little doubt about why the [theory to] which he subscribes is called the negative view of liberty [*Thomas Hobbes (Theory of freedom)*] example: 'If I am prevented by oth[ers]   therwise do, to that extent I am u[n]   nnot see because I am blind . . . it   nat I am to that degree enslaved o[r]   the view of freedom which, wheth   nisters in their pursuit of marke   d places schemes in secondary e   portable pensions. Freedom, to   on those who can afford such services.

In all these philosophies, freedom is only denied by 'coercion': a 'deliberate act' to limit or deny liberty. The person who is born blind is as free as one who is born with perfect sight. But that rule does not apply to a person who, let us say, is blinded as a punishment laid down by the brutal penal policy of a tyranny. A decision to put out the eyes of felons is taken with judicial deliberation and, as a result, their right to see has been denied and their freedom curtailed.

In between the two extreme examples, there is another sort of blindness – with a regrettably common cause. It deserves our examination. Millions of eyes are lost each year by what can only be described as deliberate negligence: the result of machinery being inadequately protected, a chemical cure being adulterated by cheap substitutes or the failure of a parent to provide proper care. In each of these cases the courts would rule that the blindness was the result of wilful human behaviour and therefore, according to the Berlin thesis, an infraction of liberty.

But the example has to be taken further. In many societies, including ours, sight is lost because of the conscious refusal of governments to make available the resources which would prevent blindness. The acts of omission which I have described, the unguarded machinery, the adulterated chemical, parental neglect and the inadequate funding of medical services, are not the result of chance. They are foreseeable consequences of precise decisions and are, in consequence, avoidable. It is difficult to understand how, even according to the negative view of freedom, they can be described as anything other than an infraction of liberty.

The blindness hypothesis may at first seem bizarre, though those who so regard it must blame Isaiah Berlin for the invention. But on closer examination its relevance to the real world becomes clear. Barely a hundred years ago we sent little boys up chimneys in the certain knowledge that they would contract cancer of the scrotum and palate. The chimney sweeps of the nineteenth century argued against the prohibition of children in chimneys on the grounds that, in a free society, the state had no right to interfere with their commercial practices. Today men and women are dying because they cannot afford, and the state does not provide, comprehensive cancer screening and swift surgery. There has been progress of a sort. But people still die because others say that to save them would involve more state interference than is morally justified. The apologists for inadequate investment in the health service say that it would be unreasonable to expect taxpayers to make a greater contribution to its success. The neo-liberals of the far right still believe that freedom requires minimum involvement of the state in the commercial as well as the private life of the nation. They are particularly opposed to the state involving itself in the way in which citizens spend their money.

They are triumphantly overt about it. Hayek's view of public expenditure, the process by which improved medical care could be provided, is at least uncompromising. It is 'an agreement by the majority on sharing the booty gained by overwhelming a minority of fellow citizens or deciding how much is taken from them'. That, he tells us, 'is not democracy' (Hayek 1978: 156). To him there is no justification in attempting to provide 'that different treatment which is necessary in order to place people who are very different into the same material position' (1978: 157). That is to say that it is wrong and pointless to disturb the market in such a way as to ensure that the poor receive the same medical attention as the rich. Hayek believes that freedom is the preservation of the pattern of wealth which is thrown up by the unfettered free market.

Say what you choose about the neo-liberals – and I intend to say a good deal which is critical – their theories are both comprehensive and consistent. Their ideas are all of a piece and possess all the seductive charm of iron laws which enthusiasts can apply without question or qualification to every situation. They also possess a second attraction to some of their devotees: a philosophy which is tailor-made for the rich and powerful. Redistribution, as an act of policy, becomes the ultimate blasphemy. In the absence of government action, authority is assumed by vested interests which build society in their own image and to their own advantage. The education system favours a privileged minority. The ethnic minorities are kept out of the white suburbs. Wages and conditions of employment are artificially depressed because as even Adam Smith, archangel of neo-liberalism, tells us: 'in a dispute the master can hold out much longer . . . In the long run the workman may be as necessary to his master as the master is to him. But the necessity is not so immediate' (Smith 1930: 169).

Of course the neo-liberals do not justify their theories by the brash proclamation that their ideology is ideally suited to the interests of the rich. They offer pseudo-philosophical justifications for the theory which turn out to be very little more than the old notion that the least government is the best government. It works out, in practice, as providing most benefit for those who need it the least. But that is not the attraction of which they speak in public. They have constructed a series of bogus justifications for their theories, most of them nonsense dressed up in pretentious language to give it a spurious intellectual respectability.

Neo-liberals argue that, by withdrawing from direct involvement in the organisation of society, the government (and the individual ministers of which it is composed) can escape all moral responsibility for the results of their inaction. Hayek tells us, almost as an afterthought, that 'it has to be admitted that the manner in which the benefits and burdens are apportioned by the market mechanism would, in many instances, have to be regarded as very unjust if it were the result of deliberate allocation to particular people . . .' (1982: 64). To Hayek any government which seeks to change the natural pattern of resource allocation is coercive, whilst the government that remains inert is absolved of all moral responsibility. The notion that governments are capable of moral abdication is patently absurd. When governments fail to act, they are responsible for the consequences of their inaction. Shooting a thousand people is worse than callously letting a thousand people starve – but only just.

The neo-liberals' second line of defence is the slippery slope argument, the notion inherent in the title of Hayek's most famous work that if you give authority a libertarian inch, it will encroach on several miles of personal freedom. It is sometimes advanced by quite sensible people: 'If everybody, because of egalitarianism approved and imposed by social democrats, has to use the same medical services, has to use the same school services . . . the citizen will be increasingly regulated by monopolies and increasingly at their service' (Gilmour 1973: 183). The implication is that the result will be poor service. Tell that to the Canadians. In Canada all parties support legislation which effectively prohibits the existence of private medicine. The health service is not, by any normal definition of that word, a monopoly. It does, however, provide a high quality service. In a moment I shall argue that some state intervention – carefully defined and directed towards specific objects – is essential to the protection and extension of liberty. I do not find that case difficult to defend. But, temporarily putting that aside, we can assert with absolute confidence that the idea of the state as Leviathan, its desire to swallow up another liberty increased by every freedom that it consumes, is simple fantasy.

We must now move on to consider a practical definition of liberty: the effective liberty which has real meaning to a generality of men and women and amounts to more than the unfettered right of the rich and powerful minority to use their power and wealth to their own advantage and against the interests of the rest of society. But before we begin the positive discussion of positive freedom, honesty requires me to pay passing tribute to the neo-liberals for two of the vital contributions which they have made to the discussion of liberty.

First, all praise to Hayek for at least firmly disowning the nonsense by which the neo-liberal ideology has been popularised by its more vulgar and unthinking proponents, namely the chance it is said to provide for all citizens to rise to great heights as long as their character, temperament and intellect allow it. It is the pretence that the system offers everyone a fair chance – equal opportunity – that makes it such an important factor in encouraging the dispossessed to accept their condition with passive good humour; it is the subject of R. H. Tawney's most famous analogy:

Intelligent tadpoles reconcile themselves to the inconvenience of their position by reflecting that, though most of them will live to be tadpoles and nothing more, the more fortunate of the species will one day shed their tails, distend their mouths and stomachs, hop nimbly onto dry land and croak addresses to their former friends on the virtues, by means of which, tadpoles of character and capacity rise to be frogs.

(Tawney 1952: 108)

The voice of the frog is clearly heard in the land every time an advocate of selective education announces that the system allows parents to choose their children's schools.

At least Hayek admits that a system which requires the naturally weak to compete for scarce resources with the naturally strong is not going to result in anything that resembles a reasonable distribution of the chance to rise or anything else. Hayek is dubious about what public claim should be made for the system which he advocates: 'It is a real dilemma to decide to what extent we ought to encourage the young to believe that when they really try they will succeed or should rather emphasise that inevitably some unworthy will succeed and some persons of worth fail' (Hayek 1982: 74).

Hayek may be ambivalent about the propriety of disguising the real effect of political and economic *laissez faire*. But to the initiated – the select few who work their way through his extended texts – he is disarmingly frank: 'It is probably a misfortune that, especially in the USA, popular writers like Samuel Smiles and Horatio Alger and later the sociologist W. G. Sumner have defended free enterprise on the ground that it regularly rewards the deserving' (Hayek 1982: 74). Conservative parliamentary candidates with a philosophical bent, please note.

The second debt which we owe to Hayek and company is even more substantial. Buried deep under the prejudiced mumbo jumbo is one profound, indeed fundamental, truth. The neo-liberals accept the relationship between freedom and economic capacity, liberty and purchasing power. That is inherent in their contention that disturbing the natural – whatever that may mean – pattern of ownership and wealth is immoral. They do, however, have the grace to feel so guilty about the outcome of that abdication that they provide justifications for the inequalities that it causes. All of them are bogus.

The first excuse concerns the poor's (supposed) dependence on the rich and deserves, if only in the cause of malicious amusement, to be examined in a little detail. The theory amounts to the view that the more food that is heaped on the rich man's table, the bigger the crumbs that fall off it and become available to the poor.

Hayek tells us that 'it is because scouts have found the goal that the road can be built for the less lucky and less energetic' (Hayek 1960: 44). Schumpeter put it more graphically, saying that it is because capitalism first brought silk stockings to queens and duchesses that they eventually became available to shop-girls. As with so many neo-liberal theories, the alternative proposition seems more convincing – rather the theory of echelon advance than the trickle-down effect. For as Hirsch argues, at least to my satisfaction, land trampled over by the rich has lost much of its fertility by the time that it is occupied by the poor. The motor car (which was an enormous boon to the rare commuter who was chauffeur-driven into London on the empty roads of 1935) is a positive detriment to that commuter's lineal successor who, stuck in the traffic jams of 1992, cannot afford the rail fare. But, once again, it is not necessary to prove the opposite case to destroy the theory that the poor need the rich to pioneer improvement. The Health Service in this country is responsible for scientific innovations which private medicine would never have been able to afford. Of course if improvement – in stockings or cures for infertility – are limited to the rich, the rich will get them first. That is all that the trickle-down effect amounts to. And it is not very much.

The second part of the notion that the poor need the rich to get richer is based on the patent error that the more that men and women in the top income decile keep for their own consumption the more they contribute to society. The present British government actually claims that the greater receipt from top tax payers, which has been recorded during the last decade, is the direct result of the highest earners being stimulated into greater effort by the reduction of the highest marginal rate to 40p in the pound. It only takes a moment's examination of a single example to realise what demonstrable nonsense that contention is. Mr Ian Vallance, Chairman of British Telecom, earns an annual salary of £536,000. Ten years ago, his predecessor earned £68,000. Does anyone seriously suggest that Mr Vallance's salary was increased because, as a result of tax cuts, he had been encouraged to work harder? The salary increased by 788 per cent – almost eight fold – because the government had created a climate in which very high salaries were acceptable. As a result, the yield from a top rate of 40p in the pound was greater than it would have been a decade before. A 50p marginal rate would have produced a greater yield still. I do not believe that Mr Vallance would have asked for a reduction in salary if the marginal rate of tax on half million pound salaries had been increased.

The Finance Bill which sets his marginal rate of tax is, whatever the percentage level, an infraction of Mr Vallance's liberty. Let us accept with Jeremy Bentham, for the sake of theoretical argument, that the term 'coercion' can reasonably be applied to a law that threatens prison to those who thieve and dispossession to those who wilfully refuse to pay their lawful debt. Certainly conscription into the armed forces is literally coercion, though most people will regard it as reasonable coercion in times of national danger and unreasonable if operated by the press gang to staff a peacetime navy. The question is how acceptable coercion is to be justified.

Bentham took the view that 'all punishment in itself is evil' but he offers an arbitrary, subjective (and therefore unacceptable) definition of tolerable coercion: 'Is it not liberty to do evil? If not, what is? Do we not say that it is necessary to take liberty from idiots and bad men because they abuse it?'[4] Bentham, of course, wanted to define evil – the condition of bad people – himself. Spinoza was even more patronisingly authoritarian: 'Children, although they are coerced are not slaves ... they obey orders given in their own interests.'[5] He believed that it was the same, or should be the same, with men and women. Fichte is even more totalitarian. The right to coerce otherwise free men and women is in the possession of a self-identified elite: 'No one has rights against reason. To compel men to adopt the right form of government, to impose on them by force is not only the right but also the sacred duty of every man who has the insight and ability to do so.'[6] Philosopher kings rule, OK.

None of those definitions of acceptable state coercion are remotely acceptable to me. For they enable those who have the power to govern to impose their will in any area which they define as suitable for the exercise of their authority. The Soviet Union – imprisoning dissidents in mental institutions – could have taken refuge in Bentham's dictum that idiots must always be restrained. Any tinpot dictator could claim that they proscribe political parties and suppress free speech according to Spinoza's dictum that they can act in the interest of their childlike subjects. Fichte's contention that the state can act to protect the assault on reason has been used by enemies of liberty from the Jacobins to the Ceausescus in Romania. We need a more objective – a more scientifically demonstrable – criterion. John Stuart Mill began to provide it.

Mill's view is simply described in terms which are, or should be, known to every schoolchild. He was in favour of personal freedom as long as one person's liberty did not cause intolerable detriment to the quality of another person's life. Restraint is never acceptable in the interests of the citizen whose freedom is restrained:

> All errors which he is likely to commit against advice and warning are far outweighed by the evil of allowing others to constrain him for what they deem to be his good. [However . . .] a person who shows rashness, obstinacy, self conceit, who cannot restrain himself from hurtful indulgences, who pursues animal pleasures, would suffer the penalties subsequent upon his action.
>
> (Mill 1962: 207, 208)

It is impossible not to suspect that Mill wants people to be free as long as they use their freedom to mould themselves on his own admirable character. And even then, the dictum that people can do as they choose as long as they do no harm is not regarded as absolute and imperative. Minor offences can be tolerated for the sake of the greater good – human freedom.

Mill had no hard and fast rules about what the state should prevent and allow. Indeed, hard and fast rules would have been in conflict with his character as well as his philosophy. He was writing at a time (1859) when Roman Catholics and non-conformists were denied the full rights of citizenship and *On Liberty* amounted to a call for the authoritarian state to abandon its intrusion into matters of private conduct and personal conviction. We can all support that. But we also need a more precise definition of the state's proper boundaries. Mill says that sale of alcohol should not be regulated but that drunken soldiers and policemen should be punished. That is a perfectly consistent view. But it is more difficult to explain why people should be prevented from drinking so much that they prejudice the peace of their neighbours but should not be prevented from owning so much that they dominate their neighbours' lives. Mill himself suggested that 'whenever there is a . . . definite risk of damage, either to an individual or to the public, the case is taken out of the province of liberty, and placed in that of morality or law' (Mill 1962: 213).

If we crudely paraphrase Mill by saying that the state cannot restrain people for what is loosely termed their own good, but may restrain them for the protection of others, we raise a number of interesting new questions. I was a member of a Cabinet which introduced laws to compel motorists to wear seat belts. Ministers who believed themselves to be disciples of Mill, quoting his authority, opposed the new law. Others argued that by not wearing seat belts, drivers were putting other people's lives at risk. The discussion widened into what is and what is not conduct which works to the detriment of other citizens. Smoking creates passive and unwilling inhalation of nicotine. Supporting private education depresses the standards of state education. Driving slowly in the fast lane holds up drivers with urgent business to transact. It may be that Mill's law only applies to direct interference, not indirect influence. Or it may be that we need a new rule – an objective rule – to determine when the state should or should not impinge on the life of its citizens.

We need a rule to determine when the state should intervene and when it should not. And I make a rash leap forward and suggest what that rule should be. The state should never intervene in the lives of its citizens when – because of its intervention – the sum of liberty is reduced, save only for those special occasions when normal liberties have to be sacrificed for the sake of national security and personal safety. The state should intervene in the lives of its citizens when, and only when, by doing so it is increasing the sum of freedom.

It may be helpful if, before we attempt an acceptable definition of the freedom which we seek to preserve, we examine an example of the sort of intervention which promotes liberty. In 1870, William Gladstone wrote to Cardinal Manning describing his determination to prevent 'the landlord from using the terrible power of undue and unjust eviction' (Morley 1903: 294). He was referring to the Irish Land Act which prevented landlords from including in their leases clauses which enabled them to negotiate tenancy agreements within brief periods of their original signature and on terms which were detrimental to the tenant farmers. It brought an end to 'rack renting' which produced, for tenants, a choice between paying exorbitant rents and leaving the land which they had worked to improve. The Irish Land Act would not have been acceptable to modern neo-liberals. For it used the power of the law to redress the economic balance between wealthy landlords and poor tenants. It broke all Hayek's golden rules. It helped in the process of making 'people who are individually very different' achieve 'the same material position as each other'.

By any standards the Irish Land Act was an 'infraction of liberty'. For the landlords were denied the liberty to exploit their tenants and, as Jeremy Bentham tells us, 'every law is an infraction of liberty . . . even if it leads to an increase in the sum of liberty'. But it is the *sum* of liberty which is important – and that the Irish Land Act increased.

In a democracy rival claims to individual liberty are certain to collide. It is the duty of a democratic government to adjudicate between conflicting demands. The adjudication is bound to limit *somebody's* liberty. In a free society, a society in which the sum of liberty is maximised, it should act to secure, protect and extend as much liberty as possible. By behaving in that way it demonstrates that the state, far from acting as an invariable enemy of freedom, can intervene to extend it. The contrary view is propaganda put about by vested interests. In Tawney's words: 'It is still constantly assumed by the privileged classes that when the state fails to act, what remains as a result of its inaction is liberty. In reality, as far as the mass of mankind is concerned, it is not liberty but tyranny' (Tawney 1964: 166). It is private tyranny: the tyranny of the monopoly that charges inflated prices, the tyranny of the drug company that sells untested products and the tyranny of the developer to despoil the environment and prejudice the planet's future.

The problem of maximising the sum of freedom has been complicated by the comparatively recent notion that when a government acts to protect freedom it has to consider more than the freedom of a favoured elite. That problem arose when the working classes decided that they too had rights which might conflict with the rights of their masters. Matthew Arnold – who, not altogether flatteringly, called the upper class barbarians and the middle class philistines – set out the dilemma: 'Every Englishman doing what he likes was convenient enough so long as there were only Barbarians and Philistines to do what they liked ... [It has] become inconvenient and productive of anarchy now that the populace wants to do what it likes too' (Arnold 1960: 313). Arnold was writing *Culture and Anarchy* at the moment in the nineteenth century when the view of freedom had just begun radically to alter. Gladstone's first administration had governed with an impeccable respect for the notion that in a free society barriers to progress, erected by an intrusive state, must be pulled down. It was the view implied and expressed by Samuel Smiles who rightly believed that George Stephenson, engineer of genius, was only able to make progress in his chosen field because his life's work was not constrained by the practices and prejudices of the old professions. Gladstone ended the purchase of commissions in the army, opened up the universities to dissenters and introduced the competitive examination for the civil service. It was an early essay in equality of opportunity and as such should be welcomed by those who want to see an end to the entrenched privilege of a favoured minority. But the breaking down of barriers, although wholly desirable, is only the first step. To quote Tawney, once again and not for the last time, 'freedom requires both an equal start and an open road'. If some competitors begin with an advantage it is foolish to pretend that the race is fair because it is run on the flat rather than over hurdles.

With the Irish Land Act, Gladstone moved on to a more positive view of freedom – the creation of a contest in which the weaker of the two protagonists was given special help. T. H. Green, writing in 1880 on the purpose and effects of that legislation, offered the definition of freedom which seems to me self-evidently right. Freedom, he wrote, is 'a positive power, a capacity of doing or enjoying something worth doing or enjoying'.[7] That definition gives freedom a practical meaning to the generality of men and women. The freedom to buy private medicine and education is not a freedom that most citizens are able to exercise. Indeed, most of my Muslim constituents have exactly the same relationship with Oxford and Cambridge that they would enjoy were those two institutions still open only to members of the Anglican Communion. Freedom to buy places in private schools offers them an equally illusory benefit. We could, however, provide them with both the right and the power to send their children to a good local authority school of their own choice, and one which is organised to respect their culture and religion – and thus extend their freedom. Combining 'the power to' with the 'right to' adds up to what has come to be called 'agency'. It is the basis of that freedom which is the only freedom worth having. Yet freedom to do what we choose (rights matched with ability, power to enjoy in practice the liberties provided by a democratic state) is still often described as a chimera.

It is claimed that positive freedom – *freedom to* – is a goal which is unattainable. Negative freedom – *freedom from* – is, on the other hand, within the grasp of any society that wishes to provide it. That contention may, in one sense, be true. It is possible for a government to exercise an almost absolute self-denying ordinance and interfere little if at all in the lives of its citizens. But if what results is not freedom in any sensible meaning of that word, what is the value of receiving it in abundance? The logic of the neo-liberals must lead them to believe in the most extreme application of the non-interventionist doctrine. Some of them are absolutely frank about it. 'Taxing people is wrong', said S E Finer, then Gladstone Professor of Government in the University of Oxford, and we must therefore assume that in his perfectly free society there would be no taxation at all – with the inevitable consequences for people whose life and health depends on tax revenue. The neo-liberals offer a number of alternative ways for such people to make their livings. Consider Rottenburg's work on *The Production and Exchange of Used Body Parts*. This work of scholarship concerns not, as you might at first imagine, motor car maintenance, but the sale of kidneys and lungs:

Since society is willing to pay people to put their lives and health at risk in hazardous occupations, it is difficult to see why it should be thought objectionable to risk impairment by the sale of tissue … Justice Cardozo said that each had property rights in his body, but a conspiracy of physicians has greatly reduced the value of those rights. Decision-making by doctors therefore means that aggregate utility is less than maximised.

Mr Rottenburg is, believe me, serious. Notice the relationship between aggregate utility (that is to say value) and freedom. Notice too the consequences of the negative freedom that the neo-liberals propose. It is, theoretically, possible to achieve it completely. Though presumably Professor Finer would accept that in a wicked world it would be necessary to allow sufficient immorality to pay for the police and the armed forces. But were we ever to achieve this theoretically achievable freedom, would it be worth having? It would be the freedom of the weak to be tyrannised by the strong and the freedom of the rich to exploit the poor. And – more important, at least for my present purpose – for the majority of citizens it would not be freedom which any reasonable person would recognise.

Freedom is the *ability* to do those things which we choose to do. A government dedicated to freedom must, therefore, do all that it can to maximise that condition for the largest possible number of people. We will never achieve that happy state in full. Nobody will ever be able to take a trip to the moon on gossamer wings. Few people will be able to own their own private airplane, yacht or Rolls-Royce. To use the phrase by which George Bernard Shaw did so much damage to the idea of positive freedom, only a minority of men and women will be free to dine at the Ritz. These are freedoms which most of us will sacrifice without much regret. All that frivolity aside, we can make *more* people *more* free to make *more* choices – choices which matter.

We can do it by organising society in the way which Tawney proposed:

... when liberty is construed, realistically, as implying not merely a minimum of civil and political rights, but securities that the economically weak will not be at the mercy of the economically strong and that the control of those aspects of economic life by which all are affected will be amenable, in the last resort, to the will of all, a large measure of equality, so far from being inimical to liberty, is essential to it ... Economic liberty implies, not that all men shall initiate, plan, direct, manage or administer, but the absence of such economic inequalities as can be used as a means of economic constraint.

(Tawney 1952: 186)

That self-evident proposition has been confused by the suggestion that positive freedom is the extension of 'social and economic rights': the right to health care, the right to decent housing, the right to social security, the right to education and, above all, the right to a job that pays a living wage. The argument against 'social rights' is that they cannot be 'rights' in any meaningful sense of the word because they can only be guaranteed when sufficient resources are available for their universal provision. No state can ever guarantee everybody a job in all circumstances. But most states can, if they choose, guarantee some even more fundamental social rights: rudimentary education, basic health care, a decent house, a minimum standard of living for all ages.

All states *can* aspire to provide them: libertarian states *will*. For the right to basic health care and to a minimum standard of living in old age are directly related to the right to life – the first principle of libertarian government. What is more, they are basic necessities which, unless they are available, deny the enjoyment of other freedoms, negative or positive. Without possessing what Professor Raymond Plant calls the capacity to meet 'a basic class of welfare needs which all citizens have in common', it is impossible to exercise the rights bestowed on its citizens by a democracy.

But, in one sense, the 'social rights' argument is a diversion. For my contention concerns absolute rights less than it concerns real opportunities. My definition of freedom is as many people as possible being enabled to make as many choices as possible. A bigger pension for every retired citizen results in an infinite number of alternative choices. So does a higher basic wage. I argue for as many rights – as much freedom – as the state can organise. There is little doubt about the best way for that desirable condition to be accomplished.

It is essentially a question of marginal utility. An extra pound produces more choices for a poor person than it provides for a person who is rich. Let me take an example which I choose for no other reason than that, when I first found it, it seemed the perfect illustration of 'agency', the philosophical jargon for the power to do what we choose to do.

Mr Gerald Ronson, in a newspaper interview several years ago, described the advantages of being a millionaire. Money, he said, made him free. If he wanted to fly to America he could use his private plane. If he chose to take a holiday he could enjoy it on his yacht. He liked work and intended to continue working. But he could retire whenever he chose. In fact, Mr Ronson possessed enough agency to guarantee him an almost limitless number of choices. If we spread Mr Ronson's agency about, by distribution among lower income families, some of his wealth would increase the sum of freedom. One man would lose the chance to sail on his own yacht, but thousands of families below the poverty line would be able to make choices which had previously been denied them: warm winter clothes, more expensive food, unlimited adequate heating. One man would have had his rights constrained by the state. But thousands would be more free. The *infraction of liberty* would, as Bentham knew to be possible, increase the *sum of freedom*. We can redistribute agency by redistributing income. That is why equality and liberty go hand in hand.

Once we accept the concept of agency – the principle that real freedom is the *ability* to do those things which we choose to do – all other questions are automatically answered: all the questions about when the state should or should not interfere in the lives of its citizens, all the questions about what form the involvement might take and all the questions about how the 'infractions' of liberty and 'coercive' decisions can be justified. At least, we can answer those questions if we accept that the protection and extension of freedom is the primary duty of the democratic state.

If the principal aim of government is the promotion of liberty and if liberty is the ability to do what we choose, the extension of agency must be the principal purpose of all policy decisions. And, since agency is extended by greater equality, a government which is committed to freedom must also be committed to greater equality. The doctrine of agency provides, for libertarians, a theory which is as all-embracing as the neo-liberal notion that *laissez faire* is the sovereign remedy for all our philosophical dilemmas. It encourages social cohesion. It is compassionate. It is conducive to a general improvement in the quality of life, the health of the nation and improved educational standards. It is also intellectually respectable.

The acceptance of the doctrine of agency requires governments to apply three precise rules which are my central thesis.

1. The libertarian state must never gratuitously interfere in the lives of the citizens which it governs: not to protect them from themselves, not to guide them towards the paths of righteousness, not to deny them the vulgar pleasures which the enlightened recognise as damaging to the human spirit.
2. It must discharge its duty of adjudication – adjudication between freedoms which conflict – on behalf of the least privileged and thus spread privilege about. When there is a legitimate dispute about rights of way, the judgement must go to the hiker who wants to walk freely rather than the duke who wants to keep his grouse moors private.
3. The state which believes in extending freedom has an obligation to redistribute both power and wealth in a way that increases the *sum of liberty*. Wealth should certainly be redistributed from the minority on whom it is concentrated to the generality of men and women who, according to the rules of marginal utility, are more likely to use it to increase their liberty. But power must also be passed out both from a centralised bureaucracy and from the private vested interest that still dominates the lives of many citizens. And – since power and knowledge go hand in hand – the state, as well as sacrificing some of its power, must also give up most of its secrets to the people.

A government which is genuinely committed to the protection and extension of liberty has an overriding obligation to place limitations on its own powers. I describe this duty – *to place limitations on its own power* – with some care. For simply promising, to itself or to its electorate, that it will act with proper restraint, will not convince a sceptical public that governments will constantly provide a voluntary check on arbitrary executives or balance the actions of an elective dictatorship against real restraints. For three hundred years the United Kingdom relied on informal limitations on the arbitrary powers which our strange constitution provides. Local government acted as a counter-weight to national government. Trade unions used their collective strength to achieve different economic aggregates from those that the Cabinet thought best for the nation. Rebellion and the prospect of rebellion in the House of Commons, from Suez to devolution, forced governments to moderate their preferred position.

During the last decade all those informal restraints have been undermined or destroyed. Recreating them is impossible. Formal checks and balances are now necessary to tie the government's hand. They come in many different shapes and sizes. But they all limit the government's power, by its division and distribution, by its dilution and diminution and by the application of positive restraint. I offer a number of examples:

1. A Freedom of Information Act limits the government's power to impose its will on the electorate by deceit.
2. Devolution creates a second focus of legislative authority which both reduces the powers of central government and acts in competition with them when the will of part of the state demands it.
3. An elected second chamber, which does more than replicate the party political discipline of the first, can hold back arbitrary or authoritarian legislation.

It has been argued with some force that a Bill of Rights protects the citizen from the tyranny of the state by providing legal redress for men and women who are tyrannised. I advise caution. Judges, obliged to defend specific liberties after the interpretation of general statements of freedom, *may* always choose the libertarian option. But I am not sufficiently confident of that outcome to move to a system in which rights depend on the courts' interpretation alone. A general statement of rights has to be reinforced with specific legislation.

What is more, a genuinely free society cannot rely on a method of protecting individual rights which requires the victim to initiate action against the oppressor. By definition, the victims who suffer most are the men and women who are least likely to be capable of such initiatives. They lack confidence. They lack knowledge. And they lack resources. A system which does not accommodate them cannot meet our needs. And it is a system which is likely to divert our attention from the third essential duty of the state. Remember liberty is not simply the absence of restraint. It is the creation of real choices. Often the key to that is economic power which a court cannot provide.

Two questions immediately arise. The first concerns how far the process of redistribution, material redistribution to create the power to choose, should go. John Rawls answers the question with two crucial definitions of ultimate intention: 'All social values, liberty and opportunity, income and wealth and all the bases of self-respect are to be distributed equally unless unequal distribution of any or all of these values is to everyone's advantage' (Rawls 1972: 62). For those who think – rightly, in my view – that general principle to be rather too general, Rawls refined it seven pages further into *A Theory of Justice*. His Difference Principle asserts: 'It must be reasonable for each relevant representative man defined by this structure (i.e. the socially just level of inequality) when he views it as a going concern, to prefer his prospects with the inequality to his prospects without it' (Rawls 1972: 69).

In short, inequality is justified and only justified when the man or woman who is the victim of inequality actually prefers the social, political or economic disadvantage of that position to the price that has to be paid for greater equality. Such a situation no longer needs to be hypothesised. It is the basis of at least some of the unrest that led to the break-up of the Soviet Union. Anyone who had read Alec Nove's *Economics of Feasible Socialism* (1983) was waiting for the second Russian revolution to happen. The position is easily described. A man, offered the prospect of three pairs of shoes, all of which are identically badly made, ill-fitting and of the same drab design and colour, is not necessarily consoled by the knowledge that everyone has three pairs of shoes of the same sort. He would probably prefer two pairs of shoes of his own choice, even if that meant that other men had more shoes than he possessed.

On the other hand, the distribution of health care is, and ought to be, governed by a quite different reaction. To say, 'I am happy about the man next door having more shoes than I, as long as I like my shoes', is one thing. To say, 'I don't mind the woman next door receiving minor surgery before I receive my immediate, essential treatment', is another. The dispossessed will always press for greater equality in medical provision. And they will be right to do so. For a two-tier service, private on the one hand and public on the other, is bound to depress the quality of service provided for the lower echelon as it improves the facilities available to the upper tier. There is no such thing as different but equal. The purchase of medical care is a calculated decision to buy advantage. Advantage for one citizen is disadvantage for another. If one patient is promoted in the queue, the rest are moved further back.

The Difference Principle solves all sorts of crucial, but incidental dilemmas. It tells us, for instance, what the libertarian view should be on markets. Choice, freedom, liberty and the Difference Principle all argue against the stupefying inefficiency of state bureaucracy, state monopolies and the agents of the state deciding the type, quality, price and output of goods which should be under the influence not of commissars but the market. The choice which the market provides is – for non-essential goods and services – itself a vital ingredient of freedom. The power that suppression of the market provides is, itself, a weapon of tyranny. The term 'commissar' was originally a description of those servants of the Soviet Union who were used to answer questions which should be asked of the market. Their ability to determine price and availability of everything from bread to sewing cotton gave them a terrible power over the people's lives.

Application of the Difference Principle would certainly have seen off the commissars. But while it is essential to go no further towards equality than that Principle allows, it may not (at least in the immediate future) be possible to apply its precept in full. We can take equality only as far as democracy allows. The real imperative is to want it, to understand its virtues, to argue for it and to turn the ideal to reality as much and as soon as we can. The blazon on our banner has to be 'Choose Equality and Flee Greed', at least that is what it must be if we really want a free society.

A brief postscript is necessary. It concerns the nature of the equality which we should seek. For equality – like freedom – has many definitions. I would not have burdened you with mine if the Prime Minister, in a rare excursion into philosophy, had not spoken of 'equality of outcome' in terms which made clear that he had no idea what it was.

I certainly want equality of outcome. But that has nothing to do with vain attempts to make everybody the same or pretending that that is either possible or desirable. Belief in equality of outcome is based on another self-evident truth. Many inequalities are not the result of genetics, even less of fate. They are the product of the way in which society is organised. Those who support a system based on class and hierarchy are perpetuating a system based on class and hierarchy. Children born into deprivation grow up with an infinitely higher risk of being permanently disadvantaged than that which is faced by children born into affluence. It is as simple as that. Socialists want first to reduce and then eliminate the organisational, institutional and social factors which make men and women *unnaturally* different. A postscript on the subject enables me to end with Tawney's explanation of equality of outcome as the objective of the good society. It is the equal start and the open road, the belief that those who fall behind in the race should not be told that they had their chance and failed but should be given a new impetus to run on. What those of us who believe in equality of outcome know to be true is that:

While natural endowments differ profoundly, it is the mark of a civilised society to aim at eliminating such inequalities as have their source, not in individual differences, but in its own organisation and that individual differences – which are the source of social energy – are more likely to ripen and find expression if social inequalities are, as far as practical, eliminated.

(Tawney 1952: 49)

Equality of outcome is, in a real and practical way – the gospel of individuality, but individuality for as many people as possible. It is the real gospel of freedom since, as is clear enough for all except the most prejudiced, equality and liberty go hand in hand.

Notes

1 The argument of this chapter was originally presented by Roy Hattersley at Glasgow University under the title 'Socialism, Liberty and the Law', 17.3.92.
2 Hobbes (1976: 10), quoted in Berlin (1958). This was Berlin's inaugural lecture as Professor of Social and Political Theory in the University of Oxford. Restated and developed in Berlin (1969).
3 Quoted in Berlin (1958: 7).
4 Quoted in Berlin (1958: 33).
5 Quoted in Berlin (1958: 35).
6 Quoted in Berlin (1958: 36).
7 T. H. Green (1880) Lecture on *Liberal Legislation and Freedom of Contract* – see Sabine (1952).

References

Arnold, M. (1960) *Culture and Anarchy*, Cambridge: Cambridge University Press.
Berlin, I. (1958) *Inaugural Lecture*, Oxford: Clarendon Press.
Berlin, I. (1969) *Four Essays on Liberty*, Oxford: Oxford University Press.
Gilmour, I. (1973) *Inside Right*, London: Hutchinson.
Hayek, F. A. (1960) *The Constitution of Liberty*, London: Routledge and Kegan Paul.
Hayek, F. A. (1978) *New Studies*, London: Routledge and Kegan Paul.
Hayek, F. A. (1982) *Law, Legislation and Liberty*, Vol. 2, London: Routledge and Kegan Paul.
Hobbes, T. (1976) *Leviathan*, London: Everyman.
Honderich, T. (1991) 'Freedom', Chapter 4 of *Conservatism*, London: Penguin.
Mill, J. S. (1962) 'On Liberty' in *Utilitaranism*, London: Fontana.
Morley, J. (1903) *Life of Gladstone*, London: Macmillan.
Nove, A. (1983) *Economics of Feasible Socialism*, London: Allen and Unwin.
Rawls, J. (1972) *A Theory of Justice*, Oxford: Oxford University Press.
Sabine, G. H. (1952) *History of Political Theory*, London: Harrap.
Smith, A. (1930) *Wealth of Nations*, London: Methuen.
Tawney, R. H. (1952) *Equality*, London: Allen and Unwin.
Tawney, R. H. (1964) *The Radical Tradition*, London: Penguin.

CHAPTER 11

Opinions: Public support for equality

WILLIAM L. MILLER, ANNIS MAY MILLER TIMPSON AND
MICHAEL LESSNOFF

Against much received wisdom, Roy Hattersley has argued not
only that freedom and equality are compatible but that the one is a
route towards the other: that a more equal society would increase
the sum total of freedom enjoyed by its citizens. He attacks the
moral basis for inequality by quoting Hayek's own remark that
'inevitably some unworthy will succeed and some persons of worth
fail' and by rejecting the argument of 'trickle-down economics' that
the (possibly) unworthy rich perform some useful service for the
(possibly) worthy poor. Like libertarians on the right he argues that
the state should refrain from doing evil, but as a socialist he argues
that it also has a duty to do some good – that it is the duty of the
state to enable its citizens to take fuller advantage of their civil
liberties. For Roy Hattersley, freedom of movement implies the
price of a ticket as well as possession of a passport.

Like Lord Armstrong's, his attitude to principle is essentially
quantitative rather than absolute. Lord Armstrong dismissed the
notion of *absolute* freedom of information but nonetheless argued
for more of it. Similarly, Roy Hattersley says his argument 'concerns absolute rights less than it concerns real opportunities'. His
view of freedom involves trading one person's loss of economic
rights against another's gains or, more especially, one rich person's
loss against several poor people's gains. Of course, that is the
moral basis for any degree of redistributive taxation – something
tacitly accepted by many who shrink from calling themselves socialists. But Roy Hattersley draws our attention to much more radically
egalitarian policies than redistributive taxation when he cites
Canada, rhetorically perhaps, as an example of a state that actively
discourages private medicine in order to achieve an equitable
distribution of high quality health care.

In this chapter we look at public opinion on five themes raised
by Roy Hattersley:

1. The moral basis of inequality,
2. The duties of the state,
3. The correlation between equality and freedom,
4. Rival definitions of equality, and
5. 'Maximising the sum of liberty'.

Table 11.1   *Who is to blame for inequality?*

	General public	Local politicians
% *agree poor are poor because:*		
they don't try hard enough to get ahead	16	9
the wealthy and powerful keep them poor	58	50
% agree men are more suited to senior jobs	16	8
% agree immigrants should try harder to be more like other British people	66	49

The moral basis of inequality

It would be convenient for those who defend inequality if they could argue that it reflected worth, effort, or even biological necessity. As Roy Hattersley points out, the more celebrated advocates of inequality do not try, but as Hayek lamented less celebrated right-wing libertarians do. What Hattersley calls 'more vulgar and unthinking proponents of neo-liberalism' argue that the poor have only themselves to blame for failing to grasp the chances that life offers. What of the public? In half our interviews (randomly selected) we asked whether 'The poor are poor because they don't try hard enough to get ahead?'. In the other half we asked whether 'The poor are poor because the wealthy and powerful keep them poor?'. Fully 84 per cent of the public and 91 per cent of politicians rejected the proposition that the poor were poor because 'they did not try hard enough'. On this Hattersley, Hayek and public opinion were all agreed that the 'vulgar neo-liberals' were wrong.

But who then *is* to blame? Hayek emphasised chance – it was no one's fault that opportunities and rewards were unequally distributed in any society. Hattersley emphasised structural arrangements in society that advantage some at the expense of others. We found that politicians were equally divided between accepting and rejecting the structural explanation, though a majority of the general public tilted clearly towards Hattersley's view and blamed 'the wealthy and powerful' for keeping the poor in poverty.

There are, of course, other forms of inequality which may also have a moral basis. We asked whether, 'By their nature, men are more suited than women to do senior jobs in business and government?'. We are well aware that the wording of this question encouraged people to express gender prejudice: it was designed to do exactly that. So it is all the more remarkable that 84 per cent of the public and 92 per cent of politicians also rejected this proposition. And it is interesting to note that the differences between the responses of men and women to this question were negligible. We also asked whether, 'Immigrants to Britain should try harder to be more like other British people?'. On this issue there was a lot less sympathy for the disadvantaged. Two-thirds of the public and just under half the politicians agreed that immigrants should try harder to assimilate themselves into the dominant British culture. So although the vast majority of the public doubts the moral basis for income or gender inequality, opinion is more divided on whether there is a moral basis for racial and ethnic inequality.

In advancing his own definition of equality, Hattersley makes clear his adherence to Tawney's notion of a civilised society. This, he says, is one that encourages equality, not by eradicating individual differences, but by eliminating those inequalities that are rooted in social organisation. We asked our respondents how important they felt it was to eliminate some of the inequalities in British society that stem, in part at least, from the organisation of social life. We asked people to give marks out of 10 to indicate how important various values were to them. The list included: 'taking care of the needy', 'guaranteeing equality between men and women', 'protecting ethnic and racial minorities', 'providing help for the disabled', 'guaranteeing equal rights for homosexuals'.

Our list was chosen to reflect a range of groups that could be seen as experiencing inequality in contemporary Britain. Our respondents' priorities were clear. They placed help for the disabled at the top of this list with an average score of over 9 out of 10. Help for the needy was not far behind with an average score of just under 9. Bottom of the list, but still with a score that indicates a degree of popular sympathy for equality, came equal rights for homosexuals with a score of 6. Gender and ethnic equality came in the middle: politicians gave 8 out of 10 to both, while the public gave slightly higher marks for the importance of gender equality and slightly lower marks for ethnic equality.

As might be expected, people were more willing to stress the importance of helping a group they deemed to be worthy than one they did not. Attitudes to whether men and women were equally suited to occupy senior jobs made a difference of about one mark (out of 10) to the importance placed upon gender equality; attitudes to whether immigrants should try harder to assimilate had a rather larger effect upon the importance people assigned to ethnic equality. Blaming the poor, however, had slightly less effect upon the importance people attached to helping the poor. Even those few who blamed the poor for their own problems still assigned 8 out of 10 to the importance they placed upon 'taking care of the needy'. Even George Bernard Shaw's 'undeserving poor' attracted public sympathy.

The duties of the state

Of course 'help' need not come from government. Those most opposed towards state socialism may nonetheless place a high

Table 11.2 **Valuing equality (marks out of 10 for importance 'to you')**

	General public	Local politicians
helping the disabled	9.3	9.1
taking care of the needy:		
among those who blame poor	8.2	8.1
among those who blame rich	9.0	9.3
gender equality:		
among those who agree men are more suited to top jobs	7.5	6.7
among those who disagree	8.4	8.0
protecting ethnic minorities:		
among those who agree immigrants should try harder	6.8	7.2
among those who disagree	8.2	8.7
homosexual equality	6.0	6.3

priority upon helping the needy by means of private and personal charity. Roy Hattersley argued that it was the duty of the state to create 'the social and economic conditions in which the greatest number of men and women are able to make choices [and] enjoy freedoms'. However, he accepted that: 'no state can ever guarantee everybody a job in all circumstances. But most states can, if they choose, guarantee some even more fundamental social rights – rudimentary education, basic health care, a decent house, a minimum standard of living'.

We asked people whether these things should, or should not, be the responsibility of government. Our question read: 'Here are a number of things which many people think are very desirable goals but, at the same time, many people feel that it is *not* the responsibility of government to provide them. Do *you* think each of the following should, or should not, be the government's responsibility?'. In this question we tried to separate out questions of desirability from government responsibility. We asked about the duties listed by Roy Hattersley: to provide education, health, housing and a decent standard of living for all. We also asked about jobs, which he specifically excluded, and about traditional duties of government – to keep citizens safe from crime and to uphold morality (clearly a traditional duty of government in a state with two established Churches, one of them headed by the monarch!) – and about more recent duties imposed upon government, 'to fight pollution' and 'ensure that big business treats its customers with fairness and consideration'. We also asked whether it was the government's responsibility to provide equality of opportunity ('equal opportunities for everyone') and of wealth ('evening out differences in wealth between people').

Over 98 per cent felt it was the government's duty to provide

Table 11.3   **Percentage believing it is duty of state to provide:**

	General public	Local politicians
Welfare-state benefits		
a decent standard of living for everyone	77	83
that everyone who wants a job can have one	78	66
adequate housing for everyone	91	90
good eduction for everyone	99	98
good medical care for everyone	98	99
all five of the above	65	62
Order, old and new		
that citizens are safe from crime	93	96
that big business treats its customers with fairness	78	76
upholding morality	65	53
fighting pollution	95	96
Equality		
evening out differences in wealth between people	51	52
equal opportunities for everyone	91	92

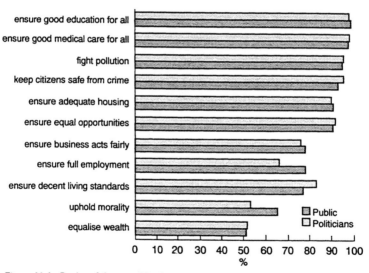

Figure 11.1   **Duties of the state (% who say government has duty to . . .)**

'good education for everyone' and 'good medical care for everyone'. While these duties seem natural in a welfare state, right-wing libertarians reject them. The United States provides universal education (to school level at least) but not yet, at the time of writing, universal health care. Over 90 per cent also felt government had a duty to provide 'adequate housing for everyone', to 'fight pollution', to ensure 'that citizens are safe from crime' and that there are 'equal opportunities for everyone'.

Considerably less, though still an overwhelming majority, felt it was government's responsibility to provide a 'decent standard of living for everyone' or ensure 'that everyone who wants a job can have one'. Among the general public about 77 per cent saw these as government responsibilities. Unlike the general public however, politicians drew a sharp distinction between living standards and jobs: 83 per cent said government had a responsibility for living standards, but only 66 per cent held it responsibile for full employment. Three-quarters of both public and politicians felt government had a responsibility to ensure that 'big business treats its customers with fairness and consideration'.

There was least support for the view that government should 'uphold morality' or 'even out differences in wealth between people'. These were more contentious issues. Only two-thirds of the public and half the politicians felt government had a duty to 'uphold morality'. Just over half felt government had a duty to 'even out differences in wealth between people'.

In fact, government guarantees on health, education, housing, jobs and living standards inevitably mean a degree of equality if they mean anything at all, but public opinion seems to focus more on the elimination of poverty than the elimination of wealth, which may imply more agreement with Hayek (though not with all his followers) than with Hattersley. Still, we should not overstate the point. Although public opinion was divided on our explicit question about equalising wealth, we found very slightly more in favour of it than against it. Even stated in the most uncompromising terms, it still commanded a bare majority.

The correlation between equality and freedom

Right-wing libertarians such as Hayek argue that there is an inevitable conflict between the ideals of equality and freedom (Hayek 1976). Roy Hattersley's central thesis is that the extension of freedom requires more equality. Opinion surveys cannot determine who is right and who is wrong, but they can reveal whether there is indeed a negative correlation in public opinion between the concepts of equality and freedom as there is in the logic of right-wing political theory. It has been widely remarked that the United States public have values rather than an ideology: that they hold to a set of inconsistent values either because they do not recognise the inconsistency or because they want to strike the best possible balance between admittedly conflicting but nonetheless desirable objectives. In particular they regard both freedom and equality as truly 'American values' (see e.g. Burns *et al.* 1981: 6–8; Hartz 1955). Similarly in Britain, our survey revealed massive support for freedom on the one hand, combined with massive support for equality of opportunity and a wide measure of social welfare on

Table 11.4 **Freedom**

	General public	Local politicians
Marks out of 10 for the importance to you of:		
guaranteeing everyone the right of free speech	9.2	9.4
tolerating different beliefs and lifestyles	7.2	8.3

Table 11.5 **Effect of commitment to freedom on attitudes to equality**

	General public		Local politicians	
Commitment to freedom =	*Low*	*High*	*Low*	*High*
% who say government has responsibility for:				
all five of jobs, housing, education, health care, and living standards	62	68	52	66
equalising wealth	48	53	43	56
equal opportunities	89	92	88	93
Marks out of 10 for the importance to you of:				
providing help for the disabled	9.0	9.5	8.4	9.3
taking care of the needy	8.3	9.0	8.2	9.1
equality between men and women	7.7	8.7	6.9	8.3
protecting ethnic and racial minorities	6.4	8.1	6.6	8.4
equal rights for homosexuals	5.1	6.9	4.5	6.8

Note:
Categories of commitment to freedom defined by the average of marks out of 10 for importance to you of 'guaranteeing everyone the right to free speech' and 'tolerating different beliefs and lifestyles', taking marks up to 8 as Low and above as High. Low and High in this context are, of course, purely relative terms.

the other, though it was divided on the explicit question of equalising wealth.

When asked to give marks out of 10 for the importance they attached to 'guaranteeing everyone the right of free speech' both public and politicians gave marks that averaged over 9 out of 10. When asked about the importance of 'tolerating different beliefs and lifestyles' the public were somewhat less libertarian but still gave marks of over 7 out of 10, while politicians gave marks of over 8. At the same time we have just recorded equally high marks for the importance of helping the needy and the disabled, protecting ethnic minorities and ensuring gender equality. Two-thirds said it was government's duty to provide all five welfare items – employment, housing, health, education and a decent standard of living for everyone; and while only just over half wanted government to equalise wealth, over 90 per cent said government had a duty to provide equal opportunities for everyone. Clearly the public values both freedom and equality.

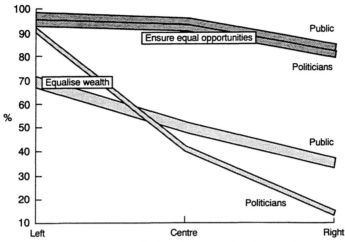

*Figure 11.2   **Ideology and equality** (% who say state has duty to . . .)*

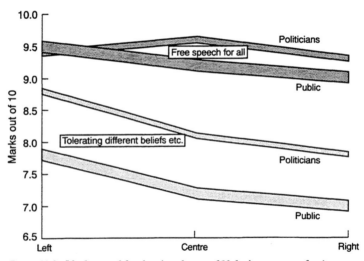

*Figure 11.3   **Ideology and freedom** (marks out of 10 for importance of . . .)*

But does the public nonetheless see the goal of freedom as conflicting with that of equality? Did people who gave a higher than average priority to freedom balance that against a lower than average concern for equality (and vice versa)? Was there a negative correlation between commitment to freedom and commitment to equality? For simplicity, let us construct an 'index of freedom' by averaging ratings given for the importance of 'free speech for all' and 'tolerating different lifestyles', taking marks up to 8 as *Low* and above that as *High*. This divides the general public roughly into two equal halves, though more politicians fall into the high

Table 11.6   Ideology, liberty and equality

Among those who place themselves on/in	General public			Local politicians		
	Left	Centre	Right	Left	Centre	Right
Equality (government duties) % who say government has a responsibility for:						
all five of jobs, housing, education, health care and living standards	80	67	44	88	56	29
equalising wealth	69	50	35	91	41	14
equal opportunities	95	93	82	97	94	81
Equality (important values) Marks out of 10 for the importance to you of:						
providing help for the disabled	9.5	9.3	9.0	9.3	9.2	8.6
taking care of the needy	9.0	8.7	8.3	9.2	9.0	8.3
equality between men and women	8.5	8.4	7.7	8.9	8.1	6.4
protecting ethnic and racial minorities	8.1	7.3	6.6	9.0	7.9	6.7
equal rights for homosexuals	6.9	6.1	4.9	8.1	6.1	4.0
Freedom Marks out of 10 for the importance to you of:						
guaranteeing everyone the right to free speech	9.5	9.2	9.0	9.4	9.6	9.3
tolerating different beliefs and lifestyles	7.8	7.2	7.0	8.8	8.1	7.8

category and fewer into the low. Among politicians there was a clear, and *positive*, correlation between this simple index of freedom and every one of our measures of equality: politicians who scored *High* on freedom, for example, were 14 per cent more favourable to social welfare, they gave 1.8 more marks out of 10 to the importance of protecting ethnic minorities, and 2.3 more marks out of 10 to the importance of equal rights for homosexuals, than politicians who scored *Low* on freedom. Those who were most committed to liberty were also the most committed to equality in all its forms. Among the general public this correlation was much weaker, sometimes very weak indeed, but never negative.

Ideology and definitions of equality

In part the positive correlation between liberty and equality reflected ideological perspectives. No one doubts that the left is egalitarian. Indeed concern for equality is often taken as a defining characteristic of the left. But liberty too is more popular on the left than on the right.

Among the public, those who placed themselves on the left were 36 per cent more likely than those on the right to regard government as responsible for jobs, housing, education, health and living standards and 34 per cent more likely to feel government should equalise wealth; among politicians the corresponding figures were a massive 59 per cent and 77 per cent.

Far smaller, but no less obvious, were the differences between left and right on 'equality of opportunity'. The phrase is used by right-wing theorists and governments to deflect demands for more equality of wealth and income: for them, *equality of opportunity* is the opposite of *equality of outcome*. But although public support for equality of opportunity was very strong across the political spectrum, it was still about 15 per cent stronger on the left. Yet more surprising to theorists of the libertarian right, though not perhaps to Hattersley, support for free speech and tolerance of different lifestyles was also a little greater on the left than on the right.

Maximising the sum of liberty

Equality can be achieved through 'levelling up' or 'levelling down'. Roy Hattersley argued that a small diminution of a rich person's freedom could produce a significant increase in the freedom of a large number of poor people. His proposal to increase freedom by increasing equality almost inevitably implies a linked combination of levelling up and levelling down. In peculiarly happy circumstances economic growth or a windfall gain such as North Sea Oil may permit the 'Pareto-optimal solution' in which everyone gets richer, or at least stays the same, while no one actually gets poorer (Pearce 1992). Such happy circumstances only encourage us to avoid or postpone the harsh test of practical commitment to greater equality; they are only relevant to arguments about absolute rather than relative wealth; and they occur a good deal less frequently than optimistic politicians hope and prophesy at election-time. We shall look at four different ways in which Roy Hattersley's followers might increase the 'sum of liberty' by increasing equality: taxation, employment quotas, parliamentary quotas, and a ban on private medicine.

Taxation for public services

Misled perhaps by the government's pre-election propaganda we did frame one question in Pareto's terms. We asked: 'If the government found that it had a surplus of cash available, which should it do: cut taxes or increase spending on public services?'. Incredible though it seems in retrospect, the question reflected the terms of public debate in the autumn of 1991 when we began interviewing. Like many others which asked similar if less optimistically phrased

Table 11.7 **Percentage for more public services rather than tax cuts**

	General public	Local politicians
all interviews	76	81
If commitment to freedom: low	69	73
high	82	84

Table 11.8 **Support for employment quotas**

	General public	Local politicians
% in favour of legal employment quotas for:		
disabled people	85	84
women	23	18
blacks and Asians	15	24

questions, our survey found a huge majority for more services rather than tax cuts. Three-quarters of the public and 83 per cent of politicians opted for more services. More important, in complete contrast to the ideas of Hayek and his followers, commitment to freedom *increased* support for public services rather than tax cuts – by around 12 per cent.

Employment quotas

There is widespread though often informal pressure for employment quotas. Formally, British law does not impose legally enforceable employment quotas, though there is increasing sensitivity to the underrepresentation of women and minorities in both public and private sector organisations. Many large employers have equal opportunities committees which act as informal internal pressure groups supported, to a degree, by the formal legal framework enshrined in the Equal Pay Act 1970, the Sex Discrimination Acts 1975 and 1986, Article 119 of the Treaty of Rome, subsequent Directives of the EC Commission, and rulings of the European Court (Hurwitt and Thornton 1989: 267–8).

We asked whether 'the law should require [large private companies/the government and civil service] to hire a fixed percentage of [women/blacks and Asians/disabled people], or should [women/blacks and Asians/disabled people] get no special treatment?'. As usual, the six different variants of the question (two employment sectors times three quota subjects) were assigned randomly to different interviews.

Focusing on the public or private sector made almost no difference to support for quotas, but focusing on gender, race or disability

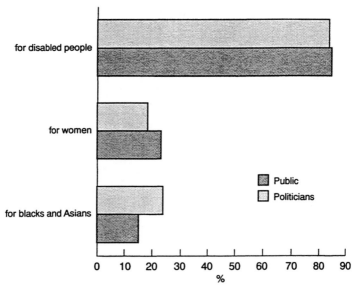

*Figure 11.4 **Percentage support for employment quotas***

had a dramatic effect. Roughly 85 per cent backed employment quotas for the disabled. By contrast, only 23 per cent of the public favoured gender quotas and 15 per cent racial quotas. Politicians were more favourable to racial quotas but less favourable to gender quotas: 24 per cent of them backed racial quotas but only 18 per cent gender quotas.

Commitment in principle to gender equality, ethnic protection, or help for the disabled more than doubled support for relevant employment quotas – from 24 per cent to 56 per cent among the public and from 25 per cent to 56 per cent among politicians. That was only to be expected. Much more significant is the pattern that did *not* occur: commitment to freedom did remarkably little to reduce support for employment quotas. Indeed quite the reverse: commitment to freedom appeared, on the surface, to *increase* support for employment quotas, not reduce it.

Simultaneously taking account of commitments to both freedom and equality however, shows that commitment to freedom did in fact reduce support for employment quotas within groups of people who held similar views about equality. This becomes clear if we construct a category of people with a *high* commitment to relevant kinds of social equality – in this case, those who gave marks of 9 or more out of 10 to the importance they placed upon gender equality, protecting ethnic minorities, or helping the disabled. Among those with a *high* commitment to the most relevant social equality, commitment to freedom reduced support for employment quotas (for corresponding social groups) by 4 per cent among the public, and 11 per cent among politicians. But this

Table 11.9 **Principles and employment quotas**

	General public		Local politicians	
% in favour of legal employment quotas:				
If commitment to relevant social equality: low	24		25	
high	56		56	
If commitment to freedom: low	37		40	
high	45		43	
	Low	*High*	*Low*	*High*
If commitment to freedom =				
If commitment to relevant social equality: low	22	27	26	24
high	58	54	65	54

Note:
Commitment to relevant social equality is defined thus: the high category consists of those who gave marks of 9 or 10 out of 10 for the importance to them of the most relevant one of the following:
gender equality (most relevant to gender employment quotas),
protection for ethnic minorities (most relevant to ethnic employment quotas),
help for the disabled (most relevant to disabled employment quotas).

small logical influence of freedom was overwhelmed by the much larger influence of equality on attitudes to employment quotas, coupled with the tendency of those with higher commitments to freedom to have higher commitments to equality as well. Statisticians will recognise this as a classic example of the 'suppressor effect' where two factors which are themselves correlated positively, commitments to freedom and equality in this case, have opposing influences on some other variable, support for employment quotas in this case.

Nonetheless it is significant for Roy Hattersley's argument about the link between equality and freedom that, even when we do take account of this supressor effect, commitment to freedom still does remarkably little to reduce support for employment quotas.

Parliamentary quotas

There have been no serious proposals for legally enforced gender or racial quotas in elections to Parliament other than those on gender contained in Teresa Gorman's 1992 Private Member's Bill. But it was a normal part of the electoral process in the old Soviet Union, and has been used for internal party elections or candidate selection in the United States and elsewhere and increasingly within Britain. The idea was also included in proposals for an elected Canadian Senate, a reform that was rejected in the 1992 constitutional referendum. Moreover, the idea of gender (but not racial) quotas gained support among those planning for a Scottish Assembly after the 1992 General Election. Only the last minute swing to

Table 11.10   **Support for parliamentary quotas**

	General public	Local politicians
% who say is is important to have more ...		
women MPs	76	77
ethnic minority MPs	59	70
% who favour legal changes to ensure this:		
among all interviews	31	14
among those who want more such MPs	47	19

the Conservatives and their subsequent election victory swept the idea of parliamentary quotas from public debate in Britain. It may return.

We asked: 'Is it important to have more [women / ethnic and racial minority] MPs in parliament?'; and, if so, 'should the law be changed to ensure more [women / ethnic and racial minority] MPs?'. As usual, each form of words was used in a randomly selected half of the interviews. Over three-quarters of both public and politicians wanted more women MPs while 59 per cent of the public and 70 per cent of politicians wanted more MPs from ethnic and racial minorities.

But when it came to changing the law, public and politicians parted company. Generally there was a lot less support for legal enforcement than for the goal of more equal social representation. Legal changes to get more women/minority MPs won the support of 31 per cent of the public but only 14 per cent of politicians. So although politicians were more favourable than the general public to the goal, they were very much more opposed to legal enforcement.

Commitment in principle to social equality increased support for the goal; and among those who accepted the goal, it also increased support for legal enforcement. The net result of these two cumulative effects was that a high commitment to social equality more than doubled support for laws to produce a more socially representative Parliament – from 21 per cent to 44 per cent among the public and from 8 per cent to 20 per cent among politicians.

Commitment to freedom had a more complex effect. Overall, it appeared to have little or no effect upon support for legal changes to ensure better social representation. That was because commitment to freedom *increased* support for the goal, yet simultaneously *decreased* support for legal enforcement, and the two effects cancelled each other out.

In combination, commitment to social equality and freedom had a powerful effect upon attitudes to legal changes that were designed to improve gender and minority representation in Parliament. Among those who actually wanted better social representation a combination of a high commitment to social equality coupled with

Table 11.11 **Effect of principles upon attitudes to parliamentary quotas**

	General public		Local politicians	
More women/minority MPs?:				
If commitment to relevant social equality =	*Low*	*High*	*Low*	*High*
% of all respondents who say it is important	56	82	60	89
% of above who support legal enforcement	38	54	13	22
% of all respondents who support legal enforcement	21	44	8	20
More women/minority MPs?:				
If commitment to freedom =	*Low*	*High*	*Low*	*High*
% of all respondents who say it is important	64	72	58	79
% of above who support legal enforcement	53	42	18	19
% of all respondents who support legal enforcement	33	30	10	15
Among those who feel it is important to have more women/minority MPs, % who support legal enforcement:				
If commitment to freedom =	*Low*	*High*	*Low*	*High*
If commitment to relevant social equality: low	42	32	14	13
high	68	47	24	22

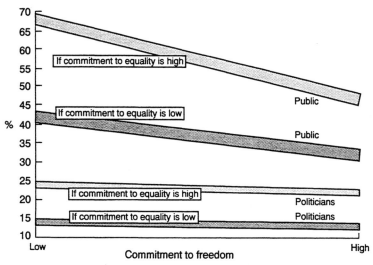

Figure 11.5 **Support for legal changes to get more women/minority MPs**

a low commitment to freedom, rather than *vice versa*, raised public support for legal changes from 32 per cent to 68 per cent (and politicians' support from 13 per cent to 24 per cent).

A ban on private medicine

Most controversially, Roy Hattersley raised the possibility of increasing the sum of liberty by banning private medicine. Having

Table 11.12 **Support for a ban on private medicine**

	General public	Local politicians
% who accept right of following to ban private medicine:		
Parliament	30	42
government	35	35
majority of people	38	38
% who themselves support ban	37	32

quoted Iain Gilmour's claim: 'If everybody, because of egalitarianism approved and imposed by social democrats, had to use the same medical services ... the citizen will be increasingly regulated by monopolies and increasingly at their service', Roy Hattersley responded: 'Tell that to the Canadians. In Canada all parties support legislation which prohibits the existence of private medicine.' It was, no doubt, a rhetorical flourish. We do not wish to suggest that Roy Hattersley personally, still less the Labour Party, currently favours a legal ban on private medicine in Britain.

Nonetheless, whether we agree or disagree with it, whether parties happen to advocate it or not, a serious case can be made for such a ban. Better services for some may, as Hattersley himself argues, be provided at the expense of worse services for others. Even if better services for the rich do not pre-empt scarce skills and resources, and do not degrade the services available to the poor in absolute terms, they certainly degrade them in relative terms and may therefore be offensive to strict egalitarians on that ground alone.

We asked: 'Suppose [Parliament / the government / the majority of people in this country] wanted to ban private medicine in order to make health services the same for both rich and poor. Should they be able to do so even though the ban would reduce the freedom of individuals to do what they want? And would you, yourself, favour such a ban?'. As usual, the three forms of wording were randomly assigned to one-third of interviews.

Overall, about a third favoured a ban on private medicine. The public were more favourable to a ban than politicians, but less willing than politicians to accept Parliament's right to impose one. Commitment to the general principle of equality of outcome increased support for a ban by 23 per cent among the public and by 38 per cent among politicians, a large effect but not an altogether surprising one. Again what is more surprising is that commitment to freedom only slightly reduced support for a ban among the public and actually raised it among politicians.

In part that was because commitment to the principle of freedom was positively correlated with commitment to the principle of equality, and equality had so much more influence towards

Table 11.13 **Effect of principles on support for ban of private medicine** (%)

	General public		Local politicians	
If commitment to equalise wealth: no	26		12	
yes	49		50	
Effect	+ 23		+ 38	
If commitment to freedom: low	39		27	
high	36		34	
Effect	− 3		+ 7	
If commitment to freedom =	Low	High	Low	High
If commitment to equalise wealth: no	28	24	12	13
yes	51	48	49	51

increasing support for a ban on private medicine than freedom had towards reducing it. But even if we look at the influence of freedom among egalitarians and non-egalitarians separately, we can still detect little or no tendency for commitment to freedom to reduce support for a ban on private medicine. The basic truth is that neither public nor politicians found commitment to freedom incompatible with support for a ban on private medicine. In the end, commitment to freedom did little to reduce support for a ban on private medicine while commitment to equality did a great deal to increase it.

Logically, it is impossible to deny the proposition that imposing equality necessarily curtails someone's liberty. Roy Hattersley does not deny that. But he argues that equality also extends someone else's liberty; so that the sum of liberty may be increased by greater equality. We have found that despite the logical trade-offs between liberty and equality these principles are correlated in public opinion: those who value liberty most are the people who also value equality more than others. We have also found that those who value liberty most, support practical egalitarian policies at least as much as others: partly because their commitment to liberty only slightly reduces their support for egalitarian policies, partly because their commitment to equality outweighs their commitment to liberty. Despite the deluge of literature from the new right, among both public and politicians in contemporary Britain, the egalitarians are at least as libertarian as anyone else.

References

Burns, J. M., Peltason, J. W. and Cronin, T. E. (1981) *Government by the People*, Englewood Cliffs: Prentice Hall.
Hartz, L. (1955) *The Liberal Tradition in America*, New York: Harcourt Brace Jovanovich.

Hayek, F. (1976) *The Road to Serfdom*, London: Routledge.
Hurwitt, M. and Thornton, P. (1989) *Civil Liberty: The Liberty/NCCL Guide*, London: Penguin.
Pearce, D. W. (ed.) (1972) *Macmillan Dictionary of Modern Economics*, 4th edition, London: Macmillan.

PART SIX

Freedom versus the Moral Community

CHAPTER 12

Argument: Defining deviancy down[1]

SENATOR DANIEL PATRICK MOYNIHAN

In one of the founding texts of sociology, *The Rules of Sociological Method* (1895), Emile Durkheim set down that 'crime is normal'. 'It is,' he wrote, 'completely impossible for any society entirely free of it to exist.' By defining what is deviant, we are enabled to know what is not, and hence to live by shared standards. This *aperçu* appears in the chapter entitled 'Rules for the Distinction of the Normal from the Pathological'. Durkheim writes:

From this viewpoint the fundamental facts of criminology appear to us in an entirely new light . . . (T)he criminal no longer appears as an utterly unsociable creature, a sort of parasitic element, a foreign, inassimilable body introduced into the bosom of society. He plays a normal role in social life. For its part, crime must no longer be conceived of as an evil which cannot be circumscribed closely enough. Far from there being cause for congratulation when it drops too noticeably below the normal level, this apparent progress assuredly coincides with and is linked to some social disturbance.

Durkheim suggests, for example, that 'in times of scarcity' crimes of assault drop off. He does not imply that we ought to approve of crime – 'pain has likewise nothing desirable about it' – but we need to understand its function. He saw religion, in the sociologist Randall Collins's terms, as 'fundamentally a set of ceremonial actions, assembling the group, heightening its emotions, and focusing its members on symbols of their common belongingness'. In this context 'a punishment ceremony creates social solidarity'.

The matter was pretty much left at that until 70 years later when, in 1965, Kai T. Erikson published *Wayward Puritans*, a study of 'crime rates' in the Massachusetts Bay Colony. The plan behind the book, as Erikson put it, was 'to test (Durkheim's) notion that the number of deviant offenders a community can afford to recognise is likely to remain stable over time'. The notion worked out very well indeed. Despite occasional crime waves, as when itinerant Quakers refused to take off their hats in the presence of magistrates, the amount of deviance in this corner of seventeenth-century New England fitted nicely with the supply of stocks and whipping posts. Erikson remarks:

It is one of the arguments of the . . . study that the amount of deviation a community encounters is apt to remain fairly constant over time. To start at the beginning, it is a simple logistic fact that the number of deviances which come to a community's attention are limited by the kinds of equipment it uses to detect and handle them, and to that extent the rate of deviation found in a community is at least in part a function of the size and complexity of its social control apparatus. A community's capacity for handling deviance, let us say, can be roughly estimated by counting its prison cells and hospital beds, its policemen and psychiatrists, its courts and clinics. Most communities, it would seem, operate with the expectation that a relatively constant number of control agents is necessary to cope with a relatively constant number of offenders. The amount of men, money, and material assigned by society to 'do something' about deviant behaviour does not vary appreciably over time, and the implicit logic which governs the community's efforts to man a police force or maintain suitable facilities for the mentally ill seems to be that there is a fairly stable quota of trouble which should be anticipated.

In this sense, the agencies of control often seem to define their job as that of keeping deviance within bounds rather than that of obliterating it altogether. Many judges, for example, assume that severe punishments are a greater deterrent to crime than moderate ones, and so it is important to note that many of them are apt to impose harder penalties when crime seems to be on theincrease and more lenient ones when it does not, almost as if the power of the bench were being used to keep the crime rate from getting out of hand.

Erikson was taking issue with what he described as 'a dominant strain in sociological thinking' that took for granted that a well-structured society 'is somehow designed to prevent deviant behaviour from occurring'. In both authors, Durkheim and Erikson, there is an undertone that suggests that, with deviancy, as with most social goods, there is the continued problem of demand exceeding supply. Durkheim invites us to

... imagine a society of saints, a perfect cloister of exemplary individuals. Crimes, properly so called, will there be unknown; but faults which appear venial to the layman will create there the same scandal that the ordinary offence does in ordinary consciousness. If, then, this society has the power to judge and punish, it will define these acts as criminal and will treat them as such.

Recall Durkheim's comment that there need be no cause for congratulations should the amount of crime drop 'too noticeably below the normal level'. It would not appear that Durkheim anywhere contemplates the possibility of too much crime. Clearly his theory would have required him to deplore such a development, but the possibility seems never to have occurred to him.

Erikson, writing much later in the twentieth century, contemplates both possibilities. 'Deviant persons can be said to supply needed services to society'. There is no doubt a tendency for the supply of any needed thing to run short. But he is consistent. There can, he believes, be *too much* of a good thing. Hence 'the number of deviant offenders a community *can afford* to recognise is likely to remain stable over time' (my emphasis).

Social scientists are said to be on the lookout for 'poor fellows getting a bum rap'. But here is a theory that clearly implies that there are circumstances in which society will choose *not* to notice behaviour that would be otherwise controlled, or disapproved, or even punished.

It appears to me that this is in fact what we in the United States have been doing of late. I proffer the thesis that, over the past generation, since the time Erikson wrote, the amount of deviant behaviour in American society has increased beyond the levels the community can 'afford to recognise' and that, accordingly, we have been redefining deviancy so as to exempt much conduct previously stigmatised, and also quietly raising the 'normal' level in categories where behaviour is now abnormal by any earlier standard. This redefining has evoked fierce resistance from defenders of 'old' standards, and accounts for much of the present 'cultural war' such as proclaimed by many at the 1992 Republican National Convention.

Let me, then, offer three categories of redefinition in these regards: the *altruistic*, the *opportunistic*, and the *normalising*.

The first category, the *altruistic,* may be illustrated by the deinstitutionalisation movement within the mental health profession that appeared in the 1950s. The second category, the *opportunistic*, is seen in the interest group rewards derived from the acceptance of 'alternative' family structures. The third category, the *normalising*, is to be observed in the growing acceptance of unprecedented levels of violent crime.

Altruistic redefinition

It happens that I was present at the beginning of the deinstitutionalisation movement. Early in 1955 Averell Harriman, then the new governor of New York, met with his new commissioner of mental hygiene, Dr Paul Hoch, who described the development, at one of the state mental hospitals, of a tranquilliser derived from rauwolfia. The medication had been clinically tested and appeared to be an effective treatment for many severely psychotic patients, thus increasing the percentage of patients discharged. Dr Hoch recommended that it be used systemwide; Harriman found the money.

That same year Congress created a Joint Commission on Mental Health and Illness whose mission was to formulate 'comprehensive and realistic recommendations' in this area, which was then a matter of considerable public concern. Year after year, the population of mental institutions grew. Year after year, new facilities had to be built. Never mind the complexities: population growth and such like matters. There was a general unease. Durkheim's constant continued to be exceeded. In *Spanning the Century: The Life of W. Averell Harriman*, Rudy Abramson writes:

'New York's mental hospitals in 1955 were overflowing warehouses, and new patients were being admitted faster than space could be found for them. When he [Harriman] was inaugurated, 94,000 New Yorkers were confined to state hospitals. Admissions were running at more than 2,500 a year and rising, making the Department of Mental Hygiene the fastest-growing, most expensive, most hopeless department of state government.'

The discovery of tranquillisers was adventitious. Physicians were seeking cures for disorders that were just beginning to be understood. Even a limited success made it possible to believe that the incidence of this particular range of disorders, which had seemingly required persons to be confined against their will or even awareness, could be greatly reduced. The Congressional Commission submitted its report in 1961; it proposed a nation-wide programme of deinstitutionalisation.

Late in 1961, President Kennedy appointed an interagency committee to prepare legislative recommendations based upon the report. I represented Secretary of Labour Arthur J. Goldberg on this committee and drafted its final submission. This included the recommendation of the National Institute of Mental Health that 2,000 community mental health centres (one per 100,000 of population) be built by 1980. A buoyant Presidential Message to Congress followed early in 1963. 'If we apply our medical knowledge and social insights fully,' President Kennedy pronounced, 'all but a small portion of the mentally ill can eventually achieve a wholesome and a constructive social adjustment.' A 'concerted national attack on mental disorders (was) now possible and practical'. The President signed the Community Mental Health Centres Construction Act on 31 October 1963, his last public bill-signing ceremony. He gave me a pen.

The mental hospitals emptied out. At the time Governor Harriman met with Dr Hoch in 1955, there were 93,314 adult residents of mental institutions maintained by New York State. As of August 1992, there were 11,363. This occurred across the nation. However, the number of community mental health centres never came near the goal of 2,000. Only some 482 received federal construction funds between 1963 and 1980. The next year, 1981, the programme was folded into the Alcohol and Other Drug Abuse block grant and disappeared from view. Even when centres were built, the results were hardly as hoped for. David F. Musto of Yale writes that the planners had bet on improving national mental health 'by improving the quality of general community life through expert knowledge, not merely by more effective treatment of the already ill'. There was no such knowledge.

However, worse luck, the belief that there *was* such knowledge took hold within sectors of the profession that saw institutionalisation as an unacceptable mode of social control. These activists subscribed to a redefining mode of their own. Mental patients were said to have been 'labelled', and were not to be drugged. Musto says of the battles that followed that they were 'so intense and dramatic precisely because both sides shared the fantasy of an omnipotent and omniscient mental health technology which could thoroughly reform society; the prize seemed eminently worth fighting for'.

But even as the federal government turned to other matters, the mental institutions continued to release inmates. Professor Fred Siegel of Cooper Union observes: 'In the great wave of moral deregulation that began in the mid-1960s, the poor and the insane were freed from the fetters of middle-class mores'. They might henceforth sleep in doorways as often as they chose. The problem of the homeless appeared, characteristically defined as persons who lacked 'affordable housing'.

The *altruistic* mode of redefinition is just that. There is no reason to believe that there was any real increase in mental illness at the time deinstitutionalisation began. Yet there was such a perception, and this enabled good people to try to do good, however unavailing in the end.

Opportunistic redefinition

Our second, or *opportunistic* mode of redefinition, reveals at most a nominal intent to do good. The true object is to do well, a long-established motivation among mortals. In this pattern, a growth in deviancy makes possible a transfer of resources, including prestige, to those who control the deviant population. This control would be jeopardised if any serious effort were made to reduce the deviancy in question. This leads to assorted strategies for redefining the behaviour in question as not all that deviant, really.

In the years from 1963 to 1965, the Policy Planning Staff of the US Department of Labor picked up the first tremors of what Samuel H. Preston, in the 1984 Presidential Address to the Population Association of America, would call 'the earthquake that shuddered through the American family in the past twenty years'. The *New York Times* recently provided a succinct accounting of Preston's point: 'Thirty years ago, 1 in every 40 white children was born to an unmarried mother; today it is 1 in 3, according to Federal data. Among blacks, 2 of 3 children are born to an unmarried mother; 30 years ago the figure was 1 in 5.'

In 1991, Paul Offner and I published longitudinal data showing that, of children born in the years 1967–69, some 22.1 per cent were dependent on welfare – that is to say, Aid to Families with

Dependent Children – before reaching age 18. This broke down as 15.7 per cent for white children, 72.3 per cent for black children. Projections for children born in 1980 gave rates of 22.2 per cent and 82.9 per cent respectively. A year later, a *New York Times* series on welfare and poverty called this a 'startling finding . . . a symptom of vast social calamity'.

And yet there is little evidence that these facts are regarded as a calamity in municipal government. To the contrary, there is general acceptance of the situation as normal. Political candidates raise the subject, often to the point of dwelling on it. But while there is a good deal of demand for symbolic change, there is none of the marshalling of resources that is associated with significant social action. Nor is there any lack of evidence that there is a serious social problem here.

Richard T. Gill writes of 'an accumulation of data showing that intact biological parent families offer children very large advantages compared to any other family or non-family structure one can imagine'. Correspondingly, the disadvantages associated with single-parent families spill over into other areas of social policy that now attract great public concern. Leroy L. Schwartz, M.D. and Mark W. Stanton argue that the real question regarding a government-run health system such as that of Canada or Germany is whether it would work 'in a country that has social problems that countries like Canada and Germany don't share to the same extent'. Health problems reflect ways of living. The way of life associated with 'such social pathologies as the breakdown of the family structure' lead to medical pathologies. Schwartz and Stanton conclude: 'The United States is paying dearly for its social and behavioural problems', for they have now become medical problems as well.

To cite another example, there is at present no more vexing problem of social policy in the United States than that posed by education. A generation of ever more ambitious statutes and reforms have produced weak responses at best and a fair amount of what could more simply be called dishonesty . . . ('Everyone knows that Head Start works'; 'By the year 2000, American students will be first in the world in science and mathematics').

None of this should surprise us. The 1966 report *Equality of Educational Opportunity* by James S. Coleman and his associates established that the family background of students played a much stronger role in student achievement relative to variations in the 10 (and still standard) measures of school quality.

In a 1992 study entitled *America's Smallest School: The Family*, Paul Barton came up with the elegant and persuasive concept of the *parent*–pupil ratio as a measure of school quality. Barton, who was on the policy planning staff in the Department of Labor in 1965, noted the great increase in the proportion of children living in single-parent families since then. He further noted that the proportion 'varies widely among the states' and is related to 'variation in achievement' among them. The correlation between the percentage of eighth graders living in two-parent families and average mathematics proficiency is a solid 0.74. North Dakota, highest on the mathematics test, is second highest on the family composition scale – that is, it is second in the percentage of children coming from two-parent homes. The District of Columbia, lowest on the family scale, is second lowest in the test score.

A few months before Barton's study appeared, I published an article showing that the correlation between eighth-grade mathematics scores and the proximity of state capitals to the Canadian border was 0.522, a respectable showing. By contrast, the correlation with per pupil expenditure was a derisory 0.203. I offered the policy proposal that states wishing to improve their schools should move closer to Canada. This would be difficult, of course, but so would it be to change the parent–pupil ratio. Indeed, the 1990 Census found that for the District of Columbia, apart from Ward 3 west of Rock Creek Park, the percentage of children living in single-parent families in the seven remaining wards ranged from a low of 63.6 per cent to a high of 75.7 per cent. This being a one-time measurement, over time the proportions become asymptotic. And this in the nation's capital. No demand for change comes from that community – or as near to no demand as makes no matter. *For there is good money to be made out of bad schools.* This is a statement that will no doubt please many a hard heart, and displease many genuinely concerned to bring about change. To the latter, a group in which I would like to include myself, I would only say that we are obliged to ask why things do not change.

For a period there was some speculation that, if family structure got bad enough, this mode of deviancy would have less punishing effects on children. In 1991 Deborah A. Dawson, of the National Institutes of Health, examined the thesis that 'the psychological effects of divorce and single parenthood on children were strongly influenced by a sense of shame in being "different" from the norm'. If this were so, the effect should have fallen off in the 1980s, when being from a single-parent home became much more common. It did not. 'The problems associated with task overload among single parents are more constant in nature', Dawson wrote, adding that since the adverse effects had not diminished, they were 'not based on stigmatisation but rather on inherent problems in alternative family structures' – *alternative* here meaning other than two-parent families. We should take note of such candour. Writing in the *Journal of Marriage and the Family* in 1989, Sara McLanahan and Karen Booth noted: 'Whereas a decade ago the prevailing view was that single motherhood had no harmful effects on children, recent research is less optimistic.'

The year 1990 saw more of this lesson. In a paper prepared for the Progressive Policy Institute, Elaine Ciulla Kamarck and William

A. Galston wrote that 'if the economic effects of family breakdown are clear, the psychological effects are just now coming into focus'. They cite Karl Zinsmeister:

There is a mountain of scientific evidence showing that when families disintegrate children often end up with intellectual, physical, and emotional scars that persist for life . . . We talk about the drug crisis, the education crisis, and the problems of teen pregnancy and juvenile crime. But all these ills trace back predominantly to one source: broken families.

As for juvenile crime, they cite Douglas Smith and G. Roger Jarjoura: 'Neighbourhoods with larger percentages of youth (those aged 12 to 20) and areas with higher percentages of single-parent households also have higher rates of violent crime.' They add: 'The relationship is so strong that controlling for family configuration erases the relationship between race and crime and between low income and crime. This conclusion shows up time and time again in the literature; poverty is far from the sole determinant of crime.' But the large point is avoided. In a 1992 essay 'The Expert's Story of Marriage', Barbara Dafoe Whitehead examined 'the story of marriage as it is conveyed in today's high school and college textbooks'. Nothing amiss in this tale. It goes like this:

The life course is full of exciting options. The lifestyle options available to individuals seeking a fulfilling personal relationship include living a hetero-sexual, homosexual, or bisexual single lifestyle; living in a commune; having a group marriage; being a single parent; or living together. Marriage is yet another lifestyle choice. However, before choosing marriage, individuals should weigh its costs and benefits against other lifestyle options and should consider what they want to get out of their intimate relationships. Even within marriage, different people want different things. For example, some people marry for companionship, some marry in order to have children, some marry for emotional and financial security. Though marriage can offer a rewarding path to personal growth, it is important to remember that it cannot provide a secure or permanent status. Many people will make the decision between marriage and singlehood many times throughout their life.

Divorce represents part of the normal family life cycle. It should not be viewed as either deviant or tragic, as it has been in the past. Rather, it establishes a process for 'uncoupling' and thereby serves as the foundation for individual renewal and 'new beginnings'.

History commences to be rewritten. In 1992, the Select Committee on Children, Youth, and Families of the US House of Representatives held a hearing on 'Investing in Families: A Historical Perspective'. A fact sheet prepared by committee staff began:

'INVESTING IN FAMILIES: A HISTORICAL PERSPECTIVE'

FACT SHEET

HISTORICAL SHIFTS IN FAMILY COMPOSITION

CHALLENGING CONVENTIONAL WISDOM

While in modern times the percentage of children living with one parent has increased, more children lived with just one parent in Colonial America.

The fact sheet proceeded to list programme on programme for which federal funds were allegedly reduced in the 1980s. We then come to a summary:

Between 1970 and 1991, the value of AFDC (Aid to Families with Dependent Children) benefits decreased by 41%. In spite of proven success of Head Start, only 28% of eligible children are being served. As of 1990, more than $18 billion in child support went uncollected. At the same time, the poverty rate among single-parent families with children under 18 was 44%. Between 1980 and 1990, the rate of growth in the total Federal budget was four times greater than the rate of growth in children's programs.

In other words, benefits paid to mothers and children have gone down steadily, as indeed they have done. But no proposal is made to restore benefits to an earlier level, or even to maintain their value, as is the case with other 'indexed' Social Security programmes. Instead we go directly to the subject of education spending.

Nothing new. In 1969, President Nixon proposed a guaranteed income, the Family Assistance Plan. This was described as an 'income strategy' as against a 'services strategy'. It may or may not have been a good idea, but it was a clear one, and the resistance of service providers to it was equally clear. In the end it was defeated, to the huzzahs of the advocates of 'welfare rights'. What is going on here is simply that a large increase in what once was seen as deviancy has provided opportunity to a wide spectrum of interest groups that benefit from redefining the problem as essentially normal and doing little to reduce it.

Normalising redefinition

Our *normalising* category most directly corresponds to Erikson's proposition that 'the number of deviant offenders a community can afford to recognise is likely to remain stable over time'. Here we are dealing with the popular psychological notion of 'denial'. In 1965, having reached the conclusion that there would be a dramatic increase in single-parent families, I reached the further conclusion that this would in turn lead to a dramatic increase in crime. In an article in *America*, I wrote:

From the wild Irish slums of the 19th century Eastern seaboard to the riot-torn suburbs of Los Angeles, there is one unmistakable lesson in American history: a community that allows a large number of young men to grow up in broken families, dominated by women, never acquiring any stable relationship to male authority, never acquiring any set of rational expectations about the future – that community asks for and gets chaos. Crime, violence, unrest, unrestrained lashing out at the whole social structure – that is not only to be expected; it is very near to inevitable.

The inevitable, as we now know, has come to pass, but here again our response is curiously passive. Crime is a more or less continuous subject of political pronouncement, and from time to time it will be at or near the top of opinion polls as a matter of public concern. But it never gets much further than that. In words spoken from the bench, Judge Edwin Torres of the New York State Supreme Court, Twelfth Judicial District, described how 'the slaughter of the innocent marches unabated; subway riders, bodega owners, cab drivers, babies; in laundromats, at cash machines, on elevators, in hallways'. In personal communication, he writes: 'This numbness, this near narcoleptic state can diminish the human condition to the level of combat infantrymen, who, in protracted campaigns, can eat their battlefield rations seated on the bodies of the fallen, friend and foe alike. A society that loses its sense of outrage is doomed to extinction.' There is no expectation that this will change, nor any efficacious public insistence that it do so. The crime level has been *normalised*.

Consider the St Valentine's Day Massacre. In 1929 in Chicago during Prohibition, four gangsters killed seven gangsters on 14 February. The nation was shocked. The event became legend. It merits not one but two entries in the *World Book Encyclopaedia*. I leave it to others to judge, but it would appear that society in the 1920s was simply not willing to put up with this degree of deviancy. In the end, the Constitution was amended, and Prohibition, which lay behind so much gangster violence, ended.

In recent years, again in the context of illegal traffic in controlled substances, this form of murder has returned. But it has done so at a level that induces denial. James Q. Wilson comments that Los Angeles has the equivalent of a St Valentine's Day Massacre every weekend. Even the most ghastly re-enactments of such human slaughter produce only moderate responses. On the morning after the close of the 1992 Democratic National Convention in New York City in July, there was such an account in the second section of the *New York Times*. It was not a big story; bottom of the page, but with a headline that got your attention: '3 Slain in Bronx Apartment, but a Baby is Saved'. A subhead continued: 'A mother's last act was to hide her little girl under the bed'. The article described a drug execution; the now-routine blindfolds made from duct tape, a man and a woman and a teenager involved. 'Each had been shot once in the head.' The police had found them a day later. They also found, under a bed, a three-month old baby, dehydrated but alive. A lieutenant remarked of the mother, 'In her last dying act she protected her baby. She probably knew she was going to die, so she stuffed the baby where she knew it would be safe.' But the matter was left there. The police would do their best. But the event passed quickly; forgotten by the next day, it will never make the *World Book Encyclopaedia*.

Nor is it likely that any great heed will be paid to an uncanny re-enactment of the Prohibition drama a few months later, also in the Bronx. The *Times* story, page B3, reported:

9 Men Posing as Police

Are Indicted in 3 Murders

Drug Dealers Were Kidnapped for Ransom

The *Daily News* story, same day, on page 17, made it *four* murders, adding nice details about torture techniques. The gang members posed as federal Drug Enforcement Administration agents, real badges and all. The victims were drug dealers, whose families were uneasy about calling the police. Ransom seems generally to have been set in the $650,000 range. Some paid. Some got it in the back of the head. So it goes.

Yet, violent killings, often random, go on unabated. Peaks continue to attract some notice. But these are peaks above 'average' levels that thirty years ago would have been thought epidemic.

LOS ANGELES. AUG. 24. (Reuters) Twenty-two people were killed in Los Angeles over the weekend, the worst period of violence in the city since it was ravaged by riots earlier this year, the police said today.

Twenty-four others were wounded by gunfire or stabbings, including a 19-year old woman in a wheelchair who was shot in the back when she failed to respond to a motorist who asked for directions in south Los Angeles.

'The guy stuck a gun out of the window and just fired at her,' said a police spokesman, Lieut. David Rock. The woman was later described as being in a stable condition.

Among those who died was an off-duty officer, shot while investigating reports of a prowler in a neighbour's yard, and a Little League baseball coach who had argued with the father of a boy he was coaching.

The police said at least nine of the deaths were gang-related, including that of a 14-year-old girl killed in a fight between rival gangs.

Fifty-one people were killed in three days of rioting that started April 19 after the acquittal of four police officers in the beating of Rodney G. King.

Los Angeles usually has above-average violence during August, but the police were at a loss to explain the sudden rise. On an average weekend in August, 14 fatalities occur.

Not to be outdone, two days later the poor Bronx came up with a near record, as reported in *New York Newsday*:

Armed with 9mm pistols, shotguns and M-16 rifles, a group of masked men and women poured out of two vehicles in the South Bronx early yesterday and sprayed a stretch of Longwood Avenue with a fusillade of bullets, injuring 12 people.

A Kai Erikson of the future will surely need to know that the

Department of Justice in 1990 found that Americans reported only about 38 per cent of all crimes and 48 per cent of violent crimes. This, too, can be seen as a means of *normalising* crime. In much the same way, the vocabulary of crime reporting can be seen to move toward the normal-seeming. A teacher is shot on her way to class. The *Times* subhead reads: 'Struck in the Shoulder in the Year's First Shooting Inside a School'. First of the season.

It is too early, however, to know how to regard the arrival of the doctors on the scene declaring crime a 'public health emergency'. The 10 June 1992, issue of the *Journal of the American Medical Association* was devoted entirely to papers on the subject of violence, principally violence associated with firearms. An editorial in the issue signed by former Surgeon General C. Everett Koop and Dr George D. Lundberg is entitled: 'Violence in America: A Public Health Emergency'. Their proposition is admirably succinct.

Regarding violence in our society as purely a sociological matter, or one of law enforcement, has led to unmitigated failure. It is time to test further whether violence can be amenable to medical/public health interventions. We believe violence in America to be a public health emergency, largely unresponsive to methods thus far used in its control. The solutions are very complex, but possible.

The authors cited the relative success of epidemiologists in gaining some jurisdiction in the area of motor vehicle casualties by re-defining what had been seen as a law enforcement issue into a public health issue. Again, this process began during the Harriman administration in New York in the 1950s. In the 1960s the morbidity and mortality associated with automobile crashes was, it could be argued, a major public health problem; the public health strategy, it could also be argued, brought the problem under a measure of control. Not in 'the 1970s and 1980s', as the *Journal of the American Medical Association* would have us think: the federal legislation involved was signed in 1965. Such a strategy would surely produce insights into the control of violence that elude law enforcement professionals, but whether it would change anything is another question.

For some years now I have had legislation in the Senate that would prohibit the manufacture of .25 and .32 calibre bullets. These are the two calibres most typically used with the guns known as Saturday Night Specials. 'Guns don't kill people,' I argue, 'bullets do.'

Moreover, we have a two-century supply of handguns but only a four-year supply of ammunition. A public health official would immediately see the logic of trying to control the supply of bullets rather than of guns.

Even so, now that the doctor has come, it is important that

criminal violence should not be defined down by epidemiologists. Doctors Koop and Lundberg note that in 1990 in the state of Texas 'deaths from firearms, for the first time in many decades, surpassed deaths from motor vehicles, by 3,443 to 3,309'. A good comparison. And yet keep in mind that the number of motor vehicle deaths, having levelled off since the 1960s, is now pretty well accepted as normal at somewhat less than 50,000 a year, which is somewhat less than the level of the 1960s – the 'carnage', as it once was thought to be, is now accepted as normal. This is the price we pay for high-speed transportation: there is a benefit associated with it. But there is no benefit associated with homicide, and no good in getting used to it. Epidemiologists have powerful insights that can contribute to lessening the medical trauma, but they must be wary of normalising the social pathology that leads to such trauma.

Conclusion

The hope – if there be such – of this essay has been twofold. It is, first, to suggest that the Durkheim constant, as I put it, is maintained by a dynamic process which adjusts upwards and *downwards*. Liberals have traditionally been alert for upward redefining that does injustice to individuals. Conservatives have been correspondingly sensitive to downward redefining that weakens societal standards. Might it not help if we could all agree that there is a dynamic at work here? It is not revealed truth, nor yet a scientifically derived formula. It is simply a pattern we observe in ourselves. Nor is it rigid. There may once have been an unchanging supply of jail cells which more or less determined the number of prisoners. No longer. We are building new prisons at a prodigious rate. Similarly, the executioner is back. There is something of a competition in Congress to think up new offences for which the death penalty is deemed the only available deterrent. Possibly also modes of execution, as in 'fry the kingpins'. Even so, we are getting used to a lot of behaviour that is not good for us.

As noted earlier, Durkheim states that there is 'nothing desirable' about pain. Surely what he meant was that there is nothing pleasurable. Pain, even so, is an indispensable warning signal. But societies under stress, much like individuals, will turn to painkillers of various kinds that end up concealing real damage. There is surely nothing desirable about this. If our analysis wins general acceptance, if, for example, more of us came to share Judge Torres's genuine alarm at 'the trivialisation of the lunatic crime rate' in his city (and mine), we might surprise ourselves how well we respond to the manifest decline of the American civic order. Might.

Note

1 The argument of this chapter originally appeared in *The American Scholar*, **62** (1), Winter 1993, pp. 17–30. Detailed bibliographic references are not available for this chapter.

CHAPTER 13

Opinions: Public tolerance of private freedom

WILLIAM L. MILLER, ANNIS MAY TIMPSON AND
MICHAEL LESSNOFF

Senator Moynihan has raised an alarm about the increasing levels of deviancy in contemporary United States society. He claims that current levels of homelessness, family breakdown, drug abuse and crime have exceeded the standards that most Americans can 'afford to recognise'. Indeed he argues that the only way Americans can cope with this 'epidemic' is to define deviancy downwards, so that previously stigmatised behaviour becomes acceptable.

In advancing this case, Senator Moynihan raises a much broader question – certainly not limited to the United States – about the way that any community establishes collective norms and defines practices as being tolerable or intolerable, be they in the public or private domain. The idea that 'the personal is political . . . denies the validity of the public/private distinction' (Randall 1991), but it is a belief shared by contemporary feminists, Roman emperors, medieval monarchs, religious fundamentalists, communist dictators and tabloid editors. Pierre Trudeau may have argued that 'the state has no business in the bedrooms of the nation' (McLaren and McLaren 1989: 9), but none of these would accept the view that moral and perhaps even legal censure should stop at the front door, or even at the door of those most private of private places: the bedroom, the kitchen, the study, or the household shrine. They focus on different aspects of what others see as a legitimate 'private space', on the division of domestic responsibilities, sexual behaviour, religious belief and practice, or intellectual enquiry. But they agree that no important aspect of life should be sheltered from public censure. The Emperor Constantine, Prince Vladimir, or the English King Henry VIII not only defined, but redefined the political correctness of religious belief and practice; and thousands perished because they made the change too early or too late. Under Stalin it was dangerous even to retire to your apartment and read the works of Lenin in the original (especially Lenin's *Testament*). These rulers were in the business of defining community norms, definitely not in the business of 'defining deviancy down'.

In this chapter we consider whether the British public has a clearly defined set of collective community norms that people feel should be adhered to in all circumstances. We also ask what makes people see some behaviour as acceptable and other practices as deviant. Although many of the problems that Senator Moynihan discusses are becoming increasingly evident in contemporary Britain and increasingly prominent in contemporary British political (and party) debate, there are other dimensions of tolerance that require attention, especially in a country that has not just one, but two, established Churches (the Church of England within England, the Church of Scotland within Scotland, although none in Wales or Northern Ireland). In this chapter, therefore, we focus on Senator Moynihan's essential concern with traditional values and with deviance, but do so through attention to specific issues of religious expression, sexual practice, and drug/alcohol consumption which are particularly relevant in contemporary Britain.

Enthusiasts

As Senator Moynihan noted the competition to define community standards, and therefore deviance, is always intense. It is not just established authorities, whether monarchs or churches or 'professionals', that hold stern views about proper beliefs and practice. Non-conformist groups within society may have convictions that are at least as strong as those of the orthodox. Within Scottish Church history those who passionately believed that they, and they alone, knew what was right were called 'enthusiasts'. It is a good term. It captures both the passion and the certainty far better than the anaemic 'moralist' derived from the Anglicisation of the Latin *mores* (customs). Enthusiast is derived from the Greek *enthousiastes* – 'possessed (or inspired) by a God' – though the Oxford dictionary defines the English term as a 'self-deluded visionary'. This is a useful ambiguity between the Greek and the English since enthusiasts see themselves as 'possessed by a God' while their opponents see them as 'self-deluded visionaries'. Of course, their God may be secular and particular groups of enthusiasts may reject overt use of the term 'God', but it is surprising how many do not, even in these latter days.

We asked a number of questions designed to measure enthusiasm. It is a very easy concept to understand but a very difficult one to measure simply because there are so many and such varied enthusiasms and it is in the nature of enthusiasts to be particularly sensitive to language and terminology. They not only believe that 'the personal is political' but that 'language is political' also. Our measures of enthusiasm, which use phrases like 'traditional ideas' or 'God's will', are therefore somewhat better indicators of conservative and orthodox enthusiasm than of revolutionary or minority enthusiasm but they do allow personal and varied interpretations of what is right.

Over 90 per cent of the public and only slightly fewer politicians agreed that 'it is very important to protect children and young people from wild and immoral ideas'. When we asked people to

Table 13.1 **Enthusiasm**

	General public	Local politicians
% who agree that it is very important to protect children and young people from wild and immoral ideas	91	87
% who give 6 or more out of 10 for importance of:		
preserving traditional ideas of right and wrong	83	80
following God's will	50	44
Average marks out of 10 for importance of:		
preserving traditional ideas of right and wrong	8.0	7.6
following God's will	5.7	5.0
% actively religious (attend more than once a year)	25	40

Note:
For further analysis we define 'enthusiasts' as those who give a mark of 6 or more for the importance, to them, of 'following God's will'.

give us marks out of 10 for how important to them it was to 'preserve traditional ideas of right and wrong' the public responded with marks that averaged 8 out of 10, and the politicians only slightly less. Over 80 per cent of both public and politicians gave us a mark of 6 or more out of 10 for the importance of preserving these 'traditional ideas'. On this evidence, 'Victorian values' seem to be widely supported, in word if not always in deed. A large majority of our respondents would surely have joined Senator Moynihan in lamenting the 'moral deregulation' of recent decades.

On the other hand people were more divided on the importance of 'following God's will'. This is the nearest to classic definitions of enthusiasm. Exactly half the public and 44 per cent of politicians gave 6 or more out of 10 for the importance *to them* of following God's will. We shall use this as our criterion for enthusiasm partly because it reflects the classic definition so closely, and partly because it proves the best statistical predictor of more specific attitudes towards private freedom in matters of sex, drugs and religion.

We also enquired whether people were connected to any organised religion and how frequently they attended a place of worship; 25 per cent of the public and 40 per cent of politicians claimed to attend more frequently than once a year. It is interesting to note that politicians were much more frequent attenders than the public though they placed less importance than the public upon 'following God's will'.

All these potential indicators of enthusiasm were positively inter-correlated at the individual level however. Those who placed more weight on following God's will also tended to place more weight on traditional ideas of right and wrong, they worshipped more frequently, and they put more importance on the need to protect children and young people from wild and immoral ideas.

Tolerance

Enthusiasts are often accused of intolerance – sometimes with justification. Sometimes they glory in it. In words attributed to Antoni Gaudi, the architect of Barcelona's unique church of the Sagrada Familia: 'There is no freedom in Heaven, because if one knows the whole Truth one completely submits to it' (Hughes 1992: 498). It was not an original thought, nor was it claimed to be so. But as evidence of intolerance it can be misleading. Enthusiasts can combine submission for themselves with tolerance for others. It is possible for believers to submit to the truth without requiring unbelievers to do the same.

We asked people to agree with the intolerant proposition that 'we should *not* tolerate people whose ideas are morally wrong'. J. L. Sullivan and others have argued that it is impossible to tolerate what we think is morally right; indeed, that it is impossible to tolerate anything which we approve (Sullivan *et al.* 1989: 60–3). According to them, the question of toleration only really arises when we are asked to refrain from action against something or someone that we find offensive, hence the phrase 'morally wrong'. Logically, it could be argued that we cannot simultaneously tolerate something and condemn it as morally wrong, but our survey question did not put that self-contradictory proposition. It distinguished clearly between the sinner and the sin, a familiar enough notion in the modern pulpit, but then put the intolerant proposition that we should condemn the sinner as well as the sin. We also framed the question in terms of intolerance rather than tolerance to avoid confusing acquiescence with support for toleration. To support toleration, respondents had to disagree with this proposition. We shall take that as our criterion of tolerance. By that measure, politicians appear more tolerant than the public: 65 per cent of politicians rejected the intolerant proposition but only 47 per cent of the public. While that difference might be attributed, in part, to the well-established tendency for the public to be more reluctant than politicians to disagree (with any proposition) other indicators confirmed that politicians were indeed more tolerant than the general public. When asked to give marks out of 10 for the importance, to them, of tolerating different beliefs and lifestyles, 90 per cent of politicians but only 73 per cent of the public gave marks of 6 or more out of 10 – and that finding does not depend upon any variations in willingness or reluctance to agree or disagree.

When we put the proposition that 'to compromise with our political opponents is dangerous, because it usually leads to the

Table 13.2 **Tolerance**

	General public	Local politicians
% who disagree that we should not tolerate people whose ideas are morally wrong	47	65
Average marks out of 10 for importance of tolerating different beliefs and lifestyles	7.2	8.3
% who give 6 or more out of 10 for importance of tolerating different beliefs and lifestyles	73	90
% who disagree that it is dangerous to compromise with our political opponents, because it usually leads to the betrayal of our own side	51	70

Note:
For further analysis we define the 'tolerant' as those who disagree with the proposition that 'we should not tolerate people whose ideas are morally wrong'.

betrayal of our own side', 51 per cent of the public but 70 per cent of politicians disagreed. Obviously there is a logical distinction between tolerance and compromise but they are sufficiently close in concept that it is reassuring to find they are also statistically related.

Once again all of these measures, this time of toleration, were positively intercorrelated. Those who, by our criterion, were more tolerant, were also more likely to accept political compromise and put more weight on tolerating different beliefs and lifestyles.

But enthusiasm and tolerance were negatively correlated. Among the public, 61 per cent combined enthusiasm with intolerance or lack of enthusiasm with tolerance; among politicians this overlap was 64 per cent. Nonetheless that left substantial numbers who combined enthusiasm with tolerance (especially among politicians) or lack of enthusiasm with intolerance. While this slippage between enthusiasm and intolerance must partly reflect the inevitable inaccuracy of our criteria of classification, it also reflects the reality of tolerant enthusiasts and intolerant unbelievers.

Enforcing morality or community standards

Intolerance need not necessarily imply legal prohibition. It need not necessarily be limited by the 'supply of stocks and whipping posts' as Senator Moynihan surmised. It can be expressed in all manner of social behaviour or even be restricted to intellectual intolerance. So we asked explicitly whether morals should be translated into laws. We put the proposition in two forms: [If something is morally wrong, then it should be made illegal/Even though something may be morally wrong, it should not necessarily be made illegal] and used each form in a randomly selected half of the interviews. Taking agreement with the first, or disagreement with the second, as an indicator of support for legal enforcement of moral codes, 47 per cent of the public but only 24 per cent of politicians favoured legal enforcement. As usual, the public showed a greater reluctance to disagree with these propositions than the politicians but, whichever form was used, politicians gave less support to enforcement than the public generally.

Elsewhere we asked whether it was the duty of government, among many other things, 'to uphold morality'. A government could do that in two ways – by upholding moral standards in its own conduct, and/or by imposing moral standards on others. Sixty-five per cent of the public but only 53 per cent of politicians said government did have a duty to uphold morality.

We can relate these opinions on legal enforcement to the basic principles of enthusiasm and tolerance. Among the public, those we have designated as enthusiasts were 26 per cent more willing (than non-enthusiasts) to translate morals into laws while those we have designated as tolerant were 31 per cent less willing (than the intolerant) to do so. Among politicians, enthusiasm had slightly less effect (21 per cent instead of 26 per cent) and tolerance had slightly more (35 per cent instead of 31 per cent). In combination these two principles were extremely powerful. Among both people and politicians, those who combined enthusiasm with intolerance were over 45 per cent more willing to translate morals into laws than those who combined tolerance with a lack of enthusiasm.

But while enthusiasm and intolerance pulled in the same direction, by the same token, enthusiasm and tolerance necessarily pulled in opposite directions and tolerance outweighed enthusiasm. Those who combined enthusiasm with tolerance were *less* willing to translate morals into laws than those who combined *in*tolerance with a lack of enthusiasm – 5 per cent less among the public and 18 per cent less among politicians.

Community and ideology

Enthusiasm and tolerance also shaped people's attitudes to community. We used four indicators of community. First we asked people to choose between the statements:

1 Our laws should aim to enforce the community's standards of right and wrong.
2 Our laws should aim to protect a citizen's right to live by any moral standard he or she chooses provided this does no harm to other people.

Just 29 per cent of both public and politicians opted for enforce-

Table 13.3 **Enforcing morality**

	General public	Local politicians
% who agree that if something is morally wrong then it should be made illegal (or disagree with the opposite proposition)	47	24
% who say that the government has a responsibility to uphold morality	65	53

% who agree that morally wrong should be made illegal

Among those whose enthusiasm is: Low	34	15
High	60	36
Effect of enthusiasm	+ 26 (= 60 − 34)	+ 21 (= 36 − 15)
Among those whose tolerance is: Low	62	47
High	31	12
Effect of tolerance	− 31 (= 31 − 62)	− 35 (= 12 − 47)

% who agree that morally wrong should be made illegal

Among those whose enthusiasm is:	Low	High	Low	High
And whose tolerance is: Low	50	69	37	53
High	22	45	8	19

Effect of combination of enthusiasm and intolerance	+ 47 (= 69 − 22)	+ 45 (= 53 − 8)
Effect of combination of enthusiasm and tolerance	− 5 (= 45 − 50)	− 18 (= 19 − 37)

ment of community standards though that was conditioned by our use of the phrase 'provided this does no harm' in the alternative proposition. Second, we asked whether: 'In Britain today there is [too much emphasis on citizens' rights and not enough on citizens' duties / too much emphasis on citizens' duties and not enough on citizens' rights] – using each version in randomly selected half-samples. Opinion was evenly divided on whether there was too much emphasis on rights rather than on duties. Third, we asked people to choose between the statements:

1 Ideally society should be like a unified body pursuing a common goal.
2 Ideally society should be like a collection of people independently pursuing their own goals.

The public were evenly divided but two thirds of politicians opted for the 'common goal'. Finally we asked whether: 'In Britain today too much emphasis is placed upon individual interests at the expense of the community's interest.' Two-thirds of the public and only slightly less of the politicians agreed. For brevity let us call these four measures of community: *Community Standards, Citizens'*

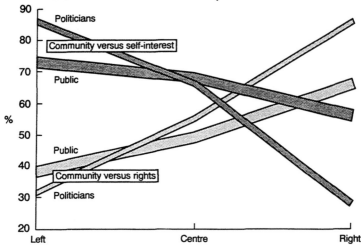

Figure 13.1 **Ideology and community**

Duties, Unified Body, and *Community Interest* respectively. They measure different aspects of the idea of community.

An analysis in terms of political ideology is revealing. The left gives most support to the *Unified Body* and *Community Interest* aspects, but the right to the *Community Standards* and *Citizens' Duties* aspects. Those on the left see community in terms of economic equality while those on the right see community in terms of conformity to standards of behaviour; the left sees community in terms of rights, and the right sees community in terms of duties. These are equally strong, though diametrically opposed, concepts of community.

Enthusiasm and tolerance do little to shape public attitudes towards the left-wing notions of community, but they have a powerful effect upon right-wing notions of community: *Citizens' Duties* and, more especially, *Community Standards*.

Among politicians, enthusiasm increased support for enforcement of *Community Standards* by 20 per cent while tolerance reduced it by 31 per cent. Among the public the same pattern was evident though each effect was only half that among politicians. Once again, the combination of enthusiasm and tolerance reduced support for the legal imposition of *Community Standards*, because that support was more sensitive to tolerance than to enthusiasm; but the combination of enthusiasm and intolerance raised support for the enforcement of *Community Standards* by 20 per cent among the public and 39 per cent among politicians.

Table 13.4 **Community**

	General public	Local politicians
% who choose: 'Our laws should aim to enforce the community's standards of right and wrong'	29	29
% who agree that in Britain today there is too much emphasis on citizens' rights and not enough on citizens' duties (or disagree with the opposite proposition)	50	55
% who choose: 'Ideally society should be like a unified body pursuing a common goal'	56	65
% who agree that in Britain today, too much emphasis is placed on individual interests at the expense of the community's interest	67	63
Effect of enthusiasm on:		
% enforce the community's standards of right and wrong	+ 10	+ 20
% there is not enough emphasis on citizens' duties	+ 5	+ 22
% society should pursue common goal	+ 8	+ 0
% there is not enough emphasis on the community's interest	+ 5	− 11
Effect of tolerance on:		
% enforce the community's standards of right and wrong	− 14	− 31
% there is not enough emphasis on citizens' duties	− 2	− 18
% society should pursue common goal	− 5	+ 5
% there is not enough emphasis on the community's interest	− 11	+ 5
Effect of combination of enthusiasm and intolerance on:		
% enforce the community's standards of right and wrong	+ 20	+ 39
% there is not enough emphasis on citizens' duties	+ 6	+ 30
% society should pursue common goal	+ 12	− 2
% there is not enough emphasis on the community's interest	+ 15	− 11

Note:
Effects calculated as in Table 13.3.

Table 13.5 **Community and ideology**

Among those who place themselves on/in:	General public			Local politicians		
	Left	Centre	Right	Left	Centre	Right
% enforce the community's standards of right and wrong	21	29	36	17	29	46
% there is not enough emphasis on citizens' duties	38	49	.66	31	55	86
% society should pursue common goal	62	58	48	78	64	49
% there is not enough emphasis on the community's interest	73	68	56	86	66	28

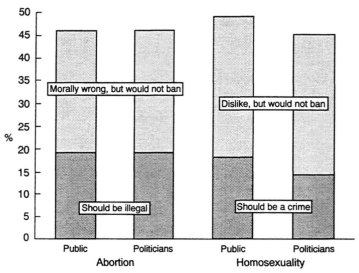

*Figure 13.2 **Moral and legal censure on sex issues***

Tolerance in practice: Three issues relating to sex

So far we have dealt with attitudes to moral enforcement or community standards at a very general, abstract level. But what do people decide in more concrete situations?

Abortion

Senator Moynihan is concerned that the rapid rise of single parenthood in the United States over the past 30 years is undermining the social fabric of American society. Members of the British Cabinet have expressed similar fears about Britain. Of course, one of the ways to reduce the growth of single parenthood, both in Britain and the United States, is through more extensive provision of state-funded abortions. That raises questions about how far a community will tolerate the provision of abortion to pregnant women simply because they do not want to mother a child: what some call 'abortion on demand'.

We asked: 'Suppose that a woman decides to have an abortion for no other reason than that she does not wish to have the child. Then in this particular case, would she be morally right or morally wrong to have an abortion?' While we recognise that in many cases there are other reasons why a woman might seek an abortion, this 'no other reason' situation poses the moral dilemma most starkly. Among both public and politicians, 46 per cent said it would be morally wrong in this case. We then asked those who said it was morally wrong whether 'irrespective of your personal views, you think the law should forbid such an abortion'. Only two-fifths of

Table 13.6 **Tolerance in practice: sex issues**

	General public	Local politicians
% who say that it would be morally wrong for a woman to have an abortion for no other reason than that she does not want to have the child	46	46
% of above who say it should be illegal	42	41
% who positively dislike gays and lesbians (i.e. give mark of 4 or less out of 10 for how much they like them)	49	45
% of above who say homosexuality should be a crime even though that would reduce the freedom of individuals to do what they want	37	31
% who support mandatory AIDS tests for:		
cooks	60	47
surgeons and dentists	81	62
Effect of enthusiasm on:		
% wrong to have abortion	+21	+22
% of above who say it should be illegal	+13	+21
% who dislike gays and lesbians	+15	+32
% of above who say homosexuality should be a crime	+13	+11
% who support mandatory AIDS tests	+15	+20
Effect of tolerance on:		
% wrong to have abortion	−6	+1
% of above who say it should be illegal	−20	−14
% who dislike gays and lesbians	−23	−40
% of above who say homosexuality should be a crime	−21	−20
% who support mandatory AIDS tests	−16	−26
Effect of combination of enthusiasm and intolerance on:		
% wrong to have abortion	+22	+15
% of above who say it should be illegal	+27	+27
% who dislike gays and lesbians	+31	+57
% of above who say homosexuality should be a crime	+26	+28
% who support mandatory AIDS tests	+27	+37

Notes:
Effects calculated as in Table 13.3.

those who had already declared it morally wrong said it should be illegal, a striking practical demonstration of a self-conscious distinction between morals and laws.

Reasonably enough, enthusiasm had a strong effect upon attitudes to the morality of the abortion decision but tolerance did not. Among politicians for example, enthusiasts were 22 per cent more willing to describe it as morally wrong but the tolerant and intolerant differed by only 1 per cent. On the other hand tolerance had a marked effect upon attitudes towards the legality of abortion. Indeed, among the public, tolerance had more influence than enthusiasm in shaping attitudes to legality. The tolerant were 20 per cent less willing to declare it illegal while the enthusiasts were only 13 per cent more willing to do so.

Sexual orientation

While the growth of single parenthood provides one indicator of sexual deregulation in Britain and the United States, the open expression of homosexuality is often seen as another. In both countries this remains a contentious issue. As part of a battery of 11 questions about how much people liked or disliked various groups we asked for a mark out of 10 to indicate attitudes towards 'gays and lesbians'. The question read: 'I am going to read you a list of groups which some people like but others dislike. Please give a mark out of 10 to show how much you like each group. If you like a group give it a score above five, the more you like it the higher the score. If you dislike a group give it a score less than five, the less you like it the lower the score.' Among the public 49 per cent indicated their dislike of gays and lesbians by giving them a score of 4 or less; among politicians 45 per cent did the same. Although this means that a narrow majority of both public and politicians indicated a neutral (score 5) or positive (score more than 5) attitude to gays and lesbians, it is the attitude of those who clearly disliked them which concerns us most in any analysis of toleration.

Among the public, enthusiasts were 15 per cent more inclined to dislike gays and lesbians, while the tolerant were 23 per cent less inclined to do so. Among politicians the effects of enthusiasm and tolerance were approximately twice as great: 32 per cent for enthusiasm and 40 per cent for tolerance. In combination therefore, enthusiasm and intolerance among politicians raised dislike for gays and lesbians by a massive 57 per cent, and among the general public by 31 per cent.

Even among those who did express dislike for gays and lesbians however, only 37 per cent of the public, and 31 per cent of politicians agreed that 'homosexuality should be a crime even though that would reduce the freedom of individuals to do what they want'. (And only a negligible percentage of those who liked gays and lesbians agreed to make homosexuality a crime.) Once again there was a great difference between the large numbers who disliked gays and lesbians and the small numbers who would make homosexuality a crime.

Enthusiasm made people more willing to make homosexuality a crime while tolerance had the opposite effect; and in combination, enthusiasm and intolerance made those who disliked gays about 27 per cent more likely to say homosexuality should be a crime. As usual however, tolerance outweighed enthusiasm in its effects upon all aspects of attitudes towards homosexuality.

AIDS

Although the spread of AIDS is not exclusively linked to questions of sexual conduct, or indeed to any departure from the most narrowly and conservatively defined 'traditional values' – as various tragic blood-transfusion scandals have proved – we found great concern about this issue among our respondents. Fully 60 per cent of the public favoured mandatory AIDS tests for cooks and 81 per cent for surgeons and dentists. Politicians were substantially less favourable to mandatory AIDS testing, however. The principles of enthusiasm and tolerance shaped attitudes to AIDS testing: a combination of enthusiasm and intolerance increased support for mandatory AIDS testing by 27 per cent among the public and 37 per cent among politicians. Of course, public concern about AIDS may, in part, reflect the limits to public tolerance of drug abuse, an issue to which we now turn.

Tolerance in practice: Issues relating to drugs

Senator Moynihan's discussion of increased drug use in America was framed in altruistic terms as part of his analysis of the deinstitutionalisation of mental patients from state hospitals. But the issue of drug use is often linked in the public imagination to that of drug *abuse*, a question we looked at in some depth. To investigate attitudes to drugs we asked whether: 'People should be allowed to [take whatever drugs/drink as much as] they like [(*null*)/provided they do not harm or behave offensively towards other people]?'. There were four variants of this question depending upon whether it asked about drink or drugs and whether the proviso was included or omitted. The four variants were randomly assigned to interviews.

Opinion was much more antagonistic to drugs than to drink, whether or not the proviso was added; and the proviso encouraged more favourable responses to both drink and drugs. Among the public, about 45 per cent more would allow unlimited alcohol than (other) drug taking; while the proviso encouraged an additional 19 per cent to accept either unlimited alcohol or drugs. At one extreme 86 per cent of the public would permit unlimited drinking provided it did no harm to others while, at the other, only 22 per cent would permit unlimited drug taking without the proviso about harm to others. Politicians had similar views to the public about alcohol but, unusually, more restrictive views than the public about drugs.

In sharp contrast to attitudes on issues related to sex, attitudes towards drink and drugs were not greatly influenced by either enthusiasm or tolerance. As might be expected, enthusiasts were more opposed to unlimited drink or drugs while the tolerant were less; and enthusiasm had slightly more effect upon attitudes to drugs than to drink; but the effects were fairly small. The overwhelming

Table 13.7   **Tolerance in practice: drugs issues**

	General public	Local politicians
% disagree that people should be allowed to:		
drink as much as they like	34	35
take whatever drugs they like	78	86
% disagree that, provided they do not harm or behave offensively to others, people should be allowed to:		
drink as much as they like	14	15
take whatever drugs they like	61	71
% support random searches in a shopping centre		
for drugs	48	32
for theft	43	28
Effect of enthusiasm on:		
% oppose free drinking (two versions combined)	+ 4	+ 5
% oppose free drug-taking (two versions combined)	+ 8	+ 9
% support random searches for drugs	+ 15	+ 18
% support random searches for theft	+ 3	+ 6
Effect of tolerance on:		
% oppose free drinking (two versions combined)	+ 1	− 11
% oppose free drug-taking (two versions combined)	− 5	− 11
% support random searches for drugs	− 12	− 30
% support random searches for theft	− 6	− 13
Effect of combination of enthusiasm and intolerance on:		
% oppose free drinking (two versions combined)	+ 2	+ 14
% oppose free drug-taking (two versions combined)	+ 11	+ 17
% support random searches for drugs	+ 22	+ 37
% support random searches for theft	+ 8	+ 16

Note:
Effects calculated as in Table 13.3.

pattern was simply widespread tolerance for alcohol and intolerance for (other) drugs by a factor of about three to one in each case.

But another question on attitudes to drugs revealed a greater influence for both enthusiasm and tolerance. We asked whether: 'In the case where there is concern about [illegal drug use/ shoplifting] in a shopping centre, do you think that [a security guard/a police officer/a shop owner] should have the right to make random searches of the bags carried by [shoppers/people who work in that shopping centre]?'. The question came in 12 variants depending upon whether it asked about drugs or theft, whether shoppers or employees were searched, and whether guards, the police, or the shop owners did the searching. For present purposes we shall distinguish only between those versions that asked about drugs and those that asked about theft. We can ignore the fact that there were six variants of each because they were perfectly matched.

Roughly 45 per cent of the public but only 30 per cent of politicians approved the idea of random searches. Civil liberties organisations oppose the idea of random searches but many of the public clearly share Senator Moynihan's concern about crime levels and support strong measures to deal with it. In 1993, for example, Strathclyde police won widespread public support for a clamp-down on weapons that used a combination of amnesty and publicity followed by random searches and other measures such as a curfew on entering (but not remaining in) night clubs and discos. It proved very effective in reducing violence. On average, our survey showed that neither public nor politicians distinguished very much between searches for theft and searches for drugs, though both were slightly more willing to accept searches for drugs. At the least, that suggests the public view 'illegal drug use' on a par with theft, and perhaps even a little worse than theft. But behind the overall similarities there lurked very different patterns of support for drug and theft-related random searches.

Enthusiasm and tolerance had twice as much effect upon atti-tudes to drug-related searches as on attitudes to theft-related searches. In fact, those who were tolerant and not enthusiasts were very slightly less favourable towards searches for drugs than for theft; but at the opposite extreme, intolerant enthusiasts were much more willing to accept random searches for drugs than for theft. So, as a result, the combination of enthusiasm and intolerance made the public 22 per cent more favourable to drug-related random searches, and politicians 37 per cent.

Tolerance in practice: Issues relating to religion

Though the concept of private freedom may conjure up issues of sex and drugs in contemporary Britain, the right to personal choice of religious belief and practice has a very long history, a worldwide significance, and an increasing relevance even here in Britain. It is frequently argued that Anglo-American concepts and traditions of toleration derive from the bloody contest between religious non-conformity and religious orthodoxy in seventeenth-century England. The growth (or perhaps just the persistence) of cults and fundamentalism, together with the increased intermingling of peoples who subscribe to different orthodoxies suggest that this is an issue that will grow in importance. It is not a relic of history.

To assess attitudes towards the extremes of non-conformity we asked whether: 'Religious freedom should [apply to all religious groups, even those/not apply to religious groups] that the majority of people consider strange, fanatical or weird?'. Each version of the question was put to a randomly selected half sample. Among the public 28 per cent opposed such widely framed religious freedom by disagreeing with the first form of this question or agreeing with

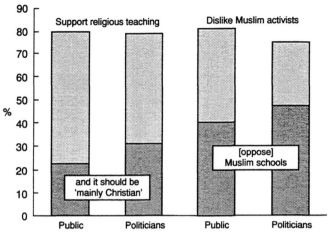

*Figure 13.3 **Support for religious conformity***

the second; and among politicians only 18 per cent. Enthusiasm had little effect upon attitudes to religious freedom but tolerance had more. Enthusiasts were scarcely any more opposed to total religious freedom than non-enthusiasts; but the intolerant were.

To assess attitudes toward orthodoxy we began by asking whether: 'There should be any religious teaching in publicly funded schools in Britain?' There was massive support, 80 per cent among both public and politicians. This time tolerance had relatively little effect upon attitudes while enthusiasm had a large effect, especially among politicians. Among the public, enthusiasts were 18 per cent more favourable to religion in schools, and among politicians 30 per cent. We then asked those who supported religion in schools whether it should be 'mainly Christian, or should it treat all the major religions equally?'. Only a minority, only 28 per cent of those members of the public and 39 per cent of those politicians *who supported religion in schools* (and, of course, significantly smaller minorities of the public and politicians as a whole), thought it should be mainly Christian. We asked that minority whether it should be 'mainly Christian, even in schools where the majority of children come from non-Christian families?', an extreme example of imposing (national) community standards. About half that minority agreed, though as a percentage of the whole sample they represent less than 15 per cent. Core support for national religious orthodoxy is therefore detectable, but small.

On the other hand support for minority religious schools was also limited. We noticed this particularly when we compared our respondents' attitudes to the provision of publicly funded schools for linguistic and religious minorities. We asked whether: '[Parents who live in Wales / Muslim parents] should have the right to have their children educated in publicly funded [Welsh-speaking /

Table 13.8 **Practical tolerance on religious issues**

	General public	Local politicians
% oppose religious freedom for strange, fanatical and weird	28	18
% who say there should be publicly funded religious teaching	80	79
% of above who say it should be mainly Christian	28	39
% of above who say so even for non-Christian areas	53	47
% oppose Welsh-speaking schools	8	12
% of above who say so even if it threatens the existence of the language	65	78
% oppose Muslim religious schools	40	47
% of above who say so even if it threatens the existence of the religion	74	80
% dislike Muslim activists	81	75
% of above who oppose Muslim religious schools	44	52
% of rest who oppose Muslim religious schools	26	31
% support a ban on ritual slaughter of animals by cruel methods even it was part of a religious tradition	79	72
Effect of enthusiasm on:		
% oppose religious freedom for strange, fanatical and weird	+ 3	+ 8
% for religious teaching	+ 18	+ 30
% for mainly Christian	+ 8	+ 16
% for mainly Christian even for non-Christians	+ 2	+ 10
% dislike Muslim activists	+ 3	− 1
% of above who oppose Muslim schools	− 3	− 14
% of above who say so even if it threatens the religion	− 4	+ 3
% ban ritual slaughter	+ 1	+ 3
Effect of tolerance on:		
% oppose religious freedom for strange, fanatical and weird	− 17	− 15
% for religious teaching	− 5	− 14
% for mainly Christian	− 8	− 11
% for mainly Christian even for non-Christians	− 10	− 17
% dislike Muslim activists	− 10	− 10
% of above who oppose Muslim schools	− 4	+ 1
% of above who say so even if it threatens the religion	− 5	− 1
% ban ritual slaughter	− 3	− 15
Effect of combination of enthusiasm and intolerance on:		
% oppose religious freedom for strange, fanatical and weird	+ 16	+ 19
% for religious teaching	+ 18	+ 32
% for mainly Christian	+ 13	+ 22
% for mainly Christian even for non-Christians	+ 11	+ 25
% dislike Muslim activists[1]	+ 10	+ 7
% of above who oppose Muslim schools	+ 2	− 13
% of above who say so even if it threatens the religion	+ 2	+ 4
% ban ritual slaughter	+ 5	+ 14

Notes:
Effects calculated as in Table 13.3.
1 Unusually, dislike of Muslim activists and opposition to Muslim schools reached their maximums among those who combined intolerance with not being enthusiasts. This is also evident in the negative effects of enthusiasm on these attitudes.

Muslim religious] schools, if they wish?'. Each version of the question was put to a randomly selected half sample. There was overwhelming support, around 90 per cent, for Welsh language schools but only 60 per cent of the public and 53 per cent of politicians supported the right to Muslim religious schools. And even that support ebbed away very rapidly if this was going to increase local taxes. We asked those who supported these special schools whether they would continue to do so 'even if it substantially increased the amount of taxes local people had to pay?'. Not only was there much higher support for Welsh-language schools, but those who did support them were much more willing to continue that support even at the cost of higher taxes. Thus, of the 60 per cent who initially supported Muslim schools, only half would do so if it meant higher taxes; while of the 92 per cent who initially supported Welsh language schools, three quarters would do so even if it meant higher taxes.

On the other side, between three-quarters and four-fifths of those who *opposed* Muslim religious schools would continue to do so even if 'as a result the continued existence of that religion was threatened'. It is specially noteworthy that politicians – who were generally more liberal and tolerant than the public, and more sympathetic to the protection and support of racial and religious minorities – were less willing to support special Muslim schools even at the cost of some threat to that religion. They were also more inclined to say that religious teaching in publicly funded schools should be 'mainly Christian'.

We had included 'Muslim activists' in our battery of groups which people might like or dislike. By giving them 4 or less marks out of 10, 75 per cent of politicians and 81 per cent of the public indicated that they disliked Muslim activists. Those who did so were much more opposed to Muslim religious schools than those who expressed neutral or positive feeling towards Muslim activists. That is hardly surprising. What is more surprising is that, among the small minority who expressed neutral or positive feeling towards Muslim activists, between a quarter and a third also opposed Muslim religious schools and that the percentage was higher among politicians than the general public. This was a pattern that we did not find on sex issues for example.

Finally we asked whether there should be a ban on the 'ritual slaughter of animals by cruel methods, even if it is part of a religious tradition'. We fully understand that particular religious groups will argue that their methods of ritual slaughter are not particularly cruel. That may be so, but in that case there is nothing to be tolerated. As we emphasised at the start, it is logically impossible to tolerate something we approve. The question of toleration only arises when we are faced with belief or conduct that we regard as false, immoral, or cruel. So, without naming any particular groups, or defining any particular practices as cruel, we asked this question to see whether people would accept a religious tradition as a valid reason for tolerating something that they, themselves, regarded as cruel. Four-fifths did not: their respect for animals outweighed their respect for religious practices. Enthusiasm had no effect upon attitudes one way or the other, but tolerance, among politicians though not the public, tilted the balance of opinion in favour of religion.

Ideology and tolerance

We have already touched upon ideology in connection with attitudes to community. It was impossible to avoid doing that because ideological perspectives were so useful in clarifying the different aspects of that concept. But it is worth looking more systematically and extensively at the relationship between enthusiasm, tolerance, private freedom and ideology. There were sharp ideological differences on both principles and practice. Among politicians, those who described themselves as right-wing were 24 per cent more likely to be enthusiasts and 31 per cent less likely to be tolerant than those on the left. Among the public, the relationships between enthusiasm, tolerance and ideology ran in the same directions as among politicians, but the scale of the differences ran at about half that among politicians.

On the first of our general measures of attitudes towards enforcement, assent to the proposition that 'What is morally wrong should be illegal', there was little difference between left and right among the public but right-wing politicians were 16 per cent more favourable to enforcement than left-wing politicians. But on our second measure, assent to the proposition that 'Our laws should enforce community standards', right-wingers were more favourable than left-wingers by 15 per cent among the public and 29 per cent among politicians.

On abortion, left/right differences were small among the public but more substantial among politicians: right-wing politicians were 14 per cent more likely to describe abortion as morally wrong and, if so, they were 14 per cent more likely to say it should be illegal. Right-wing members of the public were 18 per cent more likely to state that they disliked gays and lesbians; and among those who expressed dislike for gays and lesbians, the right was 12 per cent more likely than the left to say homosexuality should be a crime. Right-wing politicians were a massive 51 per cent more likely to say they disliked gays; though among politicians who said they disliked these groups, those on the right were only 8 per cent more likely than those on the left to say homosexuality should be a crime.

On the other hand, ideological differences on attitudes to drugs were slightly smaller among politicians than the public. Among the public, right-wingers were 10 per cent more opposed to free drug-taking and 19 per cent more willing to support random searches for drugs in shopping centres, compared to 8 per cent more and 16 per cent more respectively among politicians.

However, on religious freedom, ideological differences were, once again, larger among politicians. Right-wing politicians were 13 per cent more willing to deny religious freedom to the 'strange, fanatical or weird'; 23 per cent more favourable to religious teaching in schools; a massive 45 per cent more insistent that it should be 'mainly Christian' and not 'treat all the major religions equally'; and 29 per cent more insistent that it be Christian even 'where the majority of children come from non-Christian families'. On most of these religious issues, ideological differences among the public ran at about half those among politicians.

Those who placed themselves 'in the centre' of the ideological spectrum had views on enthusiasm, tolerance and personal freedom that were somewhere between the views of the left and the right though frequently not midway between those of left and right. More often than not, those in the ideological centre tilted towards the views of the right rather than those of the left on issues of personal freedom. That may not accord with impressions of senior Liberal Democrat politicians, such as David Steel or Roy Jenkins for example, but it should be remembered that many people other than Liberals put themselves 'in the centre'. Indeed there is an important difference between the ideological centre and the Liberal Democrats (Miller *et al.* 1990: 32–35).

People and politicians

We have shown that public attitudes on specific issues of personal freedom are shaped, sometimes very strongly, by general principles of enthusiasm and tolerance. Those who are more enthusiastic and / or less tolerant in principle are more willing to condemn and more willing to apply the law to suppress that which they do condemn. Those who combine enthusiasm and intolerance are very much more willing to condemn and suppress. But, at least according to our measures, tolerance has proved more powerful than enthusiasm, so that those who combine enthusiasm with tolerance are less willing to condemn and suppress than those who lack both enthusiasm and tolerance.

At an individual level, politicians' attitudes to specific issues of private freedom are much more closely related to their principles than those of the general public. Frequently the power of enthusiasm and tolerance to shape attitudes to specific issues seems approximately twice as great among politicians as among the general public.

On general principles, politicians were slightly less enthusiastic and substantially more tolerant than the general public. Given the

Table 13.9 **Ideology**

Amongst those who place themselves on/in:	General public			Local politicians		
	Left	Centre	Right	Left	Centre	Right
Enthusiasm	50	59	60	41	60	65
Tolerance	57	44	43	80	61	49
Morally wrong should be illegal	42	49	43	14	29	30
Laws should enforce community standards	21	29	36	17	29	46
Abortion morally wrong	47	47	46	39	48	53
% of above who say it should be illegal	33	35	38	23	35	37
Dislike gays and lesbians	40	47	58	20	52	71
% of above who would make homosexuality a crime	35	35	47	24	34	32
People should not be free to take whatever drugs they like	61	73	71	77	77	85
Approve random searches for drugs	38	48	57	21	38	37
Against religious freedom for strange, fanatical or weird	20	29	34	11	19	24
Favour religious education in schools	73	82	83	66	86	89
% of above who say it should be mainly Christian	21	25	45	21	31	66
% of above who say so even for non-Christian areas	44	52	58	25	45	54
% dislike Muslim activists	72	83	90	61	78	90
% of above who oppose Muslim schools	42	40	55	57	48	54

power of these principles to shape more specific attitudes we should therefore expect politicians to be significantly more tolerant in practice as well as in principle. In some respects they were so. The percentage of politicians who agreed that what was 'morally wrong should be made illegal' was only half that among the public. But politicians were just as willing as the public to agree that 'our laws should enforce the community's standards of right and wrong', they were only a little more opposed to making abortion and homosexuality illegal and they were *less* willing than the public to allow people to take whatever drugs they like. They were also more tolerant than the public of 'strange, fanatical or weird' religions but just as willing to back religious education in schools and even more willing to agree that it should be 'mainly Christian'. How is that possible if politicians are more tolerant and less enthusiastic in principle and if they also connect principles to practice more closely than the general public?

A partial explanation is that our measures of enthusiasm and tolerance simply worked better among politicians. Thus the politicians we have classified as tolerant proved even more tolerant in practice than those members of the public that we have designated as tolerant; while those politicians we classified as intolerant proved even more intolerant than similarly classified members of the public. But these discrepancies were not completely symmetric. The difference in practice between intolerant politicians and intolerant members of the public was greater than between tolerant politicians and tolerant members of the public. So although we classified fewer politicians as intolerant in principle, those politicians we did classify as intolerant in principle proved to be extremely intolerant in practice. For example, on the question of whether our laws should enforce community standards, 19 per cent of tolerant politicians and 22 per cent of tolerant members of the public agreed – not a great difference; but 50 per cent of intolerant politicians compared to only 36 per cent of intolerant members of the public agreed – a substantially larger difference. Consequently, although the numbers of intolerant politicians were smaller, their stronger-views made up for their lack of numbers; so that overall the public and politicians did not differ on the enforcement of community standards.

This greater intolerance in practice among intolerant politicians frequently helped to reduce the overall difference between public and politicians on practical decisions, but even that cannot explain all the findings. In particular, it does not explain the politicians' greater intolerance of drug taking. Indeed on this issue, very unusually, the politicians' markedly higher opposition to drug taking was mainly a result of strikingly high levels of intolerance in practice among those who were generally tolerant in principle: 74 per cent of tolerant politicians compared to only 67 per cent of tolerant members of the public opposed the free use of drugs; so did 85 per cent of intolerant politicians and 72 per cent of intolerant members of the public. It is no surprise to find that intolerant politicians were even more intolerant in practice than intolerant members of the public. But it is very unusual to find tolerant politicians *less* tolerant in practice than tolerant members of the public.

A tolerant society?

In conclusion, how tolerant is British public opinion? And how enthusiastic? For analytic purposes we divided the public roughly in half, into those who were, in principle, more tolerant and less tolerant. Similarly we divided them into the half who were more enthusiastic and the half who were less so. We called these halves the tolerant and intolerant, the enthusiasts and the non-enthusiasts.

But that was just an analytic convenience. We could have taken other cut points – most obviously on our 11-point scale of enthusiasm. Our 'tolerant' and 'intolerant' members of the public were only relatively, not absolutely, so. Indeed it would be pointless to try to define the tolerant and intolerant in absolute terms. The person who would tolerate everything or tolerate nothing probably does not exist. So we cannot and should not attempt to detach our numerical estimates of tolerance and enthusiasm from the definitions on which they are based nor from the practical decisions with which they correlate. The search for absolutes is doomed to failure.

Tolerance of specific beliefs and practices varies considerably with the particulars of the case. The numbers and the composition of those who will tolerate one practice are different from those who will tolerate another. And the problem of tolerance is further compounded by the confusions between approval and tolerance, and between moral and legal intolerance. We have however tried to address these confusions.

By asking whether we 'should tolerate people whose ideas are morally wrong' we attempted to distinguish between approval and tolerance. Half the public (and two-thirds of politicians) were classified as tolerant by that criterion. Of course the figure could be pushed up or down by focusing on ideas that were *profoundly* wrong, or only *slightly* wrong.

We sought to distinguish between moral and legal intolerance by asking whether what was 'morally wrong should be made illegal'. Half the public (but only a quarter of politicians) agreed. Yet less than a third supported 'laws to enforce community standards'; only two-fifths of those who said abortion was morally wrong would make it illegal; only a third of those who said they disliked gays and lesbians would make homosexuality illegal; under a third would exclude 'strange, fanatical and weird' groups from religious freedom; and only around a third of those who wanted religious teaching in schools wanted it to focus exclusively on the historically dominant orthodoxy. So over this range of activities (and any statement about tolerance must be qualified in this way) about half the public admitted to intolerance in principle though only a third of them would apply legal intolerance in practice (though there was less practical tolerance on drugs or ritual slaughter). Whether this level of tolerance seems high or low must depend upon prior expectations though it would be fair to describe public opinion as less tolerant than the current state of the law, not because there is a majority for less tolerant legislation than currently exists but because there is a large minority that is so.

Perhaps more surprising in this apparently secular age is the extent of enthusiasm and its power to shape opinion. Relatively few people now attend one of the traditional churches on any particular Sunday. On the other hand, only 19 per cent of the public (23 per cent of politicians) failed to volunteer a religious affiliation. Half the public (and only slightly fewer politicians) gave marks of 6 or more out of 10 for the importance, to them, of 'following God's will'; indeed, almost a quarter of the public gave 10 out of 10 for 'following God's will'. These marks correlate strongly both with frequency of attendance at a place of worship and with the marks given for the importance of 'preserving traditional ideas of right and wrong'. Among that quarter of the public who gave 10 out of 10 for 'following God's will', 51 per cent attended worship at least once a month, and 68 per cent also gave 10 out of 10 for the importance of 'traditional ideas of right and wrong'. There is a sizeable core of real enthusiasts in the public, and they are joined by many others who share some of their enthusiasm though to a lesser degree.

Overall support for 'traditional ideas of right and wrong' – something as nebulous yet as clear as 'Victorian values' – is very high. Over four-fifths give it at least 6 out of 10 and fully 40 per cent of the public (29 per cent of politicians) give it a full 10 out of 10. Very few, only 1 per cent of the public (and 1 per cent of politicians) give it zero. There is some resistance among the conventionally irreligious towards giving marks above zero for 'following God's will' but very little towards giving such non-zero marks for 'traditional ideas of right and wrong'. Enthusiasm, to a greater or lesser degree, is remarkably widespread and it is the tension between that pervasive enthusiasm on the one hand, and tolerance of perceived immorality on the other, that determines public attitudes to private freedom.

References

Hughes, R. (1992) *Barcelona*, London: Harper Collins.

McLaren, A. and McLaren, T. A. (1989) *The Bedroom and the State: the Changing Practices and Politics of Contraception and Abortion in Canada*, Toronto: McClelland and Stewart.

Miller, W. L., Clarke, H. D., Harrop, M., Leduc L. and Whiteley, P. F. (1990) *How Voters Change*, Oxford: Oxford University Press.

Randall, V. (1991) 'Feminism and political analysis', *Political Studies*, **34**: 529.

Sullivan, J. L., Piereson, J. and Marcus, G. E. (1989) *Political Tolerance and American Democracy*, Chicago: University of Chicago Press.

CHAPTER 14

Conclusion: Culture and constitution in conflict?

WILLIAM L. MILLER

This book has been about alternatives to freedom, defined in the Hayekian sense 'quite simply as the absence of coercion' (King 1987: 29). The attractions of freedom in this sense are obvious: no one likes being told by others (or by the state) what they should do. But we have focused upon alternatives that also have a wide and positive appeal: responsibility, accountability, equality, morality, the national interest and the sovereignty of Parliament. We now ask whether, over that range, the constitution strikes the same balance as public opinion between freedom and the alternatives. To the extent that it does not, we can say that the British constitution conflicts with British culture. Such conflict need not imply anything as dramatic as a 'legitimation crisis' (Habermas 1976) though it might imply a 'legitimacy deficit' (Beetham 1993: 369). Nor need it imply that constitutional change is likely, only that it may be desirable and perhaps not even that, for there are always two ways to resolve a conflict: perhaps the constitution is right and the people are wrong.

Defining the constitution

In Britain, unlike most other countries, it can seem as difficult to define the constitution as to define the political culture. We are more familiar with constitution as an adjective than as a noun: constitutional law, constitutional doctrine, constitutional documents, constitutional change, constitutional practice, constitutional settlement. These are all familiar enough, but the British constitution is not. And whatever the British constitution may be, even constitutional lawyers are agreed that it is decidedly not the same as constitutional law.

In the narrow sense of a document, 'the United Kingdom has no constitution' (Wade and Bradley 1987: 4). But the idea of a constitution as a single written document only became popular towards the end of the eighteenth century. 'In the 17th century it seemed possible at one point that common-law doctrines would be applied so that judges could review or restrict parliamentary statutes which did not conform to their interpretation of *right reason*' (Beloff and Peele 1980: 12) – a truly common-law constitution, self-evident to reasonable people, totally undocumented. By 1733, however, Bolingbroke could define the constitution as 'that assemblage of laws, institutions and customs that compose the general system according to which the community hath agreed to be governed' (Wade and Bradley 1987: 4). Constitutional lawyers take the view that many, perhaps most, British laws have constitutional significance to a greater or lesser degree precisely because none takes precedence as a constitution. But even Bolingbroke's definition assigns only a limited role to documents and a more recent definition seems to exclude them altogether. Beloff and Peele (1980: 10) define it as 'the sum of those norms and values which prescribe the nature of relationships between the several institutions of authority in a state and also between public authorities and individuals'. While other definitions note that there are many laws of constitutional significance, most other accounts of the British constitution also abound in expressions such as 'political practice', 'habit', 'traditional ways of doing things', 'conventions', 'customs' and 'unwritten rules'.

Can the British constitution and culture be distinct?

Indeed, descriptions of the British constitution frequently begin to sound like descriptions of British political culture, which would unfortunately preclude an analytic distinction between the two, let alone any possibility of conflict between them. Thus Wade and Bradley argue:

In a stable society constitutional law expresses what may be a very high degree of consensus about the organs and procedures by which political decisions are taken . . . In a stable democracy, constitutional law reflects the value that people attach to . . . institutions such as parliament, political parties, free elections and a free press.

(Wade and Bradley 1987: 3)

But Bolingbroke begged the question when he ended his definition with the phrase: 'by which the community hath *agreed* to be governed'; Beloff and Peele's definition does not say *whose* norms and values, if anyone's, are embodied in the constitution; and Wade and Bradley's statements about a '*stable* society' or '*stable* democracy' are strictly conditional. Writing in the late 1970s, Beloff and Peele were already suggesting that culture and constitution were not merely distinct but diverging: 'The complex web of common attitudes and beliefs which enabled British democracy to work with very few formal statements of powers, rights and obligations no longer appears to bind either the political elite or the electorate at large' (Beloff and Peele 1980: 13).

   Herbert Morrison once defined socialism as 'what Labour governments do'. He might have added, in similar vein, that the British constitution was 'what British governments do'. Tom Paine rather hopefully asserted that 'a government is only the creature of a constitution' but in reality the British constitution is only the creature of successive British governments. Constitutional lawyers express this point with only a little more professional caution: 'In the absence of a constitution to serve as the foundation of the legal system, the vacuum is filled by the legal doctrine of the legislative supremacy of parliament' (Wade and Bradley 1987: 7). In fact, government dominates Parliament and it asserts far more than merely *legislative* supremacy. Despite all the sophistry of arguments to the contrary it is difficult to deny that the British constitution is, at root, merely an empirical description of the 'standard operating procedures' of British government.

Far too often, constitutional practice, which is the practice of government, is falsely identified with the culture of the people. No one resident in Scotland could avoid noticing that in election after election, opinion poll after opinion poll, three-quarters of the electorate consistently reject present constitutional arrangements for Scotland. And yet, as long as a society does not descend into public disorder or terrorist violence too many commentators interpret public tranquillity as evidence that the operation of the constitution reflects the values of the people. Thus Birch (1986), in the seventh edition of his text on *The British System of Government* confidently asserts: 'The British system of government is determined not only by the history and social characteristics of the country but also by the political attitudes and values of the British people' (p. 13). He adds, by way of explanation: 'The British do not have a written constitution and have no wish to invent one . . . The British people appreciate the appearance of strong governmental leadership' (p. 14). In Sir Robert Peel's words they may 'abuse a Prime Minister for dictatorship and arrogance but they like being governed' (Birch 1986: 15). Birch expands on the nature of British political culture: 'Outside Whitehall the only reported case of an individual being penalised on political grounds occurred in 1956 . . . (and) the case created such a furore that it is unlikely that any similar incidents have occurred. This fact underlines the general tolerance of British society' (pp. 220–1).

All of this is based upon a false logic. The lack of a written constitution is no evidence that the people do not want one. Sir Robert Peel's speculations never were evidence about public opinion, then or now. And the somewhat implausible claim that government has been politically tolerant except in one isolated case in 1956, even if true, is not evidence that the people are tolerant: it is possible that the people are more tolerant than the constitution, and equally possible that they are less.

We can compare culture and constitution in Britain if we compare the culture of those outside government with the ever-evolving customs, practice and behaviour of those inside. They are distinct.

212 Alternatives to Freedom

Constitutional change

Moreover, times change. Public opinion may change, though any-thing based on so many individual components is likely to change fairly slowly. By contrast, the British constitution, by its nature, can change very rapidly indeed. Because so much of it consists of 'unwritten rules', mere conventions unrestricted by any legal proc-ess, it can change the moment that a government decides to behave differently. If an election defeat removes a government led by a consensus politician and replaces him by a conviction politician determined at all costs not to continue her predecessor's style of government, old conventions can be instantly and explicitly repudi-ated and replaced by new ones. That is the flexibility of which exponents of the British constitution were once so proud. Insofar as the British constitution reflects the British people's political culture it can hardly change very rapidly; but insofar as it reflects the British government's behaviour then constitutional change can be just as rapid and far-reaching as any policy change.

Of course, the experience of office may moderate that change. Politicians may favour open government more when they languish in opposition than when they revel in office. The Labour opposi-tion's 1992 manifesto proposed the Freedom of Information Act it had always opposed in government. Nonetheless, it remains true that a constitution that depends upon voluntary obedience to conventions can be changed the moment those conventions become irksome or the moment that a new government with different principles is elected. In Britain, every Parliament is a constituent assembly, every election a referendum on the constitution. So an election may change the fit between popular culture and constitu-tion overnight.

Peele accepts that the limitations on government action and the protection of citizens' liberties were weak enough before 1979 but nonetheless argues that the Thatcher period 'drew attention graphi-cally' to that weakness and exposed 'the extent to which many of the most vaunted concepts of British constitutional theory were empty' (Peele 1993: 24): 'The radical policies pursued by Conserva-tive governments after 1979 seemed calculated to strengthen the power of central government and weaken the role of any institu-tions which might act as a countervailing power to the government' (Peele 1993: 22).

Other constitutional changes owed less to change in the govern-ment's own ideology or preferred style. For over two decades, terrorism in Northern Ireland, and occasionally on the British mainland, has forced government to react. Inevitably that has done nothing to help civil liberties. On the other hand, the European Community's continued progress towards 'an ever closer union' and the developing significance of the Council of Europe's Convention on Human Rights have reduced the British Parliament's sovereignty both externally and internally to such an extent that the very concept of national sovereignty is now a matter for debate.

Constitutional debate

A growing awareness that our empirically defined constitution is fundamentally unstable and is changing substantially at the present time has helped to put constitutional issues on the public agenda. Explicit discussion of the constitution has also been encouraged by Scottish pressure for devolution and a revision of the British constitutional settlement of 1707. In the wider environment, the collapse of communism and the end of the Cold War have destroyed the certainties that muted constitutional debate. Deprived of comparison with an obviously evil empire, Western constitutions, all of them, are less self-evidently good. Moreover, the process of building new democracies in Eastern Europe and the former Soviet Union involves a critique of authoritarianism, and an on-going debate about constitutional principles, that sometimes seem to have an unintended but uncomfortable relevance to our own system.

The last great flurry of British interest in constitution-making took place in the decade after 1945 during the period of decolonisation,[1] in an atmosphere of self-satisfaction and complacency. Colonies should have written constitutions that reflected unwritten British practice insofar as local conditions would permit. There were doubts about whether colonial peoples were good enough for their new constitutions but not about whether the constitutions were good enough for the peoples. Over the last decade, however, the current constitutional debate has been more inward-looking and less complacent. Think-tanks such as the Constitutional Reform Centre, the Institute for Public Policy Research (which drew up its own proposed constitution) and even the Institute for Economic Affairs have questioned whether the British constitution is any longer good enough for the British people. Charter 88 has stridently claimed that it is not. The opposition parties have pressed for wide-ranging constitutional change. Even government has joined in with its 'Taking Stock' exercise on the State of the Union and its Citizen's[2] Charter: 'The Charter programme will be at the heart of government policy in the 1990s' (Dowding 1993: 177).

Freedom and constitutional change

Hayek's negative definition of freedom as the absence of coercion fits easily with Wade and Bradley's assertion that 'constitutions spring from a belief in limited government' (1987: 8). There are other definitions of freedom and other constitutional principles, but commitment to negative freedom and limited government have supplied the ideological drive and rhetorical theme of British governments since 1979. Yet it is a familiar paradox that they have sought to limit government by extending the role of central government and that they have sought to advance the cause of freedom by extending coercion. They have limited government and diminished the sovereignty of Parliament in their *external* aspects by accepting increasing restraints within the European Union and within the Anglo-Irish Agreement; but enlarged the role of central government and strengthened parliamentary sovereignty in their *internal* aspects by undermining, and in some cases abolishing, the intermediate institutions of civil society. Their commitment to freedom as the absence of coercion has not precluded attacks on the autonomy of trade unions, local governments or university student unions. They could claim that this has 'not been oppressive' because their 'aim has been to free individuals' from the tyranny of these intermediate institutions (Beetham 1993: 363). But their oft-repeated concern for moral and family values extends their censure from institutions to individuals and is only consistent with even the most narrow interpretation of freedom as the absence of coercion if it stops short of harassment or legal action.

We have not argued that Hayek's negative freedom is good and every alternative value is bad. Indeed it is because so many people see the good in alternative values that they are real competitive alternatives. So while some may feel the government's actions have been worse than its rhetoric, others may take exactly the opposite view: that its libertarian rhetoric has been worse than its firm actions. What we can do is compare public attitudes towards the proper balance between freedom and alternative values, with the balance struck by the laws and conventions of government. In that comparison we shall resist the very real temptation to go beyond our data. We will confine our attention to those aspects of culture and constitution which have been covered in earlier chapters.

The moral community

The European Convention on Human Rights and Fundamental Freedoms guarantees everyone the right to respect for their private life and for their freedom of religion but promptly qualifies both by accepting the right of the state to restrict these rights 'for the protection of public health or morals'.[3] We found that two-thirds of the public thought government had a duty to uphold morality and half thought that whatever was morally wrong should be made illegal, though less than a third thought the laws should enforce community standards of right and wrong. In principle, it seems that a majority would support government speaking out on moral questions and at least a very sizeable minority would accept coercive action to enforce moral standards. Politicians are more willing to separate politics and morals but the general public accepts that the two should mix, though they have reservations about coercion. The distinction between censure and coercion is carried through into practice. Half the public opposes abortion on demand and expresses dislike for gays and lesbians but not much more than one-third of those who disapprove would make either abortion on demand or homosexuality illegal.

British governments accept that they have a right, even a duty, to speak out on moral questions and to legislate on moral issues. Indeed ministers of the crown accuse the Church of being less willing than the government to take a stand on family values and sexual morality. Until the 1960s both abortion and homosexual activity (among males) were illegal. Abortion on demand remains illegal (McLean 1986: 117). On that, a large majority of the public is more libertarian than the law, though not necessarily less moralistic. Over the age of 18, a couple of years later than for heterosexual activity, homosexual activity is now legal except in the armed forces or on merchant navy ships. It is, however, hedged in with legal restrictions on soliciting and Clause 28 of the 1988 Local Government Act bans the intentional promotion of homosexuality by local governments and hence by organisations such as the schools and theatres that local government funds (Thornton 1989: 88–9). Given the division of public attitudes towards homosexuals and the fact that Clause 28, restrictive though it may be, does not make homosexual activity a crime, there does not appear to be a sharp conflict between the law and public opinion on this issue.

Similarly, laws which permit free availability of alcohol but restrictions on (other) drugs mirror public opinion.

Both Scotland and England, though not Wales, have long established state churches. Throughout Britain, state-funded schools have traditionally provided religious education of various kinds. There is overwhelming public support for this, but remarkably little insistence that it should continue to be 'mainly Christian'. At the same time a large minority would oppose setting up Muslim religious schools even if parents want it. This pattern of opinion is at once less orthodox and less tolerant than the combination of law and ministerial discretion which requires religious education to be mainly Christian in most schools but also allows parents to take their schools out of the local government system and reconstitute them as state-funded Muslim schools if that be their wish.

So on moral questions generally there is no very clear conflict between public attitudes and the law. On some issues the law and the behaviour of ministers reflects public opinion; on some the public is more libertarian than the constitution but on others less; and on others the public is too divided internally to be in conflict with anything. If there is a general tendency it is for the public to condemn much more readily than they would coerce: to permit legally what they continue to dislike or denounce as immoral; to require government to give a moral lead, but not to impose community standards by force of law.

Equality

There is close to unanimous agreement in Britain that government has a duty to ensure equal opportunities for everyone, adequate housing, good education and good medical care for everyone; and overwhelming support for the view that government has a duty to ensure decent living standards and a job for everyone who is willing to work. These are the kinds of positive social and economic rights which have been routinely written into socialist constitutions. They are excluded from liberal constitutions such as that of the United States. Most, but not all, are also included in various international covenants to which the UK subscribes – particularly the United Nations International Covenant on Economic, Social and Cultural Rights (1966) (see Institute for Public Policy Research 1991: 21). We have defined the British constitution, however, as that complex of laws and conventions, written or unwritten, that sets the bounds on government action. Government has claimed that the National Health Service is 'safe in its hands' and that social security will continue 'for ever'; but one duty of government that is overwhelmingly supported by public opinion has nonetheless been explicitly repudiated by successive governments, the duty to ensure that there is a job available for all who are willing to work.

For three decades after the war the commitment to full employment was as much a part of the British constitution as the electoral system. It was not a policy open to debate but a duty that guided ministers in their development of policy. Now it has been abandoned and there is a major conflict between culture and constitution. The constitution provides for a 'right to seek employment'; the popular culture envisages the 'right to an offer of employment'.

Although there is almost unanimous agreement that government has a duty to ensure equality of opportunity for its citizens, public opinion is sharply divided over whether it has a duty to equalise wealth and income. British governments feel under no obligation to equalise wealth and, since 1979, have been actively and openly pursuing a policy of increasing economic inequality. Whatever our personal views about such policies, the even division of public opinion means that they cannot be in conflict with political culture. The culture is too divided.

We found almost unanimous support for helping the disabled, widespread support for gender and ethnic equality and a division of opinion (tipped only slightly in the favourable direction) on homosexual equality. But, just as we found on the issues of private freedom, we found great reluctance to use the law to enforce the degree of equality that people thought was right. True, an overwhelming majority supported the idea of legal employment quotas for the disabled, but an overwhelming majority also opposed employment quotas for women or ethnic minorities. Indeed, there was much more support, though still only minority support, for a legal ban on private medicine to ensure equality of health care.

The Equal Opportunities Commission was set up under the 1975 Sex Discrimination Act and charged to 'work towards the elimination of sex discrimination' and 'promote equality of opportunity between men and women generally' (Hurwitt and Thornton 1989: 213). The act defines discrimination as direct or indirect. The NCCL Guide gives the following example of indirect discrimination that would be unlawful under the act: 'An after-school computer club open only to pupils taking an exam course in computer science could be against the law if hardly any girls took the exam course' (Hurwitt and Thornton 1989: 209). Without a minimum number of girls a school computer club would be illegal. This comes very close, as does much of the work of the Equal Opportunities Commission, to the idea of legal quotas.[4] Perhaps we should emphasise that our survey question about quotas did not specify *equal* quotas, but merely fixed quotas at any, unspecified, level; so it would cover this example very well.

There can be no doubt about public opinion. Rightly or wrongly, public opinion is strongly opposed to discrimination but at the same time overwhelmingly opposed to fixed quotas. Thus the Sex Discrimination Act conflicts with public opinion in two diametrically opposite ways. It 'did not cover social security, taxation or provision for retirement and pensionable age' (Thornton 1989: 80). According to Peter Thornton 'what little progress there has been has been forced upon the Government by cases taken to the European Court' not brought under the Sex Discrimination Act. For example, it was a European Court that found Britain guilty, in 1982, of failure to ensure that women got 'equal pay for work of equal value' (Thornton 1989: 80–1). In the 1980s maternity rights of women at work were weakened (and are only being improved in the 1990s by European directives emanating from Brussels); the real value of child benefit was reduced; and the responsibility of local authorities to provide nursery care was removed (Thornton 1989: 82). So the law, and ministerial implementations of the law, did not end discrimination, and in some cases increased it, while at the same time encouraging the use of formal and informal quotas. On both counts, that conflicts with public opinion.

Opinion on racial and ethnic discrimination is similar: the public is strongly opposed to discrimination but even more strongly opposed to employment quotas. The Commission for Racial Equality was set up under the 1976 Race Relations Act and it too, defines discrimination as direct or indirect. It explicitly allows 'positive discrimination where there have been no people of a particular racial group, or very few, doing a particular kind of work, either in the whole of Great Britain or in a region, in the previous twelve months' (Hurwitt and Thornton 1989: 197–8). The Commission issued its first Code of Practice on employment in 1984 which was not, in theory, legally binding but could be used in evidence at industrial tribunals. There is a tendency to equate disproportionality with discrimination. For example Peter Thornton notes:

The CRE is deeply concerned at mounting evidence of outright racial discrimination in recruitment and selection of young black people. The 1986 Labour Force Survey showed that the unemployment rate among black people in the 16–24 age group was 32% compared with 17% for white, with the rate for Pakistanis and Bangladeshis soaring to 43%!

(Thornton 1989: 73)

That is the language of quotas. It may be difficult to detect and eradicate 'outright racial discrimination' without resorting to the blunt instrument of quotas but that is the package, no discrimination and no quotas, that has public support.

Responsibility

Under the heading of 'responsibility' we reviewed public attitudes towards the press as a medium of free expression rather than a medium of public information. We sought to map at least a sector of the boundaries of acceptable press behaviour. In the context of an interview about politics at least, only about a third of the public would ban publication of violent pictures. About the same would ban sensational crime stories or abusive attacks on the Christian religion. 'Moderate or reasoned criticism of Anglican doctrine is not a crime' but 'immoderate or offensive treatment of the Christian faith' constitutes the legal offence of blasphemy (Hurwitt and Thornton 1989: 40). There has only been one prosecution in the last seven decades however. The operating constitution, if not the law, is therefore in accord with public opinion.

In response to criticisms that the law of blasphemy is discriminatory in a multi-ethnic multi-faith society, however, Lord Scarman suggested that it could be extended to cover any and all religions (Hurwitt and Thornton 1989: 40). It would then cover the Salman Rushdie case, for example, and prosecutions for blasphemy would become more frequent. We found more support among the public for a ban on abusive attacks upon minority religions, 44 per cent among the general public and 49 per cent among local politicians, but this even division of opinion means there was no clear public opinion on the matter. A clear majority of the public supported a ban on incitement to racial hatred, which is illegal under the 1986

Public Order Act (Hurwitt and Thornton 1989: 206) but only a narrow majority would ban incitement to religious hatred – which is not illegal under the 1986 Public Order Act (Hurwitt and Thornton 1989: 207). The contours of the law therefore follow the undulations of public opinion reasonably closely here.

Half, or slightly less, of the public would ban publication of interviews with IRA or Protestant terrorists' sympathisers. In 1988 the then Home Secretary, Douglas Hurd, issued an order to both the BBC and IBA (under the 1981 Broadcasting Act) banning the broadcast of any person 'representing or purporting to represent' a list of organisations that included the illegal IRA and UVF, the then legal UDA and the still legal Sinn Fein except where their words were spoken in Parliament or during an election campaign (Ewing and Gearty 1990: 243). Douglas Hurd's order incensed the journalists who responded by using actors to 'voice-over' silent film of relevant interviews. Eventually the actors got so good at their task that the interviews were effectively 'dubbed' with sound synchronised to lip-movements. The Scots film *Gregory's Girl* was treated similarly, synchronously dubbed from (Scots) English into (mid-West American) English, to make it intelligible in the American mid-West. In 1993 the government insisted on lower-quality voice-overs to make it clear that the audible sounds were not spoken by the terrorist sympathisers appearing on the television screen. Given the even division of public opinion, neither government nor journalists could claim the support of the public. But it is significant that two-thirds of local politicians came down on the journalists' side.

Neither Scotland nor England and Wales has a general law of privacy. In 1957 the Lord Justice-Clerk told the Court of Session: 'I know of no authority to the effect that the mere invasion of privacy, however hurtful and whatever its purpose, and however repugnant to good taste, is itself actionable' (McReadie *et al.* 1984: 532). He was discussing the complaint of a fellow judge whose conviction for a motoring offence had been exposed in a local newspaper. There are numerous laws that provide partial protection however. The laws of libel and slander may help. A 'peeping Tom' may be arrested on the grounds that he is likely to cause a breach of the peace though if he is equipped with an expensive camera and works for a national newspaper that is less likely. The Press Council, set up in 1953 and reconstituted on various occasions since then, is an industry-controlled, self-regulating body that has been criticised for lack of coercive powers. Governments regularly threaten that they will have to legislate for a statutory body with powers of coercion if the Press Council does not prevent press intrusions into private lives. Equally regularly they shrink from setting up a statutory body. The threat is itself the real instrument of government. It would be a mark of weakness if the government ever had to turn the threat into action.

A clear majority of the public would support a ban on press intrusions into the private lives 'of ordinary people' but a clear majority oppose a ban on intrusions into even the *'private* lives' of 'leading politicians'. Government attacks on press intrusion often seem to be prompted by press exposure of the private lives of politicians, ministers and the Royal Family. None of them could be described as 'ordinary people'. It is unlikely that legislation would be framed to prevent press intrusions into the private lives of ordinary people without also protecting those who were far from ordinary. We stress the word 'would', not 'could'.

Finally, the public are more opposed to publication of 'lies and distortions of the truth' than to anything else, even racial incitement. Yet government itself is one of the main culprits in this regard. Politicians promise to keep taxation down when running for election only to push it up when in office, chancellors deny that devaluation is imminent right up to the time it is announced, and prime ministers tell us that negotiations with the IRA would make them physically 'sick' when they are actually in the midst of a long-term dialogue with its leaders. Worse, government appears to have lost hold of the very concept of truth itself: 'Truth is a very difficult concept', Ian McDonald, the Ministry of Defence Official responsible for monitoring arms sales, told the Scott Inquiry (*Scotsman* 1993: 12) – and not just for permanent officials, we might add. William Waldegrave, the minister specially responsible for openness in government had to admit to that same Inquiry that he had given Parliament a false impression and that even his written statement to the Inquiry itself was wrong. Michael Heseltine, Kenneth Clarke, Malcolm Rifkind and Tristan Garel-Jones all signed 'public interest immunity certificates' to withhold – unsuccessfully as it turned out – documents vital to the defence of the accused in the Matrix Churchill trial, documents which revealed the discrepancy between the government's public statements and its private actions. In their respect for the undistorted truth, the gap between public opinion and the standard operating procedures of British government widens to a chasm. In a society in which a high proportion of the population is better educated and often, it seems, better informed than some prime ministers, this cavalier attitude to truth is more exposed and less acceptable than ever before.

The national interest

Government's most effective defence against the charge that it suppresses or distorts the truth is to argue that, while regrettable, it is necessary in the national interest. We found that half the public would ban publication of confidential government documents on the health service or on economic matters; and three quarters would ban publication of confidential government documents about defence. With an explicit appeal to the 'national interest' even more would ban publication; without such an explicit appeal, rather less. Only a minority of the public (and less than a third of local politicians) would ban publication of confidential government documents just because the government wished to keep them secret.

The government went to extreme lengths to suppress *Spycatcher*, the memoirs of Peter Wright, in which the former senior MI5 agent alleged that the security services routinely committed illegal acts not only against foreign embassies but also against left-wing political activists and even against a Labour prime minister. Although the government's case was eventually dismissed by the House of Lords at the end of 1988, it was only dismissed on the grounds that *Spycatcher* was already a best-seller throughout the rest of the world and that this made continued suppression within Britain somewhat farcical. Along the way, the Law Lords tightened censorship within Britain by extending their injunction to suppress publication of Australian court proceedings (Thornton 1989: 6). Ten thousand copies of the English language edition of *Pravda* were impounded because they contained an article about *Spycatcher*.

In 1987 Alisdair Milne, the BBC's Director General, withdrew a television documentary on the Zircon spy satellite which alleged that the government had illegally concealed its existence – and more especially its cost – from Parliament's Public Accounts Committee. In a totally unprecedented move, police officers from England were sent north to Scotland where they raided the BBC's Scottish Headquarters and seized not only the *Zircon* programme but all six films in the *Secret Society* series of which it was a part. The government defended its actions on the grounds of the national interest in secure defence but others accused it of an attempt to cover up its illegal action in misleading the Public Accounts Committee. Lord Jenkins, then a member of the House of Commons, asked what was the supreme objective for which the government were 'prepared to look as though they were running a second-rate police state, infused equally with illiberalism and incompetence' (Ewing and Gearty 1990: 151). Later, the original search warrant, supporting the raid on BBC Scotland, was quashed and the seized films had to be returned before being seized again under a new warrant.

In government circles Alisdair Milne himself was regarded as being too lax in this affair. He reports that he was informed that members of the BBC Board 'wanted my head to roll because of *Secret Society*' and at a BBC reception 'to my surprise she [the Prime Minister] effectively cut me dead' (Milne 1988: 199). Worse was to follow: less than a week after the police raids on BBC Scotland, Alisdair Milne was detained on his way to lunch, handed a sheet of paper and, without prior warning, forced to pen his resignation. He walked back to his office and told his assistant, more truthfully, 'I've been fired' (Milne 1988: 201–2). It was all handled much more ruthlessly and effectively than in Hungary.

These cases also raised the issue of 'prior restraint'. In the USA the Supreme Court had ruled during the 1971 *Pentagon Papers* affair (Ewing and Gearty 1990: 197–8), that the principle of freedom of expression, enshrined in the First Amendment to the Constitution, required that no prior restraint could be placed upon publication of government documents in peacetime. The press might be prosecuted after publication, but not subjected to restraint beforehand. At the least, that would let the people as well as the government judge the case for suppression 'in the national interest' against the case for publication 'in the public interest'. Until *Spycatcher*, that was the British practice as well. Secrets were preserved by the threat of prosecution under the 1911 Official Secrets Act, *after* publication, though – as Lord Armstrong notes – it was increasingly difficult to secure convictions under that Act. One reason for that must surely be the conflict between public and governmental perspectives on secrecy. Publications that gravely embarrass government simply fail to provoke public outrage.

A new Official Secrets Act was passed in 1989 that clarified the ambiguities of the 1911 Act and very clearly and specifically outlawed a repeat of Peter Wright's *Spycatcher* (Ewing and Gearty 1990: 173). The 1989 Act removed the unenforceable absurdity of the previous law under which it was an offence for a newspaper merely to receive secret documents, but the new Act made it a crime for it to publish their contents. It explicitly excludes the defence of 'prior publication elsewhere' or the defence of 'public interest'. Edward Heath remarked that this failed to weigh the rights of the individual against possible abuse of state power (Ewing and Gearty 1990: 203). In particular it drew a sharp contrast between accepting the government's right to quote the 'national interest' to justify secrecy, and rejecting the press's right to quote the 'public interest' to justify publication.

There is no doubt that the public does accept the need for a certain measure of secrecy, and does accept an appeal to the national interest as a justification. The question is whether the public accepts as wide a scope for secrecy as does government. Unlike government, only a minority of the public accept confidentiality – as distinct from the national interest – as a justification for secrecy. And the fact that the public put a Freedom of Information Act top of their list of 17 institutions or mechanisms for defending their rights and liberties suggests that they are not happy with the current climate of secrecy in British government.

Public accountability

Peter Thornton summed up government policy towards the media in the 1980s by claiming that 'it has imposed the greatest ever peacetime controls on broadcasting' (Thornton 1989: 3). The press and broadcasters were among the most significant of those intermediate institutions of civil society – between government and people – that underpinned Britain's pluralist democracy. He was writing before the passage of the 1989 Official Secrets Act and before the minister tightened controls on interviews with terrorist sympathisers. And, of course, he was wrong to assume that the British constitution was based upon pluralism rather than sovereignty. Perhaps British culture is pluralist and democratic, but its constitution is not.

There are three contrasting models of the proper role of the media: the libertarian, the mobilising and the public service models (Miller 1991: 200–6; Marsh 1993: 332). The *libertarian model* stresses the freedom of readers and viewers to read or view what they want, and the freedom of owners, editors and journalists to publish what they want. Under the *mobilising model*, government is the guardian of the national interest and it is the duty of the media to mobilise public support for national aims. Under the *public interest model*, the media have a duty to provide the public with objective, balanced coverage of the news, to scrutinise the actions of those in authority, and articulate the diversity of ideas and opinions that exist throughout society.

According to Marsh, although their 'rhetoric implied a libertarian view of the media, the practise of the Thatcher governments was rather different ... [and] operated with a mobilising view' (Marsh 1993: 335). Parliament and government were directly and democratically accountable to the people, they argued, while television and the press were not. It followed that television and the press should support, or at the very least not obstruct, the elected government. Thatcher and post-Thatcher governments have consistently enjoyed the willing support of three-quarters of the press, but both the IBA and more especially the BBC have felt that they had a duty to remain politically independent. Indeed the BBC operates under a Royal Charter, not under parliamentary legislation, a distinction that Professor Hankiss highlighted when he refused appointment by the Hungarian Prime Minister and insisted upon appointment by the President. The 'BBC view' of its proper role is one of public service, and its commitment to informing the public in a balanced way, its commitment to scrutinising the actions of public officials, and its refusal to act as the propaganda tool of government has frequently infuriated those in power.

We found that the public regarded television and the quality press as better mechanisms for the defence of their rights and liberties than Parliament; that despite high levels of trust in their fellow citizens they had low levels of trust in politicians; that they were overwhelmingly opposed to more government control of the press and television; and overwhelmingly in favour of more independence from government for the press and television.

Even among those on the right, under a right-wing government, two-thirds of the public backed more independence for press and television against more control by their own government. At party conferences, grass-roots activists within the governing party often seem even more antagonistic towards the BBC than their leaders. But this is not true of the grass-roots in the country, not even the right-wing of the country's grass-roots. Significantly, even those who backed several specific items of censorship nonetheless opposed government control of the media.

Parliamentary sovereignty

That brings us to the heart of the British constitution: parliamentary sovereignty or what Wade and Bradley call the 'doctrine of the legislative supremacy of parliament' which 'fills the vacuum' left by the 'absence of a constitution' (Wade and Bradley 1987: 7).

We found that although a large majority of the public agreed that it was 'important for a government to be able to take decisive action' almost everyone, 96 per cent of the public and 98 per cent of local politicians, agreed with the American doctrine that 'constitutional checks and balances are important to make sure that a government does not become too dictatorial and ignore other viewpoints'. Only half felt morally bound to obey an unjust law passed by Parliament, perhaps they remembered the Poll Tax though we did nothing to remind them of it, and two-thirds felt that important issues should be decided by referendum rather than by Parliament. Local politicians were significantly more willing to submit to Parliament however. Around half the public would accept court judgements that overruled parliamentary legislation – slightly under half if it were a British court, slightly over half if it were a European court. Significantly, they rated a judicially administered Freedom of Information Act a better defence of their rights and liberties than even the investigative journalism of the quality press.

All of this reveals a degree of public support for formal mechanisms to check government behaviour that is out of line with the British constitution's reliance upon informal mechanisms, voluntary conventions, and the innate good sense, reasonableness and self-control of government ministers.

Conclusion

Where does that leave our comparison of culture and constitution? What evidence, if any, have we uncovered to suggest that there is a conflict between them?

On moral questions we found the public swift to condemn but

slow to coerce. They differ from the law in being less coercive on abortion, less insistent upon the primacy of Christian teaching in state schools, but more opposed to minority religious schools.

On equality, similarly, they are quick to sympathise but slow to coerce. Their obstinate commitment to full employment and surprisingly high level of support for a ban on private medicine is more in keeping with a socialist constitution than a liberal one. They are sympathetic to the disabled, women, and racial minorities but – with the outstanding exception of employment quotas for the disabled – they are firmly opposed to coercive action such as either employment or political quotas. The law effectively supports these coercive mechanisms through its concept of 'indirect discrimination' but, at the same time, has had a lamentable lack of success in tackling direct discrimination.

On free expression, there is no majority for the current legal suppression of interviews with terrorist sympathisers but no majority against it either. There is a majority against press intrusions into the private lives of ordinary people but not against press intrusions into the lives of senior politicians. Although public opinion is therefore opposed to the status quo it would be even more opposed to legal changes that sheltered the rich and powerful but not the general public itself.

There was overwhelming public opposition to the publication of lies and distortions of the truth. That opposition certainly conflicts with a constitution which protects and encourages such behaviour. The public accepts the need for secrecy where national interests are clearly involved but does not accept mere confidentiality as a basis for government secrecy. Again this conflicts sharply with the constitution. There is overwhelming support for the press and television to enjoy more independence from government control.

And finally, there is unanimous support for a system of constitutional checks and balances to restrain government, and massive support for referendums to take major decisions out of the hands of Parliament. At least half would submit parliamentary legislation to judicial review and half would also submit it to the judgement of their own conscience.

This is a fair catalogue of conflicts between culture and constitution. In their relation to government the public take a liberal, almost American view. They simply do not accept the doctrine of parliamentary sovereignty: for them, it is an alien concept. Nor do they accept the government's discretion to define the national interest, or the truth, purely to suit its own convenience.

So the public does see the law as a defence against a system that makes unacceptable claims to sovereignty. But in relation to their fellow citizens they are a good deal less enamoured of legal remedies. While willing to moralise they are remarkably reluctant to support legal enforcement of community standards or, in practice, their own moral standpoints or social objectives. At the same time, they would impose on government duties which are ordinarily only to be found in socialist constitutions, notably full employment and the provision of universal, egalitarian health care.

Public opinion is therefore democratic, liberal and, in some important respects, socialist; by contrast, the constitution has a legal framework based upon monarchy, it has conventions based increasingly upon the illiberal concept of sovereignty, and, at the time of writing, it is becoming progressively less egalitarian and less socialist.

Notes

1 The Canadian constitution was not 'patriated' until 1982, however. That allowed future constitutional amendments to be made by the Canadians themselves, instead of the British Parliament. It is also likely that there will be important changes to the Australian constitution, with British concurrence, within the next decade. But it is a long time since the British felt any deep, rather than purely formal, responsibility for the constitutions of the old Dominions.

2 Note the official position of the apostrophe which we have taken from the front cover of the document itself. It pictures citizens as individuals, not as a community or collective.

3 Articles 8 and 9. The Articles and Protocols protecting rights and freedoms are reprinted in Hurwitt and Thornton (1989: 109–19).

4 The Equal Opportunities Commission acts by issuing 'Non-Discrimination Notices' which have the force of law unless overturned on appeal to an industrial tribunal or County Court within six weeks; by issuing 'Codes of Practice' which do not have force of law but can be used in evidence at industrial tribunals; and by itself applying for court injunctions, for which it has specially privileged access to the courts. This is all in addition to its powers to encourage and fund individuals who wish to take their own complaints to court (see Hurwitt and Thornton 1989: 204–5, 213, 214).

References

Beetham, D. (1993) 'Political theory and British politics' in P. Dunleavy, A. Gamble, I. Holliday and G. Peele (eds) *Developments in British Politics 4*, London: Macmillan.

Beloff, M. and Peele, G. (1980) *The Government of the United Kingdom: Political Authority in a Changing Society*, London: Weidenfeld and Nicholson.

Birch, A. H. (1986) *The British System of Government*, 7th edn, London: Allen and Unwin.

Dowding, K. (1993) 'Government at the centre' in P. Dunleavy, A. Gamble, I. Holliday and G. Peele (eds) *Developments in British Politics 4*, London: Macmillan.

Ewing, K. D. and Gearty, C. A. (1990) *Freedom under Thatcher: Civil Liberties in Modern Britain*, Oxford: Oxford University Press.

Habermas, J. (1976) *Legitimation Crisis*, London: Heinemann.

Hurwitt, M. and Thornton, P. (1989) *Civil Liberty: The Liberty/NCCL Guide*, 4th edn, London: Penguin.

Institute For Public Policy Research (1991) *The Constitution of the United Kingdom*, London: Institute For Public Policy Research.

King, D. S. (1987) *The New Right: Politics, Markets and Citizenship*, London: Macmillan.

Marsh, D. (1993) 'The media and politics' in P. Dunleavy, A. Gamble, I. Holliday and G. Peele (eds) *Developments in British Politics 4*, London: Macmillan.

McCreadie, R. A., McLean, J. and Willock, I. D. (1984) *You and Your Rights: An A to Z Guide to the Law in Scotland*, Edinburgh: T. and T. Clark.

McLean, S. (1986) 'The right to reproduce' in T. Campbell, D. Goldberg, S. McLean and T. Mullen (eds) *Human Rights: From Rhetoric to Reality*, Oxford: Blackwell.

Miller, W. L. (1991) *Media and Voters: The Audience, Content and Influence of Press and Television at the 1987 General Election*, Oxford: Oxford University Press.

Milne, A. (1988) *DG: The Memoirs of a British Broadcaster*, London: Hodder and Stoughton.

Peele, G. (1993) 'The constitution' in P. Dunleavy, A. Gamble, I. Holliday and G. Peele (eds) *Developments in British Politics 4*, London: Macmillan.

Scotsman, 8th December 1993.

Thornton, P. (1989) *Decade of Decline: Civil Liberties in the Thatcher Years*, London: National Council for Civil Liberties.

Wade, E. C. S. and Bradley, A. W. (1987) *Constitutional and Administrative Law*, 10th edn, London: Longman.

SUGGESTIONS FOR FURTHER READING

In this volume we have covered a wide range of topics related to freedom and its alternatives. For another equally wide ranging text that also combines argument and opinion see McClosky and Brill (1983). Many of our survey questions derive from their work, although we have modified them wherever that seemed advisable. Sullivan *et al.* (1989) is more limited and uses more advanced statistics – an advantage for some readers, a disadvantage for others. Parry, Moyser and Day's (1992) analysis of British public opinion touches on some aspects of the topics dealt with in this volume – but only just.

For arguments about rights, liberties, equality and tolerance the edited collections by Andrews (1991), Avineri and de-Shalit (1992), Campbell *et al.* (1986), and Meehan and Sevenhuijsen (1991) are useful, as is the review of 'new right' thinking by King (1987). Plant and Barry (1990) presents two sides of a vigorous debate, and Turner (1993) provides a balanced discussion of many viewpoints. Mendus (1989) is particularly good on the specific topic of toleration which is particularly relevant to part six of this volume. Edwards (1987) gives a detailed treatment of 'positive discrimination' which is relevant to part five.

Classic texts by Berlin (1969), Hayek (1960, 1982), Marshall (1992), Rawls (1972, 1993), and Tawney (1952) would be worth consulting in the original, not least because we have quoted (most of) them as authorities or criticised them for their errors. On a lighter note, Wright (1987) might be consulted since we have criticised it also. Rimmington (1994) includes some interesting comments by the new head of British intelligence.

Norton (1982) is a good review of the development of the British constitution up to the start of the Thatcher years. Ewing and Gearty (1990) and various contributors to Dunleavy *et al.* (1993) expresses well-informed concern at developments since then. The IPPR (1991) proposes one very detailed solution to the problems they discuss. Hurwitt and Thornton (1989) is a good account of current law and practice regarding civil liberties in all their aspects.

Several of our chapters focus on the mass media, both in Britain and elsewhere, especially in post-communist societies. Both Negrine (1989) and Curran and Seaton (1991) provide a good introduction to the issues that surround press and television in Britain. Miller (1991) analyses public attitudes towards the media and briefly outlines various normative theories about the role that the media should play in political life. For more general background on the political setting in post-communist countries see White (1993) and White *et al.* (1993). Milne (1988) provides an account of his experiences at the BBC which should be compared with the Hungarian Media War described in chapter eight.

Andrews, G. (ed.) (1991) *Citizenship*, London: Lawrence and Wishart.

Avineri, S. and de-Shalit, A. (eds) (1992) *Communitarianism and Individualism*, Oxford: Oxford University Press.

Berlin, I. (1969) *Four Essays on Liberty*, Oxford: Oxford University Press.

Campbell, T., Goldberg, D., McLean, S. and Mullen, T. (eds) (1986) *Human Rights: From Rhetoric to Reality*, Oxford: Blackwell.

Curran, J. and Seaton, J. (1991) *Power without Responsibility: The Press and Broadcasting in Britain*, London: Routledge.

Dunleavy, P., Gamble, A., Holliday, I. and Peele, G. (1993) *Developments in British Politics 4*, London: Macmillan.

Edwards, J. (1987) *Positive Discrimination: Social Justice and Social Policy*, London: Tavistock.

Ewing, K. D. and Gearty, C. A. (1990) *Freedom under Thatcher: Civil Liberties in Modern Britain*, Oxford: Oxford University Press.

Hayek, F. A. (1960) *The Constitution of Liberty*, London: Routledge.

Hayek, F. A. (1982) *Law, Legislation and Liberty*, London: Routledge.

Hurwitt, M. and Thornton, P. (1989) *Civil Liberty: the Liberty/NCCL Guide*, London: Penguin.

Institute for Public Policy Research (1991) *The Constitution of the United Kingdom*, London: Institute for Public Policy Research.

King, D. S. (1987) *The New Right: Politics, Markets and Citizenship*, London: Macmillan.

Marshall, T.H. and Bottomore, T. (1992) *Citizenship and Social Class*, London: Pluto.

McClosky, H. and Brill, A. (1983) *Dimensions of Tolerance: What Americans Believe about Civil Liberties*, New York: Russell Sage.

Meehan, E. and Sevenhuijsen, S. (eds) (1991) *Equality, Politics and Gender*, London: Sage.

Mendus, S. (1989) *Toleration and the Limits of Liberalism*, London: Macmillan.

Miller, W. L. (1991) *Media and Voters*, Oxford: Oxford University Press.

Milne, A. (1988) *DG: The Memoirs of a British Broadcaster*, London: Hodder and Stoughton.

Negrine, R. (1989) *Politics and the Mass Media in Britain*, London: Routledge.

Norton, P. (1982) *The Constitution in Flux*, Oxford: Martin Robertson.

Parry, G., Moyser, G. and Day, N. (1992) *Political Participation and Democracy in Britain*, Cambridge: Cambridge University Press.

Plant, R. and Barry, N. (1990) *Citizenship and Rights in Thatcher's Britain: Two Views*, London: Institute of Economic Affairs.

Rawls, J. (1972) *A Theory of Justice*, Oxford: Oxford University Press.

Rawls, J. (1993) *Political Liberalism*, New York: Columbia University Press.

Rimmington, S. (1994) *Dimbleby Lecture*, London: BBC.

Sullivan, J. L., Pierson J. and Marcus, G. E. (1989) *Political Tolerance and American Democracy*, London: University of Chicago Press.

Tawney, R. H. (1952) *Equality*, London: Allen and Unwin.
Turner, B. S. (1993) *Citizenship and Social Theory*, London: Sage.
White, S. (1993) *After Gorbachev*, Cambridge: Cambridge University Press.
White, S., Batt, J. and Lewis, P. G. (eds) (1993) *Developments in East European Politics*, London: Macmillan.
Wright, P. (1987) *Spycatcher*, London: Viking.

INDEX